Gandhian Perspectives on Satyagraha Movement and Non Violence

Gandhian Perspectives on Satyagraha Movement and Non Violence

Edited by

S.K. Shukla

OMEGA PUBLICATIONS

NEW DELHI-110 002 (INDIA)

OMEGA PUBLICATIONS
4378/4B, G-4 JMD House
Murari Lal Street, Ansari Road
Daryaganj, New Delhi - 110 002
Phone : (Off.)23278062,9811787417
e-mail : omega_publications@yahoo.com

Head Office :
79/23, Laxmi Garden
Near Satya Jyoti School,
Gurgaon (Haryana)

Edition : 2023

Price Rs 1195/-

ISBN : 978-81-8455-183-9

PRINTED IN INDIA

Published by Mahender Garg for Omega Publications, New Delhi-110 002
Printed at Suman Printers, Delhi-110093

CONTENTS

Preface

Amongst the thousands of tracts which focus on Gandhi and his approach to nonviolent action, one would think that all that could be said might already have been. Perhaps. Nevertheless, there seems to be very little written on satyagraha that is both brief enough and sufficiently non-superficial to lend itself to classroom use. Unless a course is devoted wholly to Gandhi (or a private reader is interested in devoting considerable effort to digesting reams of material), there is not much available for practical purposes. This short book is designed to close this gap in the literature.

The more serious researcher of Gandhian thought may also recognize how the material here presented provides a distinctive contribution to the literature on Gandhi. Few scholars have sought to examine Gandhi's satyagraha approach to conflict with respect to his own Hindu-hierarchical perspective. Writers from East and West alike have generally either shared a Western point of view that overlooks levels of meaning and degrees of development or have emphasized satyagraha primarily as a method/ technique, thus neglecting its religious roots and ideal of self-realization. My effort has sought to analyze Gandhian satyagraha according to the levels of secular, religious, and mysticat emphases which Gandhi, himself, attributed to it. By doing this, we are able to understand more clearly the vast potential Gandhi believed nonviolence held for both personal and political revolution.

That satyagraha, as soul force, is shown to ultimately rest upon the psychical powers believed by Gandhi to be associated with levels of spiritual development should disturb uo one. Of course, if Gandhi's metaphysical assumptions are correct, the revolutionary ramifications of his satyagraha approach to nonviolent action become quickly apparent: spiritually developed Daniels could, theoretically, disarm entire armies by their loving presence alone— and even prevent nuclear weapons from being fired. Yet one need not subscribe to Gandhi's faith in such psychical powers in order to still find some merit in satyagraha as a method secularized of such fantas-tic claims. Indeed, it would seem that it is one testament to Gandhi's brilliance that he was able to communicate about the potentials of his approach, relating different levels of understanding it to different audiences at different times.

This study abandons Gandhi's practice of selective communication. Here the attempt is to share with the reader the full range of meaning that Gandhi gave to his satyagraha approach. The purpose is neither to convert you to share Gandhi's faith nor to glorify his views. The purpose is to better understand Gandhian satyagraha as a whole, and thus to have further basis for reflection. Whether anyone comes to eventually more agree or disagree with Gandhi is really irrelevant. That we seek to improve our understanding in the process of seeking Truth ourselves is what is most crucial.

The present book, "Gandhian perspectives on Satyagraha Movement and Non violence" deals with this basic question in multi-dimensional manner—social, political, economic and technological, besides moral and spiritual aspects of man and the society. The book will be of great use for Gandhian researchers, development planners and welfare economists.

Editor

1

Mahatma Gandhi : Life Sketch

Mohandas Karamchand Gandhi was born on 2 October 1869 in Porbandar, India—at a time when Bahá'u'lláh had been exiled to the Holy Land as a prisoner of the Ottoman Empire. Gandhi is best known for helping to free the people of India from British rule through nonviolent resistance. He thus became one of the most respected spiritual and political leaders of the twentieth century. India honors him as "Father of the Nation" and as a Mahatma, or Great Soul.

Gandhi left India in 1888 to study law in London and returned to India in 1891 to practice. In 1893 he took on a one year contract to do legal work in South Africa. At the time, South Africa was controlled by the British. When he attempted to exercise his rights as a British subject he was abused, and soon realized that all ethnic Indians suffered similar treatment. Gandhi stayed in South Africa for 21 years working to improve the rights and conditions of ethnic Indians. He developed a nonviolent method of direct social action based on spiritual principles, which he called *Satyagraha,* also known as passive resistance. In 1915 Gandhi returned to India and within 15 years became the leader of the Indian nationalist movement. Using the tenets of *Satyagraha* he lead the campaign for Indian independence from Britain. Gandhi was arrested many times by the British for his activities in South Africa and India. He believed that it was honorable to suffer or go to jail for a just cause. He spent a total of seven years in prison for his political activities. More than once Gandhi used fasting to impress upon others the need to be nonviolent.

Through the efforts of Gandhi and others, India was granted independence in 1947, but partitioned in two—thus were born India and Pakistan. Rioting between Hindus and Muslims followed. Being an advocate for a united India where Hindus and Muslims could live together in peace, Gandhi began a fast at the age of 78 in order to stop the bloodshed. After five days, the opposing leaders pledged to stop the fighting and Gandhi broke his fast. Sadly, twelve days later Gandhi was assassinated by a Hindu fanatic who opposed his program of tolerance for all creeds and religions. He died with the mention of God on his lips.

Gandhian Ideals

As humankind struggles to find ways of living responsibly in the "global village," many of Gandhi's teachings appear pertinent again and are receiving renewed attention. The direction of his thought is challenging and points to a holistic worldview.

Truth and nonviolence, both of which are discussed in other chapters of this book, were Gandhi's most cherished principles. Gandhi writes: "Truth resides in every human heart, and one has to search for it there, and to be guided by truth as one sees it. But no one has a right to coerce others to act according to his own view of truth." Gandhi teaches that Truth is God, and that it is our sacred duty to seek it. If Truth was to Gandhi the Ultimate End (i.e. God), then *ahimsa* (nonviolence) was the perfect means of attaining that end. Gandhi writes: "Non-violence is the greatest force man has been endowed with. Truth is the only goal he has. For God is none other than Truth. But Truth cannot be, never will be, reached except through non-violence... That which distinguishes man from all other animals is his capacity to be non-violent. And he fulfils his mission only to the extent that he is non-violent and no more." From these two fundamental principles can be "derived" all of his other teachings:

Gandhi teaches that all faiths spring from the same ultimate, timeless, eternal Religion. He writes: "The root of all religions is one and it is pure and all of them have sprung from the same source, hence all are equal." "Let no one even for a moment entertain the fear that a reverent study of other religions is likely to weaken or shake one's faith in one's own." "This study of other religions besides one's own will give one a grasp of the rock-bottom unity of all religions and afford a glimpse also of that universal and absolute truth which lies beyond the 'dust of creeds and faiths'."

Sarvodaya and Collective Trusteeship

Sarvodaya is the name given to Gandhi's ideal of nonviolent socialism. Gandhi teaches that one should earn no more money than is enough to support oneself and one's family, and advocates voluntary sharing of excess wealth. While wealth should be used for the common good of all rather than for the private gain of a few, Gandhi condemns its forceful redistribution: "Wealthy people should act as trustees of the wealth. But if they are robbed of this wealth through violent means, it would not be in the interest of the country. This is known as communism. Moreover, by adopting violent means, we would be depriving society of capable individuals."

Village Autonomy

Gandhi advocates independence for the common people, not just for those who rule over them. Thus, while Gandhi is best known as a freedom fighter who brought India independence from Britain, his primary aim was independence for the grassroots of society. He writes: "Independence must begin at the bottom." "My idea of village *swaraj* [self-rule] is that it is a complete republic, independent of its neighbors for its own vital wants, and yet interdependent for many others in which dependence is a necessity."

Decentralization of Power

According to Gandhi, centralized government is inherently prone to violence. Therefore Gandhi advocates decentralization of political power. Explaining his metaphorical vision of the structure of a future nonviolent society, Gandhi writes: "Life will not be a pyramid with the apex sustained by the bottom. But it will be an oceanic circle whose centre will be the individual always ready to perish for the village, the latter ready to perish for the circle of villages, till at last the whole becomes one life composed of individuals, never aggressive in their arrogance, but ever humble, sharing the majesty of the oceanic circle of which they are integral units."

Self-reliance

Swadeshi (Self-reliance) is mainly understood to mean a protectionist technique that Gandhi employed against the mercantilistic policies of the British, whereby the masses were urged to abstain from cloth manufactured outside India, and instead to use cotton, silk, or wool cloth made in India. But Gandhi gives it a broader meaning: "*Swadeshi* carries a great and profound meaning. It does not mean merely the use of what is produced in one's own country. That meaning is certainly there in *swadeshi*. But there is another meaning implied in it which is far greater and much more important. *Swadeshi* means reliance on our own strength. We should also know what we mean by 'reliance on our own strength'. 'Our strength' means the strength of our body, our mind, and our soul. From among these, on which should we depend? The answer is brief. The soul is supreme and therefore soul-force is the foundation on which man must build."

Machines

Gandhi strongly disapproved of machinery, since in his time machines typically led to the concentration of economic and political power in the hands of a few, extremely rich people. Today, of course, the reverse appears to be possible. For example, information technology has led to decentralization, rather than centralization, of power. It would be interesting to know what Gandhi would have to say about the Internet, for he wrote: "Every machine that helps every individual has a place. But I must confess that I have never sat down to think out what that machine can be." "I would prize every invention of science made for the benefit of all." Although Gandhi's original fears about machines have proven unfounded, nevertheless industrialization and automation have not automatically led to an equitable distribution of work and leisure time.

Gandhi teaches that work should be done with pure motives, without desire for any type of reward, in a spirit of service. When work is thus performed, it becomes an act of *yajña* (sacrifice). He writes: "'*Yajña*' means an act directed to the welfare of others, done without desiring any return for it, whether of a temporal or spiritual nature. 'Act' here must be taken in its widest sense, and includes thoughts and word, as well as deed. 'Others' embraces not only humanity, but all life."

The word *Satyagraha* was coined during Gandhi's lifetime to describe passive resistance, as developed and practiced by Gandhi in South Africa. The term can be literally translated in English as "insistence on truth." *Satyagraha* was Gandhi's nonviolent method of resisting injustice and violence in their various manifestations. Essentially, it consists in nonviolent noncooperation with the protagonists of violence. As a method of last resort, Gandhi did use civil disobedience—passive resistance in its most disruptive (and violent) form. Gandhi's method of nonviolent noncooperation is a true and tried technique that has been successfully used to fight violent and systematic human rights violations in a number of states. Examples of leaders who have adapted the method include

Nelson Mandela, Martin Luther King Jr., and His Holiness the Dalai Lama.

Gandhi teaches that every human right is fundamentally related to some reciprocal responsibility towards the world. He writes: "All rights to be deserved and preserved come from duty well done. Thus the very right to live accrues to us only when we do the duty of citizenship of the world. From this very fundamental statement perhaps it is easy enough to define the duties of man and woman and correlate every right to some corresponding duty to be first performed. Every other right can be shown to be a usurpation hardly worth fighting for."

According to Gandhi, it is possible to establish *Ramarajya*, or the Kingdom of God, on earth. Indeed, he seems to have believed in its inevitability. But before this can happen, nations must renounce violence towards each other and learn to live in peace. He explains that "a world federation is possible of realization and in that case it would not be necessary for countries to maintain armed forces." "There can be no world federation of countries ruled by armies."

REFERENCES

J. E. Esslemont, *Bahá'u'lláh and the New Era,* 5th rev. ed. (Wilmette: Bahá'í Publishing Trust, 1987).

The Moral and Political Writings of Mahatma Gandhi. Ed. Raghavan Iyer (Oxford: Oxford University Press, 1986).

The Essential Writings of Mahatma Gandhi. Ed. Raghavan Iyer (Oxford: Oxford University Press, 1990).

Eknath Easwaran, *Gandhi the Man* (Petaluma: Nilgiri Press, 1983).

Bahá'u'lláh, A statement prepared by the Bahá'í International Community's Office of Public Information New York.

The Hidden Words of Bahá'u'lláh. Trans. Shoghi Effendi (Wilmette: Bahá'í Publishing Trust, 1985), 3-4.

Paris Talks: Addresses given by 'Abdu'l-Bahá in Paris in 1911-1912 (London: Bahá'í Publishing Trust, 1972), 143.

Gleanings from the Writings of Bahá'u'lláh. Trans. Shoghi Effendi (Wilmette: Bahá'í Publishing Trust, 1976), 287-288.

'Abdu'l-Bahá, quoted in J. E. Esslemont, *Bahá'u'lláh and the New Era,* 5th rev. ed. (Wilmette: Bahá'í Publishing Trust, 1987), 147.

'Abdu'l-Bahá, quoted in J. E. Esslemont, *Bahá'u'lláh and the New Era,* 5th rev. ed. (Wilmette: Bahá'í Publishing Trust, 1987), 149.

Gleanings from the Writings of Bahá'u'lláh, 259-260.

The Hidden Words of Bahá'u'lláh. Trans. Shoghi Effendi (Wilmette: Bahá'í Publishing Trust, 1985), 41.

Gleanings from the Writings of Bahá'u'lláh, 95.

'Abdu'l-Bahá, quoted in *Bahá'u'lláh and the New Era,* 160-161.

Shoghi Effendi, quoted in *Bahá'u'lláh and the New Era,* 281-282.

The Essential Writings of Mahatma Gandhi, 240-1.

The Essential Writings of Mahatma Gandhi, 160.

The Essential Writings of Mahatma Gandhi, 150.

The Essential Writings of Mahatma Gandhi, 408.

The Essential Writings of Mahatma Gandhi, 347.

The Essential Writings of Mahatma Gandhi, 358.

The Essential Writings of Mahatma Gandhi, 348.

The Essential Writings of Mahatma Gandhi, 362.

See, for example, *The Essential Writings of Mahatma Gandhi.* Ed. Raghavan Iyer (Oxford: Oxford University Press, 1990), 348.

The Essential Writings of Mahatma Gandhi, 348-9.

The Essential Writings of Mahatma Gandhi, 402.

The Essential Writings of Mahatma Gandhi, 379.

The Essential Writings of Mahatma Gandhi, 392-3.

The Essential Writings of Mahatma Gandhi, 409.

2

Satyagraha Movement in the Bombay

The Rowlatt Act (March 1919) which was 'an infringement on personal liberty and freedom' hastened further experiments of the weapon of Satyagraha in Indian Politics on a large scale. This weapon 'not only changed the technique and programme of our struggle but it basically affected our approach to politics and also the content of it'. In the first week of March, Gandhiji came to Bombay from Ahmedabad, it appears, on the invitation of Bombay leaders and organised the Satyagraha Subha of which he himself was elected the president and Mr. Horniman the Vice-President. Gandhiji already had intimated the Viceroy that he would be constrained to launch Civil Disobedience Movement if the Rowlutt act was brought into operation. The atmosphere in the Country was full of tension. Bombay was experiencing unprecedented emotion and commotion. Brisk preparation for enlisting Satyagrahis in Bombay was started. Meetings were attended by thousands. The Mulji Jethat and Morarji Gokuldas cloth markets had observed hartal on the 21st of March. Gandhiji in his appeal (24th March) had invited the attention of the workers to the fact that " the movement is essentially a religious one"; "that it is a process of self-purification and penance"; " an effort to secure redress through suffering".

The frantic efforts made by the Government of India and the Bombay Government to understand Gandhi's mind on the one hand and on the other to keep the Military ready at key places to meet eventualities, are seen in the extracts given here. They also show how heroically Bombay prepared itself for the struggle and stood by its lender Gandhiji in the days of peril and also at the time of its suspension (18th July 1919). This period was most critical for Gandhiji as well as for his lieutenants and followers. On the 30th (March) the Delhi police fired their bullets and Mahatma Munshi Ram better known as Swami Shradhananda, with bare chest, challenged the English Sergeants to shoot at him. This thrilled the atmosphere of the whole country. From the 6th to 13th (April) Bombay, Ahmedabad, Viramgaon, Nadiad and many other places in the presidency exhibited tremendous capacity to organise and. resist.

Police and military firings, resulting in the deaths of the innocent, released fury and passion. Gandhiji had rushed to Delhi at the invitation of the Swamiji where he was served with a prohibitory order which he refused to obey and was arrested and sent back. The news of his arrest poured oil on the flames. But he immediately returned to Bombay where with great difficulty he pacified the furious mobs at Paidhuni. The Amritsar shooting of the 10th and the massacre at the Jalianwala Bag created volcanic conditions in the country. The details need not be narrated here. All this was happening when the fate of the empire was hanging in the balance due to the war: war which was fought for saving democracy in which Indian soldiers and the people in general also, had made ' remarkable sacrifices'.

The police reports show how Bombay responded to Gandhiji's call. At one place they say 'it was a victory for Gandhi'. The Police Commissioner's report states that' Gandhi is a transitory figure-head !' About the Bombay leaders the report at one place says ' they are men of no weight; there is no one with 'any pretention to statesmenship.' The political atmosphere of Bombay was well prepared. In fact the people were eager for some action. The period of the three preceding years (1916-1918) was full of national activity. The Home Rule League activities and the anti-Willingdon memorial agitation had sufficiently surcharged the atmosphere of Bombay. The Railway workshop strike (July 1917) and the Postal strike had shown the new directions of labour activities. The Kaira Satyagraha had brought this new weapon once again to the forefront. People so far were used to popular agitations and demonstrations. But those weapons of political struggle were found not yielding satisfactory results. And all this was happening when the country had very heavily paid for the War. It was when the country was thus suffering under humiliation and was seized by frustrations that Gandhiji assumed its leadership.

When Gandhiji came to Bombay in the first week of March, he had discussions with Horniman, Jamnadas Dwarkadas, Shankarlal Bankar, Sarojini N'aidu, Umar Sobhani, Dr. Sathaye, Mavji Govindji, Anusuyaben and others whom he described as the ' prop of the Bombay activities'. The Bombay Chronicle is described in the police reports as the ' organ of the Satyagraha movement'. Gandhiji by July 1919 had persuaded himself to suspend the CD. movement 'for the time being', as the situation wus not congenial to satyagraha. The reports show under what breath-killing atmosphere high police officials were watching Gandhiji's movements. All influences political, personal, commercial were engaged in bringing pressure on Gandhi to stop the movement. Shrinivas Shastri, the President of the Servants of India Society, Gandhiji's revered friend, came out to declare " that Civil disobedience was against law ". Gandhiji told his workers (18th July) that' in response to the warning given by Government of India and due to the urgent desire publicly expressed by " leaders and editors I have decided not to resume Civil Resistance for the time being ". At the same time he told them that the suspension also was meant to ' hasten the end of the legislation (Rowlatt act)'. The reports describe how Gandhiji was heckled and cross-questioned in the meeting (17th July) when the decision of suspension of the movement was taken. Some even went to the length of saying that the deportation of Horniman was made possible because of the suspension. Hindustan, the Gujarat! newspaper of Bombay, styled Gandhiji as a " Murderer " or " Khuni". This shows the popular resentment against the suspension. The suspension was the bitterest pill that Gandhiji had to swallow. The reports of the interviews taken by Mr. Robertson, Secretary to Government of Bombay and Mr. Griffith, Commissioner of Police Bombay, show with what alertness and anxiety Delhi and Bombay Governments were watching Gandhiji's movements and speeches. He was ordered not to leave Bombay presidency which he could hardly tolerate. Nor did he want to embarrass the Government until peace was restored in the Punjab. He, therefore, it appears, decided to break the order and go to the South (July 1919). Mr. Griffith's interviews with Gandhiji taken under instructions from Government of India show how strong Gandhiji's convictions were and how poor were the arguments offered by Robertson and Griffith. Robertson was imploring Gandhiji not to break the law and court jail as that would remove the restraining influence on the Muslim mind. Gandhiji promptly replied that his courting arrest would help to persuade them to be peaceful. These talks appear like Gandhiji's discourses on Satyagraha, the place of pupils being occupied by top officials of the Government.

These reports also include two useful documents statements by Vinobaji Bhave and Kishorlal Mashruwala, made bejore Ahmedabad Police, when both of them were called upon to identify persons involved in the riots (April 1919). Both of them refused to piny the role. The soft speaking Kishorlalji had done it perhaps more definitely.]

THE KAIRA SATYAGRAHA, 1918

Regarding Home Rule League, 1917

A Home Rule League was established at Nadiad just after the internment of Annie Besant and in the beginning of July 1917. There were some theosophists and others who revered her and considered her an innocent personage. She soon rose in public esteem. I heard some of the lectures of the Home Rulers in the early stage of the Home Rule movement with a view to get first hand information for report to the Collector and subsequently got reports from Karkuns or Talatis and I submitted my reports from time to time to the Collector. Several meetings were held at Nadiad, and the Home Rulers used to go out in villages and preach their doctrines to the villagers. It was generally preached that Government officers are our servants (in one case people were told that mamlatdars need not be styled Rao Sahibs-as was customary with the people), that we should not fear them, that supply of carts and labour by Veth must cease, principles of equality must be established. India is fit for Home Rule and must get it, and every endeavour should be made to bring home to the people that every Indian is a Home Ruler. Some lecturers were from Bombay and Ahmedabad. The Nadiad Branch was in close touch with the Bombay League, and Home Rule literature was freely disseminated.

PASSIVE RESISTANCE CAMPAIGN, 1917-13

The above movement gained considerable force when the agitation against payment of Land Revenue was started.

A Short History of the Satyagraha Movement in the Kaira District

(a) When and how and under what circumstances the movement commenced.

The season o'f 1917-18 promised very well, but owing to heavy rains in the latter part of the season, most of the Kharif crops were seriously damaged. Recovery of the land revenue depends on the anna valuation of crops arrived at by Revenue officers. If the crops were valued at less than 4 annas no revenue is collected, but it is suspended (not remitted entirely); if the crops are between 4 and 6 annas, half the revenue is collected ; and if between 6 and 8 annas, whole revenue is collected. As it was apprehended from the very beginning that the anna valuation was going to be challenged by non-officials, the Collector had issued orders that the anna valuation should be made carefully.

Mr. Somabhai Kashibhai of Nadiad who is called ' African' first began to agitate, and printed applications dated 15th November 1917 praying for total remission of land revenue for the year began to pour in. Subsequently at a mass meeting held at Nadiad on 25th November 1917 it was resolved that the Honourable Messrs. Gokaldas Kahandas Parekh and Vithalbai Jhaverbhai Patel and others should go in a deputation before the Collector (Mr. Namjoshi). These gentlemen had an interview with the Collector at Thasra in the middle of December 1917, and the Collector promised to give the matter his best attention.

THE ANNA VALUATION

The anna valuation proposals in Nadiad Taiuka were arrived in this way :—

The Mamlatdar himself moved through most of the villages in the taiuka, and some were inspected by the Awal Karkuns. Then in the middle of December, all the Talatis, Circle Inspectors and Awal Karkuns were called, together at Nadiad, and after full discussion on the spot, it was settled that 39 villages should be put down for half suspension, one for full suspension and the rest for full collection. Nadiad and Narsanda were put down for full collection. Proposals were accordingly submitted to the Collector, who suggested certain minor modifications, but it was represented that it would entail hardship on the people : and so finally the proposals as submitted were sanctioned in toto.

GUJARAT SABHA TOOK THE ISSUE

As the orders passed by the Collector for the recovery of the land revenue were net appreciated by the agitators, the Gujarat Sabha of Ahmedabad took up the cause. The Sabha issued a printed notice dated 10th January 1918 informing the ryots that till final settlement of the question by Government they should not pay the land revenue. Under the rules, final ;orders are to be issued by the Collector. The Collector therefore warned the people to pay up the land revenue as final orders had already been issued by him. No relief was secured from the Commissioner, and Government in their Press Note dated 16th January 1918 upheld the views of the local officers on 5th February 1918. His Excellency the Governor received a deputation of the two honourable members, Mr. Gandhi and others. Their views could not stand close scrutiny in contrast with the official statistics. The question was then taken up in right earnest by Mr. Gandhi on behalf of the Gujarat Sabha. The Servants of India Society also held an independent inquiry in the matter. They (the latter) came to the conclusion that some relief was necessary in Matar Taiuka only. Meanwhile the acting Collector Mr. Namjoshi reverted and J. Ghosal, Esquire, I.C.S,, who had intimate experience of the district was reposted to Kaira. Minor alternations were found necessary in the collection orders relating to Matar Taluka, and they were made. The collector did not find it necessary to make any other changes in the collection orders.

GANDHI STARTS MOVEMENT

Mr. Gandhi carried out his campaign with Nadiad as his headquarters Nadiad was the main centre of the Home Rule movement started there in 1917 and there were several men of Nadiad who used to go out in the villages and in other talukas to lecture to the people. Mr. Gandhi visited some villages in the Nadiad Taluka and other talukas and thought that the anna valuation was below 4 annas. There were practically no Kharif crops standing at the time of his inspection, but from the account narrated to him by the people he thought that their story must be true ; he was also guided by the advice of Mohanlal Kameshwar Pandya of Kathlal (among others), and he at last challenged the annn valuation of Vadthal a village in the Nadiad Taluka, where full collection had been ordered, stating that he would stand or fall by Vadthal. I personally reasoned with Mr. Gandhi regarding this on 20th February 1918 at Nadiad in the Anathashram; but without success. A very detailed inquiry was made of the crops at Vadlhal by the Collector, and an exhaustive report was prepared and submitted by him to the Government fully vindicating the correctness of the official annawari, and bringing to light the mistakes committed by Mr. Gandhi. It may be noted that no suspensions were given in the neighbouring districts or States which were almost similarly situated, that according to the Rules relating to remissions and suspensions, these cannot be claimed as of right and that inquiry into individual cases, if any, of general hardship was not contemplated by the Rules. The Collector then notified the confirmation of his orders, and Mr. Gandhi was informed by the Commissioner that no concessions were possible.

ADVICE OF PASSIVE RESISTANCE

Thereupon Mr, Gandhi declared in a large public meeting at Nadiad on 22nd March 1918 that the people should resort to passive resistance. It may be noted that even before the actual declaration of this movement, people were instructed off and on to refrain from paying land revenue. The Government then issued a Press Note, dated 24th April 1918, confirming the Collector's action. The passive resistance propaganda gradually spread over the greater part of the district. Several pleaders and leading gentlemen from Ahmedabad and Bombay also served as volunteers, and actually helped the spread of the movement. It may be noted that Nadiad ranks foremost in political activities in the Kaira District from the beginning, and especially since the deportation of Lala Lajpatrai. The first Home Rule League branch in the district was established at Nadiad in 1917.

PRINCIPLES PREACHED BY THE SATYAGRAHIS

(b) What were the principles and doctrines preached by the authors and followers of the said movement ?

Their principles were that those whose crops were below four annas should not pay. whether able to pay or not, and whether the property be distrained or lands forfeited, or ' Chothai' lines imposed, or the defaulters imprisoned. Those who wanted to adhere to this were required to sign pledge-forms. Mr. Gandhi considered breaking of the pledge as equivalent to throat-cutting. The idea for those able to pay to join the movement was that if they paid it would not be borne out that the anna valuation was below four annas and the poor would follow in the wake of the rich and be constrained to pay. The followers of Mr. Gandhi preached that payment of land revenue should not be made under any circumstances. Whenever distraints were made, crowds of people (Satyagrahis) would turn up, ostensibly to give courage to the defaulter, but practically to browbeat the officials, and even joke and laugh at them when the distraints were unsuccessful.

THE EFFECT OF THE MOVEMENT

(c) What consequences it had and how it ended and whether it benefited the landholders and how far ?

Every method of obstruction was in fact adopted by the villagers e.g., : —

(a) Giving supplies of food or drink or shelter to Government officials was stopped.

(b) Rawanias were dissuaded from doing their service.

(c) No labourers would be forthcoming for taking out or removing distrained property.

(d) No panch would assist in drawing up punchnamas for distraint.

(e) At times houses of defaulters or property (e.g. live-stock) belonging to them would not be pointed out by any.

(f) Anyone assisting collection of land revenue would be socially ostracised (*e.g.*, Navagam Panch resolution, dated 26th April 1918 printed in Kaira Vartaman dated 8th May 1913).

(g) Labourers or rawanias brought from outside for distraints were threatened and packed off.

(h) Distrained property would not be allowed to be taken possession of.

(i) Distrained property promised to be produced at a certain date and place would not be produced.

(j) No one would bid for the property and if bidding took place it was for very low amounts, so that further distraints would have to be made and the proceedings prolonged, or the auction postponed for another date. Often the bids were on behalf of the owners themselves.

(k) Actual tendering of cash by defaulters was prevented.

(l) Live-stock would be let lose, so that they cannot be distrained for want of identification.

(m) Property of defaulters was placed at houses of those who had paid up their dues.

(n) False claims were set up to property taken in distraint.

(o) Houses were locked up purposely and sometimes shut from inside only to prevent distraints.

(p) Warnings by bugles, etc., were given to all the villagers as soon as an officer arrived, so that the people would soon take the hint.

(q) Barbers, potters, Brahmins, etc. were dissuaded from doing customary service.

Several such devices were played by the villagers. In some cases false charges were made that certain articles had been stolen in the act of distraints. There ' were some cases of active resistance and some criminal prosecutions had therefore to be launched. The Mamlatdar had even received a push himself, and the Anand Mamlatdar feared to move without the help of the Police.

The effect was the general weakening of the authority. Before the Satyagraha campaign was started, coercive measures had been taken very sparingly, but subsequently the Mamlatdars were allowed full latitude permissible by law.

Mr. Gandhi did not advocate any active obstruction or the denial of usual courtesies, but the people could not properly follow him The movement was more out of control during the absence of Mr. Gandhi to Delhi and Bijapur.

The Revenue officers exercised an amount of forbearance, but the obstinacy of the people led to an estrangement of feeling between the Government and the people.

A COMPROMISE

When most of the revenue due for collection had been actually collected the Mamlatdar met Mr. Gandhi at Uttersanda on 3rd June 1918 and discussed the situation with him that the poor were not going to be pressed for payment and there was no necessity for the continuance of his campaign. A written order was then issued by the Mamlatdar to the village officers of Uttersanda on the post asking them to explain to the villagers that the arrears of those who were really poor would stand over till the next year and the others should pay up. Mr. Gandhi agreed to this ; and he exhorted the people assembled there and then to pay up the land revenue at once and told them that the poor whose poverty would be proved to the satisfaction of the officers would not have to pay this year and that the others should pay up without any delay. The people were surprised to hear this. It appears they liked him much when he preached them not to pay as it was in their own interests, but when the question of loosening the purse arose they assumed a different attitude. It was remarkable that when Mr. Gandhi left the place, no one went even a few paces to see him off. Mr. Gandhi asked for similar orders for the whole of the district, and he was replied by the Collector that the orders applied to the whole of the district, and that they were based on the (confidential) orders issued on 25th April 1918 and repeated on 22nd May 1918 to Mamlatdars and besides they were the standing orders of Government. Mr. Gandhi thought he won a victory, while the Government thought that they did not yield in. At this time about 8 per cent, only of the land revenue was in arrears. Most of this was subsequently recovered. It may, however, be noted that even the subsequent recovery was largely due to the efforts of Revenue officers than to the direct preachings of Mr. Gandhi and his followers. At any rate the contumacy of the people did not then receive any support from Mr. Gandhi, and this facilitated matters.

The landholders did not derive any substantial benefit from the agitation. They however, certainly became bolder than ever, e.g., in the gathering held by the Commissioner, N. D., on 12th April 1918, at Nadiad, several people told him in his face that they were not going to pay and were prepared to suffer.

PEOPLE'S FAITH IN GANDHI SHAKEN

The feeble response of the people to Mr. Gandhi's subsequent efforts for recruiting, however, shows that self-sacrificing spirit did not sufficiently develop and that the Passive Resistance movement became popular as it was in the interest of the ryots. Some even said that Mr. Gandhi had been won over when he asked people to pay up. Some expressed their dislike in that they had after all to pay the land revenue and worries and ' Chothai' in addition. It may be noted that when the movement was in its full swing, forefeiture notices that had been issued were hailed with joy and rejoicings. Also when some of the prisoners concerned in Satyagraha cases were released they were garlanded, taken in a procession and highly praised.

The movement naturally entailed hard work on the Talatis, and they were discontented with their lot, and owing to the agitation were emboldened to go out on strike (in May 1919).

Perhaps the Dharalas who committed dacoities in 1918 and 1919 first took courage because of the general impression created amongst them about the weakness of the authority as an indirect consequence of this Passive Resistance.

ROWLATT BILL SATYAGRAHA IN BOMBAY

The following events between May 1916 to January 1919 give us the background of the establishment of the Satyagraha Sabha in Bombay under the leadership of Mahatma Gandhi. The newly started Home League was the leading force in all these events, which prepared the ground for the April Satyagraha. The events in brief were as under:

1. The Maharashtra Home Rule League was started in May 1916 and Mrs. Basant's Home Rule League in September 1916. The two leagues co-operated in the election of delegates to the Lucknow Congress of 1916. The Home Rule League was also to secure the election of Mrs. Besant as president of the 1917 Calcutta Congress.

2. During June and July 1917 a military labour Camp had been opened at Dadar. Articles appeared in the Chronicle criticising this camp. It was alleged that Military Sepoys had committed outrages on the women of the neighbourhood. The Government of Bombay passed an order under the Defence of India Act prohibiting any further reference to the subject.

3. In July 1917 there was a scare among the merchants of the Mulji Jetha market that British Soldiers were abducting Indian Women.

4. In July 1917 there was a strike at G. I. P. Railway workshops at Matunga and Parel. The Home Rule League guided the strikers.

5. On 19th September, 1917 there was Postmen's strike sponsored by Home Rule League.
6. In 1918 was started Kaira Satyagraha supported by Home Rule League.
7. In November 1918 Anti Willingdon address agitation sponsored by B. G. Horniman, J. Dwarkadas, Omer Sobhani and M. A. Jinnah.
8. January 1919 Great Mill Strike in Bombay.

The Bombay Government in a statement contained in Special Department File No. 521 (1AJ of 1919 has styled these events as "preliminary skirmishes in Bombay". The following extracts from the statement give the government history of the April Satyagrah campaign

THE SATYAGRAHA CAMPAIGN

"With this brief sketch of the preliminary skirmishes in Bombay, we arrive at the opening of the Satyagraha Campaign which culminated in the disturbances of April. In February the so-called Rowlatt Bill had been introduced in the Imperial Council, and ultimately, notwithstanding opposition, both within and without the Council, became law as the Anarchical and Revolutionary Crimes Act. When it was clear that Government was determined in its attitude, warnings and threats of agitation such as had not been paralleled in India were indulged in by extremist politicians. On the 24th of February Messrs. Horniman, Jamnadas Dwarkadas,

Omer Sobhani, Mrs. Naidu and some others went from Bombay to Ahmedabad and met Gandhi. As a result of their deliberations Gandhi sent a strongly worded telegram to His Excellency the Viceroy stating that if Government proceeded with the Rowlatt 3ills it was their intention to resprt to Passive Resistance. On the 26th of February the Chronicle published a message from its correspondent in Delhi, dated the 25th February, which was worded as follows:

" In reply to an enquiry as to when Mr. Gandhi would start for England as a member of the Congress Deputation, he had wired to the Honourable Pandit Malaviya as follows:—

' I have no confidence in deputation. Rowlatt Bills block all progress.'

PROCESSION AND MEETING

On the 28th of February a large public meeting was organised by, the Home Rule League in the mill districts of Bombay. Messrs. Horniman, Jamnadas, Omer Sobhani and other prominent Home Rulers went in procession to the meeting. This procession was clearly intended to attract the notice of the millhands, but in this respect it largely failed in its purpose. At the meeting every speaker endeavoured to persuade the audience that the Rowlatt Bills were intended to rob them of their personal liberty and freedom and to enable the bureaucracy to govern despotically. It was announced that Mahatma Gandhi was about to preach Passive Resistance, and the audience was urged to be prepared to protest at' any cost, if they were not willing to be enslaved.

THE SATYAGRAHA SABHA

Chronicle announced the inauguration of Passive Resistance against what it termed the " Black Bills " and published Mr. Gandhiji's Satyagraha Vow. Throughout the following weeks the chronicle was devoted, day after day, to a campaign of extraordinary vehemence in favour of Passive Resistance. On the 1st of March Mr. Gandhi arrived in Bombay where he was continuously visited by Messrs. Horniman, Jamnadas Dwarkadas, S. G. Banker, Dr. D. D. Sathye, Dr. M. B. Velkar, Mrs. Naidu, Mrs, Anusuyabai of Ahmedabad, Mavji Govindji and other Home Rulers. The employees of the Mulji Jetha cloth market were invited to join the movement and to sign the vow at S. G. Banker's residence. The Satyagraha Sabha was organised with Mr. Gandhi as President, Mr. Horniman as Vice-President, and the leading Home Rulers on the Committee.

MODERATES OPPOSE

The inauguration of the Passive Resistance movement called forth a manifesto from the leaders of the Indian Moderate Party who had joined with the extremists in their opposition to the Rowlatt Legislation. In this manifesto they made it clear that they were not prepared to follow the Extremists in this movement. The members of the Home Rule League, now merged in the Satyagraha

Sabha, met this manifesto with ridicule, and the cleavage between the two Indian political schools of thought which had temporarily combined thus manifested itself again. It may be noted that Mr. Shrinivas Shastri, President of the Servants of India Society, was among those who regarded Passive Resistance against other laws as ridiculous and dangerous.

MAHATMA MUNSHIRAM'S SPEECH

On the 8th of March rumours were circulated in Bombay that Government intended to apply the Rowlatt Bills to Muhammadan agitators in connection with the Turkish question. From the 10th onwards numerous strongly worded leaflets and pamphlets urging the people to join the passive Resitance movement were widely circulated. At the same time a very vigorous campaign of speech making was conducted—Mr. Horniman, Mrs. Naidu, Mr. Jamnadas and other prominent members of the Home Rule League being as usual the chief speakers. On the 14th of March Swami Shradha-nand, otherwise known as Mahatma Munshiram of the Gurukul at Kangri near Hardwar, made a noteworthy speech. His wording was often obscure, his meaning being apparently helped out by his gestures. This speech was fanatical in tone, and the general effect was one of hostility to Government and its officers. It contained the following quotation from " Krishna's words to Arjun ":

" You cannot control the result, you can only control your action, do your work and leave the result to look after itself. Whether the Government will give in or not under pressure of the Satyagraha agitation is not our lookout. It is their affair. Our concern is in starting the campaign."

It is not without significance that the account of this speech published in the Chronicle of the 16th was edited in such a manner as to minimise its effect.

MARKETS CLOSED

On the 19th of March came the news of the passing of the " Rowlatt" Act. On receipt of this information some 50 merchants of the Mulji Jetha cloth market sent in a written request to the Secretary of the Native Piecegoods Merchants Association of Bombay to convene a meeting to consider the question of closing the market as a protest. In response to this request the Secretary called a meeting for the 20th. It was held in the market hall in the afternoon, and it was then decided to close the market on the 21st for one day. As a result the Mulji Jatha Market closed on the 21st. The Luckmidas Khimji and Morarji Gokuldas Markets followed suit. There was no excitement in this connection. This incident is interesting as furnishing an instance of a spotaneous hartal very different in its effects from those organised by the political leaders.

THE DAY OF HUMILIATION AND PRAYER

The news of the passing of the Act was followed by a stream of excited articles and leaders in the Chronicle which now struck a note of despair coupled with determination to suffer. On the 25th of March Mr. Gandhi announced in the Chronicle that Sunday the 30th of March would be a day of fast and prayer. Shortly afterwards he announced without any explanation of the change that his intention was to fix the 6th of April as the day of penance. The reason for this change has never come to light, but it is remarkable that the new date was adopted nearly everywhere in India, except in Delhi and a few other places.

The following is the text of Mr. Gandhi's letter to the Press announcing his ideas as to the way in which the day of humiliation and prayer should be observed. It is dated March the 24th from Madras, which place he visited in connection with the campaign :—

"Satyagraha, as I have endeavoured to explain at several meetings, is essentially a religious movement. It is a process of purification and penance. It seeks to secure reforms or redress of grievances by self-suffering. I therefore venture to suggest that the second Sunday after the publication of the Viceregal assent to Bill No. 2 of 1919 may be observed as the day of humiliation and prayer. As there must be effective public demonstration in keeping with the character of the observance, I beg to advise as follows :—

"A twenty-four hours fast counting from the last meal on the preceding night should be observed by all adults unless prevented from so doing by consideration of religion or health. The fast is not to be regarded in any shape or form in the nature of a hunger-strike or designed to put any pressure upon Government. It is to be regarded for Satyagrahis as a necessary discipline to fit them for the civil disobedience contemplated in their pledge and for others as some slight token of the intensity of their wounded feelings.

"All work except such as may be necessary in the public interest should be suspended for the day. Markets and other places should be closed. Employees who are required to work even on Sunday may only suspend work after obtaining previous leave. I do not hesitate to recommend these two suggestions for adoption by public servants for, though it is an unquestionably right thing for them not to take part in political discussions and gatherings, in my opinion they have the undoubted right to express upon vital matters their feelings in the very limited manner herein suggested. Public meetings should be held on that day in all parts of India not excluding villages at which a resolution praying for the withdrawal of the measures should be passed. If my advice is deemed worthy of acceptance the responsibility will lie in the first instance on various Satyagraha Associations for undertaking the necessary work of organisation but all other associations will, I hope, join hands in making this demonstration a success".

In a special evening edition on the 1st of April the Chronicle first published in Bombay the news of the rioting in Delhi and the use of fire arms by the troops."

RIOT ON 11TH APRIL 1919 IN BOMBAY : POLICE VERSION

THE SECRETARY TO GOVERNMENT,

Special Department, Bombay.

POLICE COMMISSIONER'S OFFICE :

Bombay, 19th April 1919.

Sir,

I have the honour to report on the rioting in Bombay on Friday 11th April.

1. I enclose the Head Office diary and the C. I. D. diaries connected with the events of Friday

11th April giving the detailed reports of passing events as they were received on the telephone.

2. I add the following remarks on the salient features of the rioting, and the events which

immediately preceded it.

EVENTS IMMEDIATELY PRECEDING THE RIOTING

3. I shall not here discuss the general aspects of the violent agitation which has been going on for. some years in the press and on the platform in innumerable articles and speeches designed to bring Government into hatred and contempt. They have been reported to Government from week to week. It is necessary however to refer to the gradual approach to the present point of culmination in the Satyagraha movement, in which the Bombay Chronicle as an organ and its Editor, Horniman, as an individual have played leading parts. After the spectacular success of the

demonstration of Black Sunday (April 6th) reported last week, the leaders of the movement decided, as Gandhi's speeches had foretold, that they had shown their power sufficiently, and that their Satyagraha had penetrated the masses sufficiently for them to proceed to the next step, the open violation of laws. To understand the real nature of this movement, of which Gandhi is the transitory figurehead, it is necessary to study in detail the character and speeches of the men who have come to the surface in connection with it, as well as the large political movements which have preceded it both in Bombay and elsewhere in India. Speaking generally, it may be said that Gandhi, Jamnadas Dwarkadas, Umer Sobhani, Horniman and the rest of the Satyagraha leaders are either agitators pure and simple or men of no weight. There is no one with any pretentions to statemanship among them.

4. I enclose reports on recent speeches at meetings held in Bombay on the 4th, 5th and 6th at which Gandhi was present.

GANDHI'S SPEECH

On the 4th was a meeting of mill-hands near the Elphinstone Mill at which Raut, a jobber, Gandhi, Mrs. Naidu, Horniman and Dr. Savarkar were the speakers. The meeting was clearly designed to spread the movement among the mill-hands ; and, though the speakers were more guarded in their remarks than they have sometimes been, and though Gandhi told the mill-hands not to come out

on Sunday unless they could obtain leave from their masters, there is nothing to refute that. (Gandhi told me at an interview on the 11th that he had no intention of bringing the mill-hands into the movement" probably for many a long day ".). In his speech on this occasion Gandhi made it clear that he desired the mill-hands to stop work on Sunday the 6th and that he hoped that the result of Sunday would be to secure strength to break the laws.

5. The keynote of Mrs. Naidu's speech is " We are all

poor people earning a few annas a day. We do not understand politics. We understand what we mean by our honour. In fighting the Rowlatt Bills we are fighting for our honour (izzat) ". She told the mill-hands that the Rowlatt Act trampled underfoot their right of independence, and that by passing it Government made them slaves.

6. Savarkar's speech is distinctly inciting.

7. On the 5th, Gandhi spoke at a ' meeting of the residents of Dana Bunder' at Baroda Street, Wari Bunder, Bombay. He said that Satyagraha, a new principle in politics, aims at reaching the goal and admits of no acceptance of anything less. (He did not make it clear what the goal was but he said " We have resolved to fight for our goal on the strength of truth even until we are overpowered by death. We shall die but we shall fight for our goal").

8. He remarked on dissensions which had up to then prevailed and said that from the next day (Sunday) a new policy would be adopted. He evidently referred to the plan for the Hindu-Mohammedan fraternisation in the Sonapur Musjid. He said that Sunday was preparation for breaking laws—" any laws we like and in such manner as we think fit", and the " The Rowlatt Act is a wrong one we propose to break it". No disorder must take place. At Delhi the mistake of using force was made. However Delhi acquitted herself well and would be immortalised in history. Munshiram and Ajmal Khan displayed ' bahaduri'.

It is important to note that this speech was not reported in the " Chronicle ".

MEETING ON THE 6TH APRIL AT CHOWPATTI

9. On the 6th at the morning meeting at Chowpatti Gandhi was the only speaker.

The following three points are important: —

(1) He gives the reason for not taking the Swadeshi vow on that day in that place as being that it is not advisable to have two irons in the fire.

(2) He attacks the authorities over the rioting at Delhi and says "the more heartless the authorities the more welcome, as Satyagrahis have resolved to die for truth.".

(3) He says no laws were to be broken that Sunday as the people were not trained sufficiently.

10. The question is what reasons induced Gandhi to postpone the Swadeshi vow. It would undoubtedly have been dangerous to his purpose as being likely to lead to an outbreak of racial feeling. His main purpose was to secure an effect by interfering with public life to the greatest possible extent on that day without causing disorder which would lead to action by the authorities before the movement had time to grow. It is for a similar reason that a Sunday was chosen. It was the day for the maximum of effect with the minimum risk of friction.

11. There are reasons for supposing that the bringing of the Swadeshi phase of the movement into prominence has been forced on Gandhi and the leaders by the Extreme element before they are prepared to do so.

THE SONAPUR MEETING

12. The next meeting of importance was that at the Sonapur Musjid which was followed by rowdyism and the holding up of tramcars as mentioned last week. The real facts of this meeting have not been fully ascertained yet. But it is beyond dispute that the speeches, particularly that of Mrs. Naidu, were very exciting. It is said that her reference to the martyrdom of Immam Hussain brought tears to the eyes of some among her audience—and this from the lips of a woman and a Hindu. There was no direct incitement to violence, no out spoken directions to take definite action. On the other hand the usual cautions not to use violence were not given. This fact is more than significant.

THE FRENCH BRIDGE MEETING

13. At the meeting at French Bridge on the evening of the 6 th Jinnah, Sir Dinshaw Petit, Natarajan and Baptista were the speakers.

Their speeches were more in the nature of constitutional politics than those of any other meeting of this campaign.

Mr. John Scurr, who was present, is mentioned by Baptista as a " Stalwart of the Labour Party". He is an official of the British Auxiliary of the Home Rule for India League.

THE NEXT STEP : THE BREAKING OF LAWS

14. Sunday's success was immediately followed by the publication of' proscribed' literature and the publication of an unregistered ' newspaper'. Gandhi sent me a copy of the paper and Umar Sobhani and Mrs. Naidu called at my bungalow in my absence with copies of ' Hind Swaraj '. Unfortunately neither of these moves brought their authors within the four corners of the law, and no action has therefore been taken by the Police. Reprints of the four pamphlets have been sold during the week on the streets of Bombay. The opinion spread rapidly that Gandhi was openly breaking the law and that Government was powerless to deal with him. The Bombay Chronicle, the ' Satyagraha organ ', made it clear that the breaking of the Press Act as only a preliminary to serve as training for breaking other laws.' It was clear to everyone that eventually if the movement progressed as it had commenced the Satyagrahis hoped to increase the following as they widened the circle of laws which it was their pleasure to break, until they were in a position to paralyse the whole administration. Moderate and loyal Indians began to show signs of general alarm. More than one implored the authorities to take action.

15. Gandhi left Bombay for Delhi on the 8th (Tuesday).

16. On the 9th April he issued a message in connection with the vow of Swadeshi in the Hindustan newspaper to the following effect: —

Although the people were very eager to take the Swadeshi vow, he felt that they had not fully grasped the difficulties that lay in the way of the observance of that vow. To take the vow in respect of all articles was an impossibility. He was of opinion that the Swadeshi vow could safely be taken in respect of cotton, silk and woollen clothes of daily wear. To observe successfully this vow to this limited extent would entail various hardships. The people had committed "a grave sin by encouraging the use of foreign clothes. There would be hardly any difficulty about the supply of cloth made in the country. Honesty and abstinence were essential qualities for the observance of the vow. It was also necessary to burn all foreign clothes and to observe the Swadeshi vow suggested by him, to purify the people from the grave sin committed by them in using foreign cloth. They should also understand the difference between " Swadeshi" and " Boycott". The former was a religious aspiration and the natural duty or every individual while the latter was a sort of punishment and a malicious aspiration." Boycott" would bring harm to the public. The Satyagrahi should not take part in the movement. According to him the limited Swadeshi vow could be properly taken as under:—

"In the name of God from this day I will make use of cloth made of cotton, silk or wool of India for my purpose. I will abstain from using foreign cloth and I take a vow that I will burn to ashes all the foreign clothes that I have."

He hoped that many men and women would try to keep this vow. There should be no haste in taking it. His earnest desire was to see the foundation of Swadeshism deeply rooted. He was of opinion that such movements could easily be pushed when the Satyagraha movement was in full swing.

It is to be noted that this vow was not published or mentioned in the chronicle till a much later date.

GANDHI'S ARREST : THE EFFECT OF THE NEWS

17. On the 10th the Bombay Chronicle published a Special Supplement announcing his arrest. Satyagrahis immediately went through the streets calling upon people to shut their shops. Mahom-medans were seen taking part in this movement. The cloth merchants of the Mulji Jetha Market met to arrange for the closing of shops. The Colaba Cotton bazar closed. It was proposed to close the Share Bazar for 8 days and to raise subscriptions for the employees during that period. The value of certain shares such as the Simplex Mills fell immediately.

DISORDER AND RIOTING

18. About 10 p.m. crowds collected near Pydhowni and commenced to interfere with tram cars. They were dispersed by the Police without any difficulty.

19. On Friday morning there were unmistakable signs of trouble brewing. Shops were closed and crowds were seen loitering about in the neighbourhood of Phydhowni, Buleshwar and Abdul Rehman street.

20. By 10 a.m. reports had been received that trams were being stoned and passengers forced to alight on Kalbadevi Road and at Buleshwar and that shops which had kept open were being stoned at Maharbourie. The local Police were able to deal v/ith the situation until 11-30 a.m., when things became critical. I sent Mr. Sharp out to reinforce the Police at Pydhowni with 25 Armed Police, and ordered out a posse of the Mounted Police. I also asked the General Officer Commanding to establish a military reserve at Head Quarters and to order a Squadron of Cavalry to come down Parel Road and Frere Road from their camp at the Race Course. Meanwhile reports had come in to the effect that trams were being stoned and labour carts overturned on Frere Road. I despatched 25 Armed Police to

that area under a European Officer who were able, without much difficulty, to restore order.

21. Mr. Sharp however, reported from Pydhownie that the temper of the crowds in that locality was extremely ugly and that they were getting out of hand. The Mounted Police were compelled to charge on four or five occasions, but the effect of this manoeuver was very transitory and the crowds returned to the charge with redoubled fury. On receipt of this information I proceeded to Pydhownie" with 2 platoons of Indian Infantry while 2 platoons marched up Abdul Rehman street to the same point. The focus of the disturbance gradually moved from Pydhownie down Abdul Rehman street and finally remained at the junction of Abdul Rehman street and Nagdevi street. At this point the mob was extremely rowdy. Large boulders were repeatedly placed on the tram lines and the cars were heavily stoned. An attempt had previously been made to overturn the lorry in which the Armed Police reinforcements were proceeding to Pydhownie by flinging a heavy wooden sleeper in front of the lorry, and this manoeuvre was over and over again repeated with a view to derailing tram-cars. The mob steadfastly refused to obey the orders of the Magistrates to disperse, but contented themselves with retreating to a safe distance whence they could stone the Police with impunity. The Mounted Police made a few more charges, but the result was very evanescent. Matters culminated at about 3 p.m. when the stoning became very violent. Vigorous batton charges by the unarmed Police, who effected a number of arrests, afforded some temporary relief, but it was clear that the mob was growing in numbers and becoming more violent. I, therefore, asked that Cavalry patrols should be sent out in the hope that the crowds would be forced into movement."

GANDHI'S RETURN TO BOMBAY

22. There had been ample grounds to justify the use of fire-arms at many stages during the riot, but I was anxious

to delay taking this extreme step to the utmost limit in the hope that news of Gandhi's return to Bombay and of his release from custody would have a calming effect. This news was being bandied about from 2 p.m. but at first it was not credited.

GANDHI AT PYDHOWNIE

23. At about 2-30 p.m. Umar Sobhani appeared in Abdul Rehman Street in his motor. His arrival was the signal for a great demonstration. He asked my permission to announce to the crowds that Gandhi was in Bombay, a free man, and that he would address a public meeting at Chowpatti that evening. I gave permission for the proposed meeting and Umar Sobhani announced the fact from the running board of his car. There was at once a general cry ' to Chowpatti', but few moved. At this juncture the Cavalry patrol arrived. Their appearance was the signal for a fresh out burst of stone-throwing and a number of troopers were hit. The cavalry continued to patrol the streets for some 2 hours and were on occasions compelled to charge the mob, particularly when they were belabouring a British Officer and two troopers who had been unhorsed. Shortly after this incident Gandhi himself appeared at Pydhownie in a motor car. His attempt to control the crowd was futile and his appearance had little or no effect on their rowdyism. He announced that he was shortly to address a gathering at Chowpatti and left Pydhownie for Abdul Rehman street. A cordon of Armed Police had, earlier in the day, been drawn up across the road at this point with orders to permit no one to enter Abdul Rehman street. When Gandhi was held up, the crowd were extremely angry and the Police Officer in charge of the armed Police, seeing the road clear and the cavalry in possession, used his discretion and allowed him to pass. When the cavalry saw the exeited crowd coming down they assumed that the Police had been overwhelmed and charged the crowd. Gandhi escaped from his motor into a neighbouring house and the crowds dispersed in all directions. Reports show that the crowd was at this moment

in a state of frenzy. They were dancing along with Gandhi's car, waving their arms and shouting with all the appearance of fanatics. From this point, the disturbance gradually lessened in intensity until about 5 p.m. when conditions became more or less normal in this locality.

DISORDERS AT GIRGAUM

24. At 5-15 p.m. reports were received that the crowd was attacking tram-cars on Girgaum and Charni Roads. Police reinforcements were despatched from the local reserve and order was quickly restored, 4 arrests being made. After this episode the Tramway Company withdrew their cars to the sheds, where military guards were posted.

25. Meanwhile reports show that a crowd of enormous proportion was assembling on Chowpatti sands and was eagerly awaiting Gandhi's arrival. Adequate military arrangements were made in the locality to deal with any development that might arise, but there was no display of force beyond the customary Police arrangements for regulating heavy traffic of such a nature. The meeting passed off without incident, Gandhi being the only speaker. The crowd was on the whole very orderly. A large proportion were mere sight-seers, hundreds of whom streamed away to the City after seeing Gandhi arrive without waiting for the actual meeting.

INTERVIEW WITH GANDHI

26. After the cavalry charged the mob at Pydhownie Gandhi came to see me at my Head Quarters and complained that the charge was unprovoked and had embittered the situation. The facts were, as I explained to him, that the cavalry had been very heavily stoned, had shown great forbearance and had finally charged when they might have used fire-arms. Gandhi then proceeded to discuss the general situation with me. He would not admit that he had been convinced that hisSatyagraha " experiment" was a failure in view of the behaviour of the crowds in Bombay. I then told him of what had happened at

Amritsar and he was genuinely upset when I convinced him that his movement had degenerated into a bitter racial feud accompanied by arson and murder. Jamnadas Dwarkadas, who was with him, was also visibly perturbed at the news. I extracted from Gandhi a promise that he would not, in view of the serious consequences of his propaganda, do anything to induce the mill-hands to join and, further, a promise that he would see that his Agents did not make any attempt to stir up unrest in that quarter. Gandhi said that he would have to reconsider his position in view of what he had seen and heard and announced his intention of proceeding to Ahmedabad in order to see whether he could be of any assistance in restoring order.

It is interesting to note that while Gandhi has regularly adopted the pose of the interesting invalid when addressing meetings, the Officer in command of the Armed Police reports that he showed wonderful agility and nimbleness in escaping from his car when the cavalry were charging.

THE MOHAMMEDANS INCITED BY HINDU AGITATORS

27. One outstanding feature of the rioting is that Hindus and Mohammedans combined to attack the Police and the troops with showers of stones. There is no doubt that the Mohammedans were deliberately incited by the Hindus who, I am convinced from information obtained from various sources, spread the report that the Rowlatt Bills were intended to enable Government to coerce the Mohammedans and prevent them from giving trouble so as to facilitate the dismemberment of Turkey ; that shouts of" Hindu-Musselman ki jai" were repeatedly raised by the crowd, is not without special significance.

The total number of rioters arrested was 40 of whom 23 were Hindus, 11 Mohammedans and 1 Christian. Three Police constables were severely injured and went to hospital. Many were slightly hurt by stones.

The squadron of cavalry suffered 16 casualties of whom

4 were severely injured and went to hospital. It is greatly to their credit' that they contented themselves with charging the mob instead of firing on them.

An appreciable amount of damage was done to a number of tram-cars.

I would bring to the favourable notice of Government the conduct of the Police of all ranks at Pydhownie. Both Officers and men had an extremely trying day and their tact, patience and forbearance is deserving of all praise. The unarmed Police displayed courage in a marked degree and repeatedly attacked with the baton angry crowds who outnumbered them many times over. The mounted Police were, as usual, invaluable, while the Armed Police displayed an excellent sense of discipline in the forbearance they exercised while being heavily stoned. The burden of responsibility fell mainly upon Mr. Sharp and I cannot speak too highly of the manner in which he acquitted himself. From all accounts Mr. Sharp had ample justification for firing on the crowd on repeated occasions before my arrival at Pydhownie and the fact that he succeeded in dealing with the situation without taking this extreme step rebounds greatly to his credit.

I have the honour to be,

Sir, Your most obedient servant.

(Signed) \

F. C. GRIFFITH,

Acting Commissioner of Police.

ROWLATT BILLS PROTEST SATYAGRAHA IN GUJERAT

I enclose herewith the Satyagraha pledge regarding the Rowlatt Bills. The step taken is probably the most momentous in the history of India. I give my assurance that it has not been hastily taken. Personally I have passed many a sleepless night over it. I have endeavoured duly to appreciate Government's position but I have been unable to find any justification for the extraordinary bills. I have read the Rowlatt Committee's report. I have gone through its narrative with admiration Its reading has driven me to conclusions just the opposite of the Committee's. I should conclude from the Reports that secret violence is confined to isolated and very small parts of India, and to a miscroscopic body of people. The existence of such men is truly a danger to Society. But the passing of the Bills, designed to affect the whole of India and its people and arming the Government with' powers out of all proportion to the situation sought to be dealt with, is a greater danger. The Committee utterly ignores the historical fact that the millions in India are by nature the gentlest on earth.

Now look at the setting of the Bills. Their introduction is accompanied by certain assurances given by the Viceroy, regarding the civil service and the British commercial interests. Many of us are lilled with the greatest misgivings about the Viceregal utterance. I frankly confess I do not understand its full scope and intention. If it means that the civil service and the British commercial interests are to be held superior to those of India and its political and commercial requirements, no Indian can accept the doctrine. It can but end in a fratricidal struggle within the Empire. Reforms may or may not come. The need of the moment is a proper and just understanding upon the vital issue. No tinkering with it will produce real satisfaction. Let the great Civil Service Corporation understand that it can remain in India only as its trustee and servant not in name but in deed, and let the British commercial houses understand that they can remain in India only to supplement her requirements and not to destroy indigenous art, trade and manufacture and you have two measures to replace the Rowlatt Bills. They, I promise, will successfully deal with any conspiracy against the state.

Sir George Lowndes simply added fuel to the fire when he flouted public opinion. He has forgotten his Indian

History or he would have known that the Government he represents has, before now, surrendered its own considered opinion to the force of public opinion.

It will be now easy to see why I consider the Bills to be an unmistakable symptom of a deep-seated disease in the governing body. It needs therefore to be drastically treated. Sub-terranean violence will be the remedy applied by impetuous, hot-headed youths who will have grown impatient of the spirit underlying the Bills and the circumstances attending their introduction. The Bills must intensify the hatred and ill-will against the state, of which the deeds of violence are undoubtedly an evidence. The Indian Covenanters by their determination to undergo every form of suffering make an irresistible appeal to the Government towards which they bear no ill-will and provide to the believers in the efficiency of violence, as a means of securing redress of grievances, with an infallible remedy and withal a remedy that blesses those that use it and also those against whom it is used. If the convenanters know the use of this remedy, I fear no ill from it, I have no business to doubt their ability. They must ascertain whether the disease is sufficiently great to justify the strong remedy and whether all milder ones have been tried. They have convinced themselves that the disease is serious enough, and that milder measures have utterly failed. The rest lies in the lap of the gods, I am yours, etc.

3

Mahatma Gandhi in South Africa

Introduction

Mohandas K. Gandhi, commonly known as Mahatma (Great Soul) Gandhi, arrived in South Africa in 1893 on a one-year assignment to assist an Indian merchant in a civil suit. However he ended up spending 20 years there, attempting to ensure *national dignity*[1] for his people, the Indians, who made up less than 3 percent of the population. Shortly after arriving in South Africa a number of incidents convinced him that action was necessary - for example he was thrown off a train and denied hotel rooms, simply for being Indian. Indians were denied the vote in some states and subjected to a curfew in others. The brutality of the British towards the Indians was evident in indentured Indian labourers being given the option to return to India after five years or remain as *serfs*[2] in South Africa. If they wanted to remain free in South Africa, they had to pay an annual tax of three pounds for themselves and each dependant - the equivalent of six months pay.

When Gandhi left South Africa in 1914, the annual tax had been abolished and by 1920 the government agreed to stop indentured labour from India. Furthermore Indian marriages were validated, having been nullified in March 1913.

So after Mahatma Gandhi's stay in South Africa, *national dignity* had been restored peacefully to his people but how far was this Gandhi's achievement and how and with whose help had it been achieved? This essay seeks to explain this by examining Gandhi the person, the concept of *satyagraha*, the *satyagraha* campaigns and the role of individuals as well as the Indian community in South Africa. An understanding of these factors helps in evaluating the extent of Gandhi's influence.

Historical Context

Until the late 19th century South Africa 'was a typical agricultural colony'[3] and then its 'fabulous mineral wealth was discovered'[4] - diamonds and then gold. Mines opened and to 'recruit the necessary skilled labour'[5] mine owners 'had to offer relatively high wages to experienced immigrant miners, mainly from Britain, Australia and the United States, achieving profitability by using particularly cheap unskilled local (black) labour,'[6] who were subdued by military force. In spite of this a minority élite emerged amongst each non-white group in South Africa.

'The Indians ... occupied an ambiguous position. They were among the exploited and among the exploiters. Most were very poor, having come as indentured labourers under a brutal system that was very close to slavery ... A smaller but more prominent group of Indians came voluntarily to engage in trade.' [7]

This ambiguity was also evident in their rights as they had gradually been stripped of their status as full citizens and denied voting rights.

'The Franchise Amendment Bill of 1896 prohibited any Indians from registering [to vote] in the future, while allowing those already on the rolls to remain. In a few years this eliminated the Indian vote entirely.' [8]

It is worth noting that at this time the black community was also denied the right to vote and participate in their own country as full citizens. They made up 67 percent of the population.

Gandhi, the Man

Gandhi has been described as 'the architect of (the) mighty united front in the struggle of Indians in South Africa.'[9] What type of person was Gandhi that he eventually achieved success as well as peace with his people's opponents?

Gandhi's Honesty

Gandhi was obsessed with truth and from a young age this was his *sole objective.* Secrecy did not feature in Gandhi's life and he 'practised as he preached'. Gandhi was a shy man and although at one point he thought it was a hindrance, he later realized:

> *My shyness has been in reality my shield and buckler. It has helped me to grow. It has helped me in my discernment of truth.*[10]

Because he was trustworthy, people were convinced by his actions and encouraged to follow. His humility made him easier to approach, understand and respect. Gandhi was a 'key political actor' but occupied an 'almost religious position'.[11] He was able to link his politics with his principles and religious beliefs:

> *...my devotion to Truth has drawn me into the field of politics and ... those who say that religion has nothing to do with politics do not know what religion means.*[n]

Gandhi's Humility

Gandhi sacrificed greatly for his people demonstrating that: *All my actions have their source in my inalienable love of humankind.*[13] He believed that an aspirant after a life devoted exclusively to service must... accept poverty as a constant companion Gandhi's willingness to sacrifice everything, his selflessness, made him indispensable to the Indian liberation movement in South Africa especially in a world where 'politics and corruption have become almost synonymous.'[15] Gandhi's inspiration welled up from his absolute faith in the power of love: *What barrier is there that love cannot break?*[16] He felt that service had to be given with *a spirit of joy*[17] and that dispossession of material goods would lead to *all the treasures of the world*.

Gandhi's Weaknesses

Despite the saint-like descriptions of Gandhi, there are aspects of his character that belie this image and present Gandhi as a typical 'Victorian Indian'[19]. He was excited at the prospect of British education, he wanted to be accepted by the British, he enlisted the help of Europeans at any opportunity and he shared many of their prejudices. For example, in 1904, he wrote:

> It is one thing to register natives who would not work... but it is another thing - and most insulting - to expect decent, hard-working, and respectable Indians, whose only fault is that they work too much, to have themselves registered and carry with them registration badges.[20]

This may explain why Gandhi never involved himself in the black South Africans' struggle for freedom and equality.

Another aspect of his character demonstrating that he was 'only human' was his attitude to his wife. He had always expected her to be subservient and autonomously broke his marriage vows for his own vow of celibacy. In the film *Gandhi,* there is a scene where he chides his wife when she refuses to clean latrines (a task reserved for a lower caste) and even strikes her. He was considered 'overbearing'[21] when dealing with her - a surprising reflection of his conservatism in this sphere.

The Concept of satyagrah

Satyagraha is the Gandhian ' philosophy of peace, tolerance and non-violence'[22] and is 'a most civilised and humane form of resistance to injustice, with a willingness to suffer rather than hurt, to love rather than hate the adversary... [23] Gandhi explained the term *satyagraha* thus:

> *Truth (Satya) implies Love, and Firmness (Agraha) engenders and therefore serves as a synonym for force...*

> *that is to say, the Force which is born of Truth and Love or Non-violence...* [24]

Satyagraha was 'an instrument toward negotiating from a power base'[25] and Gandhi 'understood that successes fuelled the engines of resistance rather than dampened them'[26] so always made 'potentially achievable demands'.[27]

The most difficult part of *satyagraha* was *civility* which required *an inborn gentleness and desire to do the opponent good.*[28] The *satyagrahi* must *bid goodbye to fear,*[29] trusting the opponent and never regarding him as the adversary. There is no scope for hatred in *satyagraha* except towards the unjust law itself.

There were two types of *satyagraha* in Gandhi's campaigns. The first, civil disobedience, entailed breaking the law and usually purposely ending up in prison, making the statement:

'I care so deeply about this matter that I'm willing to take on legal penalties, to sit in this prison cell, to sacrifice my freedom, in order to show you how deeply I care.'[30]

Gandhi did not aim to win by overwhelming but by converting the opponent and bringing about 'a change of heart'. Shepard, on the other hand, believes 'there is a change of heart but it's more in the public than in the opponent.'[31] He also believes that there is an element of coercion thereafter from the public, not directly from Gandhi's camp. However the outcome was that Gandhi influenced his opponents.

The second type of *satyagraha* was non-cooperation which meant 'refusing to co-operate with the opponent, refusing to submit to the injustice being fought.'[32] This is based on the realization that 'the power of any tyrant depends entirely on people being willing to obey.'[33] The tyrant may threaten the people with prison or guns but 'the power still resides in the obedience.'[34]

Gandhi, like other non-violent activists, understood violence's negative side-effects:

> *Brute force will avail against brute force only when it is proved that darkness can dispel darkness.*[35]

Violence usually leaves the two sides enemies.

Satyagraha in Practice

The Indian community in South Africa was relatively small and insignificant in relation to the power base of the government at the time. This may be why Gandhi's philosophy was so effective - it was not a mass movement but pressure from a small group of determined individuals. A nuisance more easily dealt with than resisted.

However, whether this approach would work for other, larger groups of oppressed peoples is questionable. John L. Dube, first President of the South African Native National Congress (ANC), an admirer of Gandhi, when asked why the black people did not use the same approach said:

> '... if I lead my people along this dangerous path, we shall be destroyed. The Indian labourers ... come from an ancient culture ... A leader like Mr Gandhi could awaken their latent divinity...and they could demonstrate an extraordinary capacity for self-suffering. Our Negro people will not be able to control their tempers in a similar situation. They will hit back in self-defence and that is all the excuse the whites need to wipe us out. If my people kill one white man in their excitement, thousands of my countrymen will be killed ... we do not have the capacity to take up a passive resistance struggle. The Indians alone are capable of it.'[36]

Certainly other liberation struggles which attempted to use non-violence have nevertheless resulted in violence. Martin Luther King was assassinated, as was Gandhi, himself, in his later struggle in India.

Nelson Mandela, an icon of liberation in the twentieth century strongly believes in the power of *satyagraha:*

'We must never lose sight of the fact that the Gandhian

philosophy may be a key to human survival in the twenty-first century.'[37]

However, considering the long and violent 'road to freedom' for black South Africans, this seems idealistic rather than realistic.

The Satyagraha Campaign

There were three phases in the *satyagraha* campaign and during the first Gandhi stated what was expected:

> A satyagrahi must be afraid neither of imprisonment nor of deportation. He must neither mind being reduced to poverty, nor be frightened, if it comes to that, of being mashed into a pulp with a mortar and pestle.[38]

This emphasizes that *satyagraha* was not the same as passive resistance - the latter implies *weak and helpless*[39] while in the former, although a *satyagrahi* will never kill, he is strong and willing to die for the cause. In January 1908, during the first campaign, 150 Indians went to prison in defiance of the Act and a compromise was reached between Gandhi and General Smuts.

However, government refused to repeal the Act and the second phase of *satyagraha* began during which over 2000 people were imprisoned, many repeatedly. This phase was suspended when the Union of South Africa was formed, in anticipation of a negotiated settlement but once again the *satyagrahis* were disappointed.

During the third phase of *satyagraha* (September 1913) women were invited to join since they had been degraded to the rank of concubines since Indian marriages in South Africa were no longer considered legal. At this time there was a protest march of 2200 people and Gandhi was jailed for the fourth time. In solidarity there was a spontaneous strike by all Indian workers in Natal, the biggest strike the country had ever seen which led to thousands being confined and imprisoned. That these people acted so bravely demonstrates their increasing determination, their faith in Gandhi and belief in the power of *satyagraha*.

The Power of the People

Gandhi has been elevated to the status of saint but his success in South Africa has to be considered in relation to other significant players and the Indian community itself.

Support from Individuals

The campaign received financial and material support from a number of individuals including Herman Kallenbach and Sir Ratan Tata. Kallenbach purchased Tolstoy Farm in 1910 putting it at the disposal of the *satyagrahis*. This farm became their base, encouraging a simple life: 'self-reliance ...discipline (and) self-esteem.'[40] Gandhi was extremely grateful to Kallenbach:

> We have serious doubts as to whether the struggle could have been prosecuted for eight years... if there had been no Tolstoy farm.[41]

Sir Ratan Tata was inspired by Gandhi and donated funds (worth £5000, a considerable sum then) to support the campaign.

Gandhi received support and guidance from Gopal Krishna Gokhale whom he regarded as his 'political guru'[42] and Gokhale saw Gandhi as his 'heir apparent.'[43] Gokhale was 'President of the Servants of India'[44] and 'one of the two main leaders of the Indian National Congress, the leading political party in India.'[45] In 1912 Gokhale visited South Africa to 'help find solutions to the Indian problem there.'[46] The government received him with ceremony and during his visit Gandhi was his secretary. The South African government was 'ever sensitive to public opinion in India'[47] but ultimately failed to honour their undertaking to change the law. In fact Gokhale's visit was followed by a ruling of the Cape Colony Supreme Court, that 'only Christian marriages were legal in South Africa'[48] making Indian wives concubines and their children illegitimate.

Gokhale then 'sent Reverend Charles Andrews, a Christian missionary from India, to assist Gandhi.'[49] This meant that 'the number of white people who contributed increased dramatically'[50] and, ironically, this advanced the *satyagraha* campaign because the prejudiced South African government were more likely to take notice. More political support came from Lord Ampthill when Gandhi visited England in 1910. He was a former governor of Madras and acting Viceroy of India.

Amongst the supporters from British backgrounds was Henry Polak, a Jew, Gandhi's great friend and 'trusted aide'.[51] He features in Gandhi's autobiography as an important influence and he lent Gandhi John Ruskin's book, 'Unto this Last'[52] which apparently changed his life overnight and resulted in the Phoenix settlement[53]. When Gandhi visited England in 1910, Polak visited India 'to appraise the Indian public regarding the situation in the Transvaal.'[54]

The person Gandhi relied on the most was Sonia Schlesin, also from Europe, who was his secretary and 'ran the *satyagraha* movement virtually single-handed'[55] when Gandhi and his other trusted people were imprisoned.

These were some of the individuals outside the South African Indian community who offered Gandhi and his *satyagrahis* positive support in many ways but there were also individuals who were significant at the time and had great influence on the process of empowerment but they were not on his side.

People in Power

General Smuts, in effect, represented the opposition to Gandhi's *satyagraha* campaign since he was the go-between for General Botha, the South African Prime Minister, and Gandhi. Whilst he was described as 'a genius with outstanding qualities, ... whose great spirit guided and influenced the course of world events,'[56] he betrayed Gandhi on more than one occasion.

In 1907 a registration bill was proposed requiring all Indians to be registered and to carry their identity cards with them at all times.[57] Gandhi did not register and many

Indians followed suit. Gandhi was sentenced to two months in detention and he appealed to General Smuts to not pass the bill, 'in return the Indians would volunteer to register.'[58] Smuts broke his promise and the first large-scale *satyagraha* campaign was started with the burning of 2000 registration forms.

The second time Smuts betrayed Gandhi was when he made a promise to Gokhale to remove the tax for the indentured labourers but failed to do so. However, Smuts had to consult other members of parliament and was reportedly unable to convince them. Whilst there is no doubt that Smuts hindered the freedom of Indians in South Africa, he did so with his own version of the truth:

> 'You must do the decent thing that you see you can do next, and whatever you do you must respect the dignity of the human being.' [59]

Gandhi made an outstanding impression on Smuts and, years later, he said of Gandhi:

> ' It was my fate to be the antagonist of a man for whom even then I had the highest respect...He never forgot the human background of a situation, never lost his temper or succumbed to hate, and preserved his gentle humour even in the most trying

situations. His manner and spirit even then, as well as later, contrasted markedly with the ruthless and brutal forcefulness which is the vogue in our day.'. [60]

This was an unprecedented achievement of Gandhi's - he gained the highest respect of his prime adversary and in so doing succeeded in the *satyagraha* campaign.

The Indian Community

However significant these individuals were there would have been no campaign without the support of the Indian community. The bravery and determination of the community as a whole were epitomized by Gandhi's stories of martyrs published in *Indian Opinion:*

> 'Valiamma, the young girl who refused to seek release from prison despite serious illness died soon after completing her sentence; and Harbat Singh, an illiterate 70 year old worker who insisted on serving imprisonment.'[61]

Gandhi said of the Indians in the third *satyagraha* campaign:

> The whole community rose like a surging wave. Without organisation, without propaganda, al l - nearly 40 000 - courted imprisonment.[62]

Considering that the total Indian population in South Africa was approximately 75 000, this was significant. As Gandhi said:

> I believe that no government can exist for a single moment without the co-operation of the people, willing or forced, and if people suddenly withdraw their co-operation in every detail, the government will come to a standstill.[63]

By their concerted and sustained campaign of non-violent resistance to injustice the people gave the government no option but to reform their policies and thus ensured that their *national dignity* was maintained. However, Gandhi was the catalyst - a fearless and inspiring leader who was more than willing to test his theories in 'the clash and conflict of life.'[64]

Evaluation

In this essay I have illustrated the extent of Gandhi's influence in the *satyagraha* campaign in South Africa. Clearly Gandhi was crucial. In examining the contribution of others who aided the *satyagraha* campaign it is apparent that they were all inspired by Gandhi.

Also, one cannot ignore the historical context of the campaigns - the political background in South Africa which polarised the black and white communities as well as the British and the Boers and the larger issue of Apartheid, all indirectly helped to advance the cause of the relatively insignificant Indian minority.

I judge the success of the movement by comparing the situation for Indians in South Africa in 1893, when Gandhi first arrived there, with the result when Gandhi left. However although by 1914 the law concerning the Indians had been changed, the prejudices of the white population were probably still entrenched. Essentially any change is a process which cannot be circumvented - you can change legislation overnight but changing attitudes takes time. Gandhi wrote in 1928:

> When one considers the painful contrast between the happy ending of the Satyagraha struggle and the present condition of the Indians in South Africa, one feels for a moment as if all this suffering had gone for nothing, or is inclined to question the efficacy of Satyagraha as a solvent of the problems of mankind... there is a law of nature that a thing can be retained by the same means by which it has been acquired... If, therefore, the position of Indians in South Africa has now suffered deterioration, that argues the absence of Satyagrahis among them... Individuals or bodies of individuals cannot borrow from others qualities which they themselves do not possess.[65]

What Gandhi probably did not acknowledge at the time he wrote the above was that he, and not *satyagraha,* was the essential factor - the catalyst - in acquiring freedom for the Indians in South Africa. After Gandhi arrived the Indian community's level of consciousness concerning their rights rose and with his departure, it evaporated. This is harsh but they certainly lost heart - Gandhi had been their courage.

The main problem that I encountered in my research was that in most sources Gandhi's role tended to eclipse any other factors in the success of the *satyagraha* campaign. Carr describes this as the 'Bad King John theory of history' whereby 'individual genius'[66] is seen as 'the creative force in history.'[67] So the social and economic forces active at this time - the synchronicities - are given little recognition and the significance of other individuals - like the *satyagrahis* - is underplayed. As Carr points out it is difficult to draw a distinction between the behaviour of people as individuals and as members of a group, because one inevitably affects the other.

Gandhi tends to be portrayed as a saint but his role needs to be looked at in historical context. The blacks - the majority - were particularly oppressed when Gandhi began *satyagraha* in South Africa, and were only freed from their oppression as recently as 1992. Many have criticised Gandhi for racism due to his exclusive focus on the fate of the Indians. Quotes from Gandhi reinforce this point of view:

> Ours is one continual struggle against a degradation sought to be inflicted upon us by the Europeans, who desire to degrade us to the level of the raw Kaffir whose occupation is hunting, and whose sole ambition is to collect a certain number of cattle to buy a wife with and, then, pass his life in indolence and nakedness.[68]

Gandhi appears as prejudiced as those who oppressed the Indians. In fact, one could suggest that Gandhi benefited from the status quo since the 'Indian problem' seemed manageable to the South African government against the backdrop of the oppressed black majority.

Mark Shepard interestingly points out that although Gandhi is often called 'the father of non-violence',[69] 'Gandhi and his Indian colleagues ... were well aware of other non-violent struggles before they adopted such methods themselves.'[70] Some of the more impressive of these took place among the blacks in South Africa itself. So Gandhi did not invent non-violent action but rather was 'the first ... to declare it and then to consciously apply it on a large scale.'[71]

Finally, I acknowledge the limitations of the sources available to me. Much of the material used was based on

Gandhi's own writings and while this provided insight, it also often gave a biased perspective.

Conclusion

Gandhi was an amazing man, one of the few people whose actions, deeds and words were constantly in agreement with each other. Gandhi had 'the marvellous spiritual power to turn ordinary men around him into heroes and martyrs'[72] and thus the legend of 'Mahatma' was created. Even Albert Einstein elevated Gandhi by saying:

'Generations to come, it may be, will scarce believe that such a one as this ever in flesh and blood walked upon this earth.'[73]

So undoubtedly Gandhi played a vital role in the *satyagraha* campaign - he captured the imagination of the people and has continued to do so.

In reality, though, many other factors contributed to the success of the campaign and in some ways, Gandhi may have unwittingly exploited the political situation in South Africa at the time. After all, the South African government could not afford to let the spirit of resistance spread and needed to deal with the relatively minor 'Indian problem' as quickly as possible. Also, in Gandhi's own words:

> Truly speaking, it was after I went to South Africa that I became what I am now.[74]

So in some ways, Gandhi's experience in South Africa was just preparing him for his future career in India. One may suggest that South Africa played a significant role in the creation of Gandhi, the man and the myth.

REFERENCES

1. Gandhiji and Africans in South Africa, p. 4.
2. Louis Fischer, The Essential Gandhi, p. 3 8, term adopted to describe the unpaid labourers in South Africa.
3. James D. Hunt, Gandhi and the Black people of South Africa, p. 2.
4. *Ibid*.

5. Nigel Worden, The Making of Modern South Africa, p. 44.
6. *Ibid.* p. 45.
7. *Op.cit.* Hunt, p. 4.
8. *Ibid*
9. Gandhiji and Africans in South Africa, p.2.
10. *Op.cit.* Fischer, p. 25, taken from M.K.Gandhi, Experiments.
11. Alec Erwin, Gandhi, Workers and The Struggle For Liberation in South Africa, p. 5.
12. M.K.Gandhi, The Story of My Experiments with Truth, p. 453.
13. Mark Shepard, Mahatma Gandhi and His Myths, p. 14. taken from M.K.Gandhi, Nonviolent Resistance.
14. *Op.cit.* Fischer, p.53, taken from M.K.Gandhi, Satyagraha in South Africa.
15. George Woodcock, Gandhi, p. 13.
16. Op.Cit. Fischer, p.42, taken from M.K.Gandhi, Experiments.
17. *Ibid.* p.42
18. *Ibid.* p. 56, taken from M.K.Gandhi, From Yeravda Mandir.
19. *Op.cit.* Hunt, p. 18.
20. Gandhi and Racism.
21. Lorna Wredford, Mahatma: Man of the ages, Man of the times.
22. Gandhi and South Africa, p. 1.
23. *Ibid.*
24. *Op.cit.* Fischer, p.77, taken from M.K.Gandhi, Satyagraha in South Africa.
25. *Op.cit,* Erwin, p. 4.
26. *Ibid.*
27. *Ibid.*
28. *Op.cit.* Gandhi, p.394

29. *Op.cit.* Fischer, p.81, taken from M.K.Gandhi, Satyagraha in South Africa
30. *Op.cit.* Shepard, p. 8.
31. *Ibid.*
32. *Ibid.* p. 9
33. *Ibid.*
34. *Ibid.* p. 10.
35. *Op.cit.* Fischer, p.80, taken from M.K.Gandhi, Indian Opinion, July 12, 1913.
36. *Op.cit.* Hunt, p. 15.
37. Op.Cit.Gandhi and South Africa, p. 1, Nelson Mandela in his speech opening the Gandhi Hall in Lenasia, September 1992.
38. Ibid. taken from The Collected Works of Mahatma Gandhi, Volume 20.
39. *Op.cit.* Fischer, p.78, taken from M.K.Gandhi, Satyagraha in South Africa.
40. Surendra Bhana, The Tolstoy Farm: Gandhi's Experiment in "Cooperative Commonwealth,' p. 5.
41. *Ibid.* p. 1
42. About Gopal Krishna Gokhale, p. 1.
43. The Triumph of Satyagraha, p. 3.
44. *Ibid.*
45. *Ibid.*
46. *Op.cit.* About Gopal Krishna Gokhale, p. 3.
47. *Op.cit.* The Triumph of Satyagraha, p. 3.
48. *Ibid.*
49. *Ibid.*
50. *Ibid.*
51. *Ibid.*
52. This book is a critique of classical economies - it is anti-capitalist and promotes a simple life.
53. Gandhi purchased a farm near Phoenix in 1904 and it was named the Phoenix Settlement. This farm was purchased

in order to establish a communal settlement. It was 'based on the ideals of communal living whereby all persons irrespective of their social standing and occupation would receive an equal wage. They were to contribute to the common good and welfare of the settlement.' Information taken from K.Chetty, Phoenix Settlement.

54. *Op.cit.* The Triumph of Satyagraha, p. 3.
55. *Ibid.*
56. Rose de la Hunt, A Man and his Vision.
57. Burning the registration forms, struggle against the 'three pound tax' and for recognition of Indian marriages.
58. *Ibid.*
59. *Op.cit.* Rose de la Hunt.
60. *Op.cit.* Fischer, p.98, taken from Louis Fischer, Life of Gandhi
61. E.S.Reddy, The First Martyrs of Satyagraha, p.1.
62. Op.Cit. Gandhi and South Africa, p.3, taken from M.K. Gandhi, The Collected Works of Mahatma Gandhi, Volume 20.
63. *Op.cit.* Shepard, p. 10, taken from M.K. Gandhi, Nonviolent Resisitance
64. George Woodcock, GANDHI - The Political, Personal and Practical Revolutionary,
65 *Op.cit.* Fischer, p.98, taken from M.K.Gandhi, Satyagraha in South Africa.
66. E.H.Carr, What is History? p.45
67. *Ibid.*
68. *Op.cit.* Hunt, p. 5.
69. *Op.cit.* Shepard, p. 4
70. *Ibid.* Taken from 'The Politics of Non-violent action' by Gene Sharp.
71. *Ibid.* p. 6.
72. *Op.cit.* Gandhi and South Africa, p.3, stated by Gopal Krishna Gokhale, visiting South Africa in 1912
73. *Op.cit.* Fischer, p. 323.
74. *Op.cit.*Gandhi and South Africa, p. 1.

4

Satyagraha : Meaning and Bases

In a meeting of immigrant Indians, held in the imperial threatre of the South African town, Johannesburg on 11 September 1906, which had been convened by Mohandas Karamchand Gandhi, a young Indian barrister, a resolution was adopted to carry on a non-violent agitation for the withdrawal of the discriminatory and humiliating registration ordinance against the Indians which was to be passed into an Act by the Transvaal government. This non-violent agitation, initially called passive resistance and afterwards Sadagraha and Satyagraha which was first carried on by Mahatma Gandhi in South Africa and achieved some success there was launched in the Indian sub-continent under his leadership through Indian National Congress after his return from South Africa. This movement made India free and Mahatma Gandhi the Father of Nation. Satyagraha, meaning firmness for the cause of truth is as old as human culture. It has all along been a value or virtue in domestic life and inter-personal relations. The uniqueness of Mahatma Gandhi lay in the fact that he used it as a technique for mass mobilisation, for political movements against the injustice of a government. The strength of Satyagraha lay not in application of physical force or brute force but in the application of soul force or moral power. Gandhi preached and practised the glory of moral power and believed, that a single individual, if morally strong, is capable of bringing about transformation in the environment in which he lives. This was a new concept quite contrary to the Western political tradition which relied upon external rather than internal restraints, on institutional rather than ethical limits to control those who held reins of power. Gandhi believed in the importance of private morality in public life and emphasised in the traditional Hindu manner the ethical and not institutional restraints. How did he develop courage and capacity for launching the unique movement, called Satyagraha ? From his point of view the capacity for self control that grew in him while working as a volunteer during Zulu rebellion and Boer war and as the inmate of Phoenix Settlement led him to organise Satyagraha against Registration Ordinance and go to jail. As some scholars have observed, "Phoenix and the Brahmacharya vow were indispensable pre-conditions for his first great non-violent resistance campaign." As he himself said later, "Without Brahmacharya the Satyagrahi will have no lustre, no inner strength to stand unarmed against the whole world ...; his strength will fail him at the right moment" (Harijan 13 October 1940).

The scholars have traced various sources Indian and Western, such as Jainism, Upanishads, Gita, Patanjali's Yogasutra (which he read in 1903), Bible (New Testament), Tolstoy, John Ruskin and Henry David Thoreau from whom Gandhi might have possibly drawn his ideas on Satyagraha. Once in conversation with Joseph Doke, one of his earliest biographers Gandhi told about the early influence of a Gujarati poem by Shamal Bhat. The substance of the poem is - "If a man gives you a drink of water and you give him a drink in return, that is nothing. Real beauty consists in doing good against evil." The story of the mythological Maharaja Harishchandra's adherence to truth and sacrifices, it is said, had deep influence on his mind in childhood. Gandhi appears to have been greatly influenced by the moral character of a Gujarati jewel merchant and poet, named Raichandbhai. Next to him, three Western thinkers - Leo Tolstoy, Henry David Thoreau and John Ruskin exercised decisive and formative influence on him through their writings. Deeply influneced by Tolstoy's Kingdom of God Is within you Gandhi called himself a follower of the former and had correspondence with him. Tolstoy wrote to Gandhi, prophesying that the movement in South Africa which Gandhi was leading "was destined to bring a message of hope to the down-trodden people of the earth." About Satyagraha Tolstoy wrote to Gandhi, "that which is called passive resistance is in reality nothing else than the teaching of love uncorrupted by false interpretations. That love which is striving for the union of the human soul and the activity derived from it is the highest and only law of human life; this law was proclaimed by all - by the Indian as by the Chinese, Hebrew, Greek and Roman sages of the world. I think this law was most clearly expressed by christ who plainly said, "In love alone is all the laws and prophets." On another occasion Tolstoy wrote to Gandhi, "The renunciation of all opposition by force ... means the law of love unperverted by sophistries. Love or in other words the striving of men's souls towards unity and submissive behaviour to one another that results there from represents the highest and indeed the only law of life .... any employment of force is incompatible with love as the highest law of life and .... as soon as the use of force appears permissible even in a single case, the law itself is immediately negatived."

Henry David Thoreau the American anarchist who used the term 'civil disobedience' in one of his speeches in 1849 propounded the theory that maximum of cooperation should be extended to people and institutions which lead towards good and non-cooperation should be followed when they promote evil. Unlike Gandhi Thoreau advocated not only passive but also active and violent resistance to the American Government in the struggle against slavery.

From John Ruskin's Unto This Last which Gandhi read in South Africa he derived the following ideas :

1. That the good of the individual is contained in the good of all.
2. That a lawyer's work has the same value as the barber's in as much as all have the same right of earning their livelihood from their work.
3. That a life of labour, i.e. the life of the tiller of soil and handicrafts man is the life worth-living."

Gandhi's concept of Satyagraha has been criticized (by materialists as well as spiritualists), misunderstood and misused. Some who professed disbelief in Gandhian Satyagraha carried on parallel movements following the fath of violence during freedom struggle. Some people found Gandhi's constant reference to 'God', 'truth' and 'non-violence' 'nauseating' and 'stinking'. Gandhi's Satyagraha is "truth in its dynamic form unattended with violence." Though initially he used the expression 'passive resistance' to designate his movement, subsequently he pointed out the following differences between 'passive resistance' and Satyagraha :

1. Love has no place in passive resistance. It will have no place in Satyagraha.
2. Passive resistance is frequently a precursor of armed resistance. Satyagraha precludes armed resistance.
3. Passive resistance cannot be offered against one's own kith and kin. Satyagraha can be offered even against those one loves.
4. The idea behind passive resistance is to worry and harass the opponent. Satyagraha precludes any such idea.

Satyagraha is the soul force which one can develop and use by the practice of truth and non-violence and faith in God. Now a days many use Gandhian methods like strike and *dharana* without following the norms which Gandhi prescribed for a Satyagrahi such as

1. A Satyagrahi must be truthful. Gandhi regarded truth as synonymous with God.
2. A Satyagrahi must be non-violent. While he himself might suffer, he would not inflict any pain or penalty on the opponent.
3. A Satyagrahi must not adopt unfair means for the achievement of his goal however noble. For him means justify end.
4. A Satyagrahi must have control over senses and palate.
5. A Satyagrahi must be fearless. Fearlessness means fearing and frightening none. Gandhi preferred violence to cowardice, and regarded cowardice as the worst form of violence.
6. A Satyagrahi must not steal.
7. A Satyagrahi should not possess property and make provisions for future.
8. A Satyagrahi must not hesitate to do physical work for earning his bread. He should follow the principle enunciated by Jesus Christ in New Testament - "In the sweat of thy brow shalt thou eat thy bread."
9. A Satyagrahi should be a votary of swadeshi i.e. dedicate himself to the service of his immediate neighbours. According to Gandhi, "The broad definition of swadeshi is the use of all home-made things to the exclusion of foreign things, in so far as such use is necessary for the protection of home industry, more specially those industries without which India will become pauperised."
10. Since all religions converge to the same goal, the Satyagrahi must respect all religions. He must practise tolerance. "Tolerance gives us spiritual insight which is as far from fanaticism as the north pole from the south. True knowledge of religion breaks down the barriers between faith and faith."

11. **A Satyagrahi must not treat anybody as untouchable.**

"None can be born untouchable as all are sparks of one and the same fire."

A Satyagrahi's path is not an easy one. It is beset with throns and thistles. As Mahatma Gandhi once said, a Satyagrhi has to pass through five difficult phases : "First people will greet you with indifference; next they will ridicule you; then they will abuse you ; next they will put you in jail or even try to kill you. If you go through these five stages successfully, you will get to the most dangerous phase — when people start respecting you. Then you can become your own enemy unless you are careful."

Gandhi considered Satyagraha to be a positive movement. During the struggle for freedom he placed before the Satyagrahis a constructive programme. He is reported to have said that "if once constructive work was accomplished there would not be any need left for outward Satyagraha." But in pre-independence situation, because of the compulsion of overthrowing foreign rule the Satyagraha movement had assumed a somewhat negative character and many had accepted Satyagraha as a matter of policy and not of creed.

Now since India is independent and democratic, there are ample scope and necessity for the implementation of constructive works through the methods of Satyagraha followed by Gandhi. In todays Indian society we see contrary trends. While some efforts are being made for constructive work, violence and disruptive forces sometimes seem to threaten the very foundation of our social fabric. In such a situation constructive work needs to be intensified as the only remedy for social maladies. As pointed out by K.G. Mashruwala constructive work will create "proper conditions for the urge for goodness, inherent in man to grow and gather strength to effectively check the forces of violence and to put on the right track man's age-long endeavour to eradicate poverty, ignorance, filth, disease, narrow-mindedness, inequality and open or concealed slavery which make his earth a living hell."

The Bases of Satyagraha

The term "satyagraha " was coined by Gandhi in South Africa to express the force that Indians there used. It was conceived as a weapon of the strong and excluded the use of violence and hatred in any shape or form. Satyagraha is a relentless search for truth and a determination to teach truth through nonviolent means. It literally means holding on to truth. So it is a truth-force. Gandhi calls it the soulforce.3 It can be used by individuals as well as communities. It is also a law of universal application. It is not based on the force of arms, but on the force of truth and love. We are usually aware of two kinds of forces-physical force and spiritual force. We are generally acquainted with the physical force. It consists of violence. It is a weapon of the brutes. Man is more familiar with the physical force which Gandhi was opposed to. The spiritual force is an invisible one. So he described it as truth-force. Therefore, saytagraha pre-supposes self-discipline, self-discipline, self-control, and self-purification.

According to Gandhi, a Satyagrahi is a fearless person. He will never submit to any arbitrary action. He who has attained the Satyagrahi's state of mind will remain victorious under all conditions. So it is belief in the power of spirit, the power of truth, the power of love by which man can overcome evil through self-suffering and self-sacrifice. His Satyagraha related to two things; it enjoins upon man the duty to eradicate evil and, positively, it reminds him of his obligation to serve the community.

Satyagrah is a very powerful nonviolent method of direct action. A satyagrahi exhausts all other means before he resorts to satyagraha. He also uses it as his last weapon against injustice after having exhausted all other possibilities of persuasion and conciliation. It emphasizes four basic ideas: (i) it is essentially the use of soul-force, (ii) it eliminates the use of physical-for him, the practice of

Satyagraha was an evolving science. He preached and practiced it for over three decades. We know Satyagraha is still evolving gradually.

According to Gandhi, is a philosophy of life. It is the religion by which he lived It is also the religion where he wanted all men to live by it. The veteran Gandhian, Dr R.R. Diwakar, says: "Satyagraha is a new way of life. It has several features. For him, Truth and Nonviolence are as hills. But truth through nonviolence alone is really a new feature. Secondly, the application of this principle to every walk of life and all human affairs, and to fight evil and injustice to establish truth and justice, is also one of the new features.

Satyagraha as a weapon of social control is eternal and creative. Its creativity is inherent in its basis of ahimsa and moral persuasion. The Satyagrahi would adopt satyagraha as a weapon and insist of truth being established. He resists all unjust authority and the source of evil. But the aim of Satyagraha is destruction of evil, not the evildoer; sin, not the sinner, whom actually a satyagrahi loves to liberate from the grip of evil or sin. A satyaghahi does not crave or indulge in for personal gain or glorification, or to humiliate anyone. The entire social life is impossible without satyagraha which is a true religion.5 It is not only employed against rulers and ruled,6 but also society and government.7 it is a practical philosophy. It is a weapon with a spiritual and ascetic temper. In fact, it is the soul force attainable by self-purification. It can be utilized in any situation to reach one's goal through nonviolent means. It implies adherence to truth and love. So also the term 'self-purification' singnifies the need for a proper education to create such an attitude of mind.

It is a sin to suffer unjust behaviour at the hands of another person or organization or society. Hence he did not hesitate to carry on tireless crusade against injustice, both in South Africa and India. Therefore Satyagraha may be understood as a technique for resolving conflicts and a method for fighting evil. As been explained by Joan V Bondurant: "Satyagrah became something more than a method of resistance to particular legal norms; it became an instrument of struggle for positive objectives and for fundamental change."

According to Gandhi, Satyagraha is practicable in every situation. The satyagrahi becomes mentally strong by enduring physical suffering. In this contex Gandhi wrote: "I see that Satyagraha is assured of divine help, and that in testing a Satyagrahi, the creator imposes on him at every step only as much burden as he can bear".9 There are no limitations to self-sacrifice. It may stretch to the extent of imprisonment or even death. So great suffering is highly correlated to great relief. The suffering is undergone in the purest form of Satyagraha. There are different forms of satyagraha. These forms may be employed in a satyagraha campaign. These were most commonly employed during the freedom struggle in India under leadership of Gandhi. There are three forms of Satyagraha, namely: (a) non-cooperation, (b) civil disobedience, and (c) fasting.

Non- cooperation means renunciation of the benefits of a system with which we are associated. It involves voluntary suffering in the process of resisting evil. Secondly, it consists of civil disobedience which involves direct contravention of specific laws like non-payment of taxes and so on. The spirit of civil disobedience consists in defying all those laws which are considered unjust. It is an act of civility since it is opposed to all forms of violent and uncivilized behaviour. It is an act of civility since it is opposed to all forms of violent and uncivilized behaviour. It involves disobedience to the unjust. But, it involves obedience to a higher moral law, truth and justice. 10 It advocates civilesed way of life. It opposes all uncivilized acts uncivil and violent. On the other hand, disobedience is to be civil. Finally, fasting is the most potent form of Satyagraha. It is suffering and Self-inflicted. There is a distinction between satyagrahi fasting and duragrahi fasting. Fasting is the highest expression of the prayer of a pure and loving heart. It is a means of resisting injustice and converting the evil-doer. A living faith in God is indispensable. There is no room for lack of faith, anger, impatience or selfishness. These make the fast violent. Gandhi said: "...in addition to truth and nonviolence, a satyagrahi should have the confidence that Good will grant him the necessary strength and that, if there is the slightest impurity in the fast, he will not hesitate to renounce it at once. Infinite patience, firm resolve, singlemindedness of purpose, and perfect calm must of necessity be there. But since it is impossible for a person to develop all these Qualities at once, no on who has not devoted himself to following the lays of ahimsa should undertake Satyagrahi fast",11 Thus these three important forms of satyagraha should act in the application of Satyagraha.

Philosophy is defined as the pursuit of truth. This is par excellence a succinct and sufficient definition of philosophy and accepted by all. Satyagraha is also relentless search for truth. So it is both truth-force and soul-force. We may

observe in this 'truth', there is a great force in it, since Gandhi called it God. It can be used by individual as well as communities. It is also known as the law of universal application. But it is not based on the force of arms but force of truth and love.

The philosophy of satyagraha is a new way of life. For Gandhi, truth and nonviolence areas old as hills, whereas truth through nonviolence is really a new way of life. It is a weapon of social control and is eternal and creative. Its creativity is inherent in its basis of ahimsa and moral persuasion. The satyagrahi would adopt Satyagraha as a weapon and insist on truth being established. That is why he resists all unjust authority and source of evil.

5

The Ethics of Satyagraha and Ahimsa

The Gandhi-King Connection

In his determination to find a method to end the oppression of his people and create the socio-political and economic conditions for justice, Martin Luther King, Jr. read Henry David Thoreau's classic "Essay on Civil Disobedience" while he was a student at Morehouse College. King later became familiar with the work of the Russian pacifist, Leo Tolstoy, who based his pacifism on the resist-not-evil ethic of Jesus' teachings in the Sermon on the Mount. However, we can be sure that it was to Mohandas K. Gandhi (1869-1948) that King owed the greatest debt in his search for the best method for meaningful social change.

Although helped by Thoreau and Tolstoy, King was most influenced by Gandhi, who was himself much indebted to the ideas of Tolstoy. As a result of the confluence of values taught by his parents and grandparents, teachings of the black church, and basic ideas of the philosophy of Personalism as taught by Borden Parker Bowne (1847-1910) and his disciples at Boston University, King ultimately found in Gandhi more than a method for social change. He found the equivalent of a worldview, a way of thinking, relating, and living in God's world. As with Gandhi, nonviolence became King's way of life and was for him consistent with the idea that the universe is friendly to value, especially the highest of all values, viz., persons.

King characterized Gandhi as "the little brown saint of India."[2] Indeed, he considered Gandhi to be "one of the half-dozen greatest men in world history."[3] Looking back on the Montgomery movement, King said that "Christ furnished the spirit and motivation and Gandhi furnished the method."[4] In addition, Gandhi, more than any person in history, according to King, lifted "the love ethic of Jesus above mere interaction between individuals to a powerful and effective social force on a large scale. Love for Gandhi was a potent instrument for social and collective transformation."[5]

Interestingly, during the early phase of the Montgomery bus boycott King was not completely sold on Gandhian nonviolence. While a student at Crozer Theological Seminary, King drove to Philadelphia to hear Mordecai Johnson, then President of Howard University, deliver a sermon on Gandhi.[6] Although inspired by Johnson's sermon, King remained doubtful about pacifism and nonviolence.[7] As a Ph.D. candidate at Boston University he was fortunate to have the Personalist, Walter George Muelder, then Dean of the School of Theology, help him clarify Reinhold Niebuhr's critique of Gandhi's method of pacifism. Muelder's own pacifism was no secret.[8]

However, throughout most of the more than year long struggle in Montgomery, King understood himself to be primarily influenced by the principles of the Sermon on the Mount. The basic principle, love, was the regulating ideal. This suggested to King that there was no place in the boycott for violence, even by those who had been treated most inhumanely by bus drivers and the bus company. Only as the days unfolded in Montgomery, and after Bayard Rustin and Glenn Smiley[9] joined the protest, did King begin to make explicit appeals to Gandhian principles.[10]

King visited the land of Gandhi in February 1959 and

returned in the spring.[11] He had begun seminary in 1948, the year Gandhi was assassinated. Therefore the two men did not meet in this life. However, it is significant that King met Prime Minister Jawaharlal Nehru who was the political leader of the Indian Independence Movement. Nehru and Gandhi had been close friends. Although he accepted nonviolence as a strategy for social change, he did not believe it reasonable and politically feasible to be completely devoted to it as Gandhi had been.[12]

King's wife reports that upon their return to the states he was more dedicated than ever to Gandhi's ethic of nonviolence.[13]

The Dean of Organized Collective Nonviolent Resistance

Gandhi was given the title of *Mahatma* by his long time revered friend, Rabindranath Tagore. The name means '"The Great Soul in beggar's garb."'[14] Although Gandhi chose to wear only a loin cloth in order to be at one and in solidarity with the poor of India, he himself cherished neither the title of Mahatma nor of saint. By his own admission he preferred to think of himself as a Satyagrahi,[15] or a disciple of Truth.[16] Gandhi was too aware of his own humanity and limitations. He considered himself no more a messenger of God than any other human. Nor did he claim to be a teacher. And yet he acknowledged that he could not "prevent admirers from addressing him as teacher or Mahatma.[17]

Of small physical stature, Gandhi was a giant in the things that mattered most, e.g., character, faith in the possibilities of humanity, belief in the power and fundamentality of love at both the interpersonal and collective levels, and commitment to the achievement of justice. In all these things he towered above his contemporaries. It was Gandhi who gave birth to, and endeavored to perfect what may be called *the great experiments in love,* which included his ongoing efforts to perfect the principles of *satyagraha* and *ahimsa,* to be discussed more thoroughly momentarily.

Although considered by many of his contemporaries to be a saint seeking to be a politician, Gandhi said that this was not an accurate description of him. In fact, he was not seeking to be a politician at all. By his own admission he was *a politician seeking to be a saint,* for to him "saint" was too sacred a word to be applied to any human.[18]

Gandhi's ethical system is fundamentally person-centered. That is, its primary focus is the moral and spiritual development of the individual.[19] To develop in this way requires a disciplined and indomitable will in the individual person. It also requires a steady diet of the moral-spiritual disciplines. The individual is to purify the inward self, thought, and conduct. That is, the inner self must be as pure as the outer acts of the self. Gandhi himself was the quintessential model of such a person. But in addition, he rejected the notion that any group of people, e.g., Indians or Europeans, is innately superior to any other.[20]

Gandhi's first experiments in what came to be known as Satyagraha or Nonviolence occurred in South Afrika over a twenty year period, and later in India. Arguably his greatest contribution is his method, a truly "epochal social invention," for the eradication of social evil. Homer Jack made the poignant observation that Gandhi's method of Satyagraha "is *war without violence."*[21] (emphasis added) Although not a Christian, but a great admirer of Jesus' teachings in the Sermon on the Mount, Gandhi declared Jesus to be not only "the Prince of Peace," but the first Satyagrahi. As the Prince of nonviolence, Jesus, according to Gandhi, was "the most active resister known perhaps to history. His was nonviolence *par excellence."*[22]

In addition, as noted previously Gandhi was much influenced by the work and example of Count Leo Tolstoy. "Tolstoy's *The Kingdom of God is Within You* overwhelmed me," Gandhi wrote. "It left an abiding impression on me." Gandhi admired "the independent thinking, profound morality, and the truthfulness of this book...."[23] Further study of Tolstoy convinced Gandhi of "the infinite possibilities of universal love."[24] There is, in addition, some significant extant correspondence between the two men during the Indian struggle in South Afrika.[25] Tolstoy was absolutely committed to the resist-not-evil ethic of the Sermon on the Mount, and so too was Gandhi. Indeed, for Gandhi the Sermon on the Mount contained the whole of Jesus' message.[26]

Gandhi was unquestionably *the dean of organized collective nonviolent resistance to evil.*[27] He was not the first to appeal to and implement the method of nonviolence. He was, however, the first to organize massive collective nonviolence campaigns,[28] and more passionately than any of his contemporaries argued that it was much more than a method for social change.

And yet this frail, giant "braveheart" was himself felled by an assassin's bullets. I can see the headline: THE DEAN OF NONVIOLENCE, MORTALLY WOUNDED BY AN ASSASSIN. At the age of seventy-eight and while in route to evening prayer on Friday, January 30, 1948, Gandhi was shot three times.

Biographer Louis Fischer reports that at his death Gandhi was all that he had wanted to be: "a private citizen without wealth, property, official title, official post, academic distinction, scientific achievement, or artistic gift."[29] And yet in character, moral disposition, and sense of commitment to the sacredness of persons, Gandhi was much more than all of these things combined. Albert Einstein's was an apt description.

Gandhi had demonstrated that a powerful human following can be assembled not only through the cunning game of the usual political maneuvers and trickeries but through the cogent example of a morally superior conduct of life. In our time of utter moral decadence he was the only statesman to stand for a higher human relationship in the political sphere.[30]

Indeed, one wonders where such a statesman may be found anywhere in the world, fifty years after "the little brown saint from India" was assassinated.

In light of who Gandhi was and what he tried to accomplish, not through brute force, but through the force and strength of love in the hope of making the entire world a better, more hospitable place to live, it is appropriate both that we remember and honor him, and that we examine his meaning and the relevance of his work for today and tomorrow. This is particularly important when violence and injustice reign supreme in cities, villages, and hamlets throughout the United States and the world. Although I do not think it is necessary that we agree with every detail of the ethics of Satyagraha and Ahimsa, I do think it necessary that we understand that to think of reality or being as value-fused, or to think of the universe as being friendly to persons and values as I do, means that in the deepest sense the only reasonable option is nonviolence - even when we opt for violence! I say this, recognizing as I do, my own struggle with the relevance of Gandhian ethics at a time when the conscience of church and world is almost nil. In light of this there is little evidence or reason to believe that nonviolence as a method for social change, let alone as a way of life, is a viable option. For on at least one level in order for nonviolence to be successful it must be possible to appeal to the conscience of the opponent, who might well be conscienceless. And yet I remain convinced that if there is to be any hope at all that the United States will survive as a nation, the ethics of Satyagraha and Ahimsa must at least be our guiding ideal.

Satyagraha

Gandhi had been involved in the struggle to free the Indian people in South Afrika for many years before he finally came to the best way to describe their struggle. He and the people frequently referred to their approach as "passive resistance." But increasingly Gandhi could see that this was misleading and confusing, for it implied that they were not actually engaging in substantive actions against social injustices. Gandhi admitted that initially he did not understand the implications of the term "passive resistance." But increasingly he could see that it did not describe the Indian movement in South Afrika.[31] Although they described the struggle as passive or non-resistance during this period, in reality they were resisting, although nonviolently. This was different from the passive resistance practiced by the British suffragettes and those opposed to the Education Act of 1902. For passive resistance in these cases was also compatible with mild forms of physical retaliation.[32] Said Gandhi: "Whilst it avoids violence, being not open to the weak it does not exclude its use if, in the opinion of a passive resister, the occasion demands it."[33] Gandhi's passive resistance was incompatible with all forms of violence. In addition, Gandhi's is a weapon for the strong, while that of the suffragettes was conceived as a method for the weak. These differences were all the more reason that Gandhi felt compelled to find a name that more accurately described the Indians' movement.

It was precisely the confusion of the meanings of the terms *non-resistance* and *nonviolent resistance* that prompted Reinhold Niebuhr's sharp critique of Gandhi's pacifism.[34] As noted previously, Gandhi himself became aware of this confusion. He knew from his own involvement in the struggle against the South Afrikan government that he was intentionally resisting the forces of evil, although without the use of violence. The term "passive resistance" did not accurately depict their struggle. Therefore, when he used the term "non-resistance" to describe his peoples' struggle he really meant to convey the idea that they were in fact resisting, but without using physical force. They had actually been doing for a long time what they did not initially have an adequate name for. In his autobiography Gandhi wrote: "The principle called Satyagraha came into being before that name was invented." He could see that passive resistance meant something different to he and his people and the

English. It was not a term for the weak or for cowards, as was suggested by some of his South Afrikan friends. Nor was it permissible to ever take up arms.[35] In 1920 Gandhi said that he rejected "the word 'passive resistance' because of its insufficiency and its being interpreted as a weapon of the weak."[36]

There was clearly an internal struggle being waged within Gandhi himself as he sought to name and further clarify the meaning of what he and the Indian people were involved in. There was no doubt in his mind that they were engaged in active struggle against unjust institutions and practices. But an increasing challenge was how best to name the struggle. In other words, what term best describes what the Indian people were involved in in South Afrika? Indeed, even Reinhold Niebuhr could say that although Gandhi "confuses the moral connotations of non-resistance and non-violent resistance, he never commits himself to pure non-resistance."[37] That is, Niebuhr was aware that no matter how confusing was Gandhi's earlier designation of the Indian peoples' struggle, they were clearly engaged in resisting social injustice.

Gandhi tried desperately to come up with a more adequate and precise name to characterize the Indian struggle. Unable to do so on his own, he made it into a contest. There would be a prize for the person(s) who proposed a name which best characterized the struggle. Gandhi wrote in his Autobiography: "As a result Maganlal Gandhi [Gandhi's cousin who worked with him about ten years during the South Afrika campaign] coined the word 'Sadagraha' (Sat = truth, Agraha = firmness) and won the prize. But in order to make it clearer I changed the word to 'Satyagraha' which has since become current in Gujarati as a designation for the struggle."[38] Truth Firmness or Sadagraha was a vast improvement over the term passive resistance, Gandhi thought. Satyagraha is even clearer. For Gandhi it is as different from the passive resistance of the suffragettes in the United Kingdom as the North Pole is from the South.[39]

But what does Satyagraha mean? *Satya* means truth, which is very similar to love. Both truth and love are elements of the soul. *Agraha* means firmness or force. This implies the activity of resistance or struggling against. Satyagraha may therefore be characterized as *Soul Force, Love Force,* or *Truth Force.*[40] It is a clinging to truth, no matter what. Under no circumstances can the Satyagrahi hide or keep truth from the opponent. Such a one is obligated at all times to be honest, open, and frank in dealings with opponents. One can demonstrate the power or force of truth only if she dedicates herself to truth. No matter the cost, one must follow the truth, even as he endeavors to be truthful.[41]

Unlike passive resistance or non-resistance, Satyagraha involves conscious, sustained action or resistance against injustice and oppression. Gandhi considered Satyagraha, "the matchless weapon," to be "a direct corollary of nonviolence and truth."[42] Therefore he could say that nonviolence "is an extremely active force. It has no room for cowardice or even weakness." Nonviolence is for the disciplined and strong, and therefore "does not admit of running away from danger and leaving dear ones unprotected." Given a choice between violence and "cowardly flight," Gandhi preferred violence.[43]

Truth "is the spiritual or metaphysical basis of nonviolent resistance."[44] Indeed, for Gandhi, "Truth is God."[45] Nonviolence, therefore, is built on or grounded in Truth or Love. Therefore it makes sense to say that Gandhian nonviolence is *an experiment in Love or Truth.* For the believer in God this must mean that the foundation or the ground of nonviolent resistance is God. For if God is Love or Truth as proclaimed in the Bible, by Gandhi, and by many philosophers and theologians, then it is reasonable to say that God is the ground of nonviolence. This logically leads to the idea that God expects that harm and injury will not be done to persons in the world. According to this line of thought it stands to reason that nonviolence ought to be the sole morally acceptable way of living in God's world.

For it alone is consistent with the ethics of respect for persons and their inherent dignity, which is highlighted in the teachings of the eighth century prophets, Jesus Christ, and Mahatma Gandhi.

On one level Satyagraha is the means to eradicating injustice through the use of Soul Force, rather than through violence or physical force. Gandhi believed that the Satyagrahi derives her power from God, which follows from the idea that nonviolence is grounded in God. Such a one is firmly committed to full-blown nonviolence and all that it requires, including absolute obedience to and dependence on God. Although on one level a method or strategy for social change, thoroughgoing nonviolence is, on a deeper level, a way of living and relating in the world. It is essentially a faith one lives. I shall return to this important idea momentarily.

Steadfast obedience and dependence on God will help the disciple of nonviolence to develop the courage and fearlessness[46] needed both to stay the course and to wear down his opponents in the social struggle through the use of love. "'A Satyagrahi bids good-bye to fear,' said Gandhi. 'He is therefore never afraid to trust the opponent. Even if the opponent plays him false twenty times, the Satyagrahi is ready to trust him the twenty-first time, for *an implicit trust in human nature is the very essence of his creed.*'"[47] (emphasis added) Truth, therefore, is vindicated not by inflicting suffering on one's opponent, but on one's self. The opponent "must be weaned from error by patience and sympathy."[48] Patience may mean long, protracted, self-suffering. For it will be recalled that Gandhi's is essentially a person-centered ethic. At any rate, the ultimate aim of nonviolence is to convert the enemy into a friend, which, as Gandhi found, is no easy task. And yet Gandhi himself claims to have done this very thing with South Afrikan officials such as General Jan Smuts.[49]

It is also important to keep in mind that the effectiveness of Satyagraha is not dependent upon numbers, nor upon the attitude and moral sense (or lack thereof) of the opponent. Instead, it depends upon the degree of commitment, determination, and firmness of the individual Satyagrahi. If just a handful, yea, one person, commits herself to the true spirit of nonviolence as a way of life, Gandhi believed the ultimate outcome of the struggle would be victorious.[50]

This element of Gandhi's experiment in love calls for a willingness to endure physical brutality in the social struggle without retaliating in self-defense. There must be fearlessness as well as a will to suffer. One must, as Martin Luther King, Jr. maintained, be willing to "meet physical force with soul force." But Gandhi knew, as King would learn years later, that the practice of Satyagraha is a *discipline*. This means both that it has to be taught to aspirants, and that it has to be internalized to the point that it becomes an integral part of who one is. The person without the *attitude* or *disposition* of nonviolence cannot be expected to consistently meet physical force with love force. This is an attitude or state of being that is developed in persons who consciously work to develop it. The people have to qualify or prepare themselves for campaigns of nonviolent civil disobedience, for example. This comes only through intensive training, sacrifice, and the will of the would-be Satyagrahi to internalize the spirit and attitude of nonviolence.

According to Gandhi the "man who, when faced by dangers, behaves like a mouse, is rightly called a coward. He harbours violence and hatred in his heart and would kill his enemy if he could without hurting himself. He is a stranger to nonviolence."[51] Furthermore, the ethics of nonviolence leaves no openings for vengeance. "Nonviolence presupposes ability to strike. *It is a conscious, deliberate restraint put upon one 's desire for vengeance.*"[52] (emphasis added) One has to be in the position of willing or intending not to do violence. She must have the option or choice of responding violently or nonviolently. To know that she can defeat the opponent by inflicting violence on him, but to choose not to because of her commitment to a higher force is morally commendable, especially when she retains love in her heart for the opponent. "...Nonviolence...does not mean meek submission to the will of the evil-doer," said Gandhi, "but it means putting one's whole soul against the will of the tyrant."[53]

It is part of the human instinct to react in a self-defensive manner in the face of danger. But think about this for a moment. If a man approaches an innocent person and commences beating him fiercely about the face and head only because he wishes to do so, what should be the victim's response? Some would say that if the victim had the smallest grain of common sense he would immediately retaliate and do whatever is necessary to repel the attacker. And I would say that ordinarily this would be acceptable.

But the ethics of Gandhian nonviolence requires a quite different response. If the victim is a Satyagrahi, and thus has been trained in the discipline of nonviolence, he should willingly and lovingly submit, and endure the vicious attack with Soul Force and be willing to forgive his attacker, even as Jesus forgave his persecutors. The faith of the disciple of nonviolence should be in God, who will provide the power and strength needed to endure the unearned suffering. Gandhi was quite to the point of the matter when he said: "'The Satyagrahi must always be ready to die with a smile on his face, without retaliation, without rancor in his heart.'"[54] By now we can see that Satyagraha is not for the weak and timid, but the strong and fearless.

Satyagraha is the opposite of passive resistance. It involves direct, nonviolent action by an individual or group. The Satyagrahi wishes to rid society and the world of its social evils by way of Love Force rather than by violent means. Proponents depend upon God for their power and strength. Once they catch the spirit of Satyagraha they are willing to die at the hands of opponents rather than defend themselves. Nonviolence is active, and not passive, in the sense that it directly confronts evildoers and evil social structures. It is also dynamic in the sense that the disciple of nonviolence is always engaging in mental and spiritual training in order to be prepared to do what Soul Force requires.

The man who adopts the weapon has to direct it against the evil, not the evil-doer, a very difficult thing to do without a *continuous process of self-purification*. At the same time, he has to see that it does not inflict violence on the other side, but is content to invite suffering on himself. Suffering, deliberately invited, in support of a cause which one considers righteous, naturally purges the mind of the satyagrahi of ill-will and removes the element of bitterness from the antagonist.[55]

Since the process accompanying nonviolence will often be long and slow, proponents must have the faith, strength, and determination to endure to the end. Truth must be combined with nonviolence in order for there to be an effective weapon for justice. In addition, the proponent of nonviolence must be ready at all times to suffer and die if need be. "If asked how he could be certain he had discovered Truth when listening to the 'Voice within,' Gandhi would reply that one's readiness to suffer would tell."[56]

Ahimsa

Gandhi did not come to Ahimsa late in life, but was taught its basic meaning as a boy.[57] His views on it were influenced by his study of the major religions of the world. However, his most mature view of Ahimsa was a result of his own efforts and experiments to determine its true meaning and nature.[58]

Ahimsa goes hand in hand with Satyagraha. Indeed, the two terms imply, complement, and reinforce each other. Gandhi argued that from the time history first began to be recorded humankind had "been steadily progressing towards *ahimsa.*"[59] There is such an integral relation between Ahimsa and Truth that it is impossible to separate one from the other. They are like two sides of a single coin. And as seen previously, Gandhi identifies Truth with God.

Ahimsa literally means the non-injury and the non-destruction of life, and thus points to the necessity of nonviolence. It is a comprehensive principle which is grounded in the unity and interrelatedness of all life, which is why the claim is made that injury to any person is injury to all persons. On the other hand, Himsa has just the opposite meaning. It is the undermining and-or destruction of life. Indeed, it is impossible for human beings to avoid engaging in himsa. For inasmuch as persons must eat in order to survive, this means the destruction of either plant or animal life. In other words, in order for life at any level to subsist it generally needs to feed on something living. Reflecting on this point, Gandhi said: "The very fact of his living - eating, drinking and moving about - necessarily involves some *himsa,* some destruction of life, be it ever so minute."[60] Elsewhere he said that "all life in the flesh exists by some violence."[61] But while there is no way to avoid the destruction of life at some level, *one who is committed to the principle of Ahimsa consciously and relentlessly strives for self-restraint and compassion regarding all life, and most especially human life.*

Gandhi maintained that two significant elements of Ahimsa are *truth* and *fearlessness,* which we also met in the discussion on Satyagraha. One can neither be a Satyagrahi nor a practitioner of Ahimsa if she is a coward, and-or fails to hold firm to truth. "The practice of *ahimsa* calls forth the greatest courage."[62] That the disciple of Ahimsa must love his enemies necessarily implies that he must be devoted to nonviolence. He will always be of the mind to sacrifice his self for the other, and therefore will not even entertain the thought of doing harm to another. Instead, he will willingly give his own life if need be.

Ahimsa stresses the *unwillingness* to cause injury to

life, even when we unintentionally injure a person in some way, as is the case when Satyagrahis engage in a nationwide non-cooperation campaign against a corporation. The campaign may be against corporate executives and owners, but when workers are out of work because of the campaign they and their families may also be made to grieve and suffer because of lack of income. Satyagrahis do not intend to injure others, even when injury is the concrete result of their nonviolent actions. The point is that if forced to decide whether to injure another person or one's self, the disciple of Ahimsa will always choose either to injure self or to allow self to be injured by the opponent. And yet we will see that Gandhi was not a legalist in this regard.

Although there is a coercive element inherent in Gandhi's concept of nonviolent resistance, a point that Reinhold Niebuhr made in his critique of pacifism,[63] and which Gandhi himself acknowledged, the Satyagrahi must not resort to the use of intentional physical or psychological coercion as a means of punishing the opponent. Indeed, because Gandhi did not wish to punish his opponents, he did not hesitate to withdraw from a nonviolent campaign when he believed "that other forces had changed his opponent's position, making him unfairly vulnerable." One such decision was made not long after Gandhi announced that on January 1, 1914, he would lead a mass march from Durban, Natal, in order to dramatize the Indian peoples' desire to regain lost rights. But before the march could take place white employees of the South Afrikan railroads went on strike. Gandhi reasoned that to proceed with the march in light of this development would place the government at a disadvantage at a time when much of its energy, efforts, and resources would be directed toward resolving the strike. Since the ethics of Satyagraha and Ahimsa does not intend to take advantage of, wound, embitter, or destroy a foe, Gandhi, to the chagrin of many, called off the march. Proponents of Gandhian nonviolence seek "to convince the opponent's brain and conquer his heart," said Gandhi. "They never take advantage of the government's difficulty or form unnatural alliances."[64]

In Gandhian nonviolence, then, Ahimsa means more than "non-killing." Gandhi made the point well. "It really means that you may not offend anybody; you may not harbour an uncharitable thought, even in connection with one who may consider himself to be your enemy. To one who follows this doctrine there is no room for an enemy."[65] The disciple of Ahimsa may not injure another either by her thoughts or her words. Therefore Ahimsa means that one is not to offend or injure another physically, psychologically, or emotionally. This is why Gandhi rejected the legalistic and traditional meaning of Ahimsa, which emphasized only the avoidance of physical injury or death. The legalist's view "has drugged our conscience," said Gandhi, "and rendered us insensible to a host of other and more insidious forms of violence, like harsh words, harsh judgments, ill-will, anger, spite, and lust of cruelty...."[66] The non-injury or non-killing of life forms is an aspect of Ahimsa, but the legalists failed to see that it is not the most important. The principle of Ahimsa is violated "by every evil thought, by undue haste, by lying, by hatred, by wishing ill to anybody. It is also violated by our holding on to what the world needs."[67] One might say, then, that keeping love and justice from persons in the world is a violation of Ahimsa, for the denial of these causes harm or injury. Therefore Gandhi argued that in order to be a potent force nonviolence must begin and end with the purification of the mind.[68]

One who is "saturated with the spirit of *ahimsa*" is capable of taming not only the wildest beast, but the wildest person.[69] Therefore, the purist argues that the reason an enemy is not won over is because the Satyagrahi was not saturated enough with Ahimsa. Instead, her nonviolence "did not spring from a living faith," but rather "was but a policy, a temporary expedient." The mind and spirit of the Satyagrahi was not disciplined and purified enough. Refusal to retaliate is not sufficient to meet the requirements of Ahimsa. She must also be free of angry thoughts and speech.[70]

To be a true Gandhian one must develop a "living faith" in nonviolence. Such a faith, even in one individual, will cause the spirit of Ahimsa to grow until it fills the world. Such an individual may inspire an entire people by his example and might even prompt in an enemy a changed heart and mind. Gandhi's faith was "that we will realize the vital *ahimsa.*"[71] This requires that nonviolent action always be accompanied by a nonviolent spirit, attitude, and thoughts. Ahimsa of this type vastly increases the chance that the intended goal of winning over the enemy will occur.

Non-injury or the refusal to hurt any living thing is most assuredly a part of Ahimsa. But Gandhi maintained that this is "its least expression. The principle of Ahimsa is hurt by every evil thought, by undue hate, by lying, by hatred, by wishing ill to anybody."[72] Negatively, then, Ahimsa means non-injury to any living thing.

Positively, "Ahimsa means the largest love, the greatest charity. If I am a follower of Ahimsa," Gandhi said, "I *must love* my enemy."[73] Gandhi's view of Ahimsa is novel in the sense that it is much more than a fundamental theological or philosophical principle. "It is the rule and the breath of my life,"[74] Gandhi wrote. It is the only reasonable way of life, of living in the world.

Thoroughgoing nonviolence means that one must harbor no ill-will toward persons. The ethics of Satyagraha and Ahimsa rejects the use of violence of all kinds, "in any shape or form, whether in thought, speech, or deed," said Gandhi.[75] Nonviolence is the equivalent of pure love. Gandhi believed love to be "the strongest force the world possesses and yet it is the humblest imaginable."[76] God, he held, "dwells in the heart of every human being," and this was the basis on which Gandhi claimed to love all persons, not merely his own people.[77]

Conclusion

From my reading and writing on Gandhi I have come to a much deeper appreciation for the man and his work. And yet I know in my heart of hearts that I am not yet - and perhaps may never be - a thoroughgoing Gandhian. The reason for this, I believe, is the same reason that most of us are not. That is, I lack the courage and possess insufficient faith in humankind at this hour in history. As much as I want to believe in the fundamental goodness of persons and to trust persons unqualifiedly, too much has happened - indeed happens - that has made mine a very tentative faith in this regard. It is difficult to trust even an individual these days, let alone human beings in the mass. Not I alone, but very many of us - even when we won't admit it! - possess tremendous fear of the unilateral dropping of the proverbial guard. And in my own case part of the difficulty is that in addition to my knowledge and experience of the many times my people have been betrayed by powerful privileged Whites in and out of religious institutions, I am much influenced by Reinhold Niebuhr's doctrine of human nature, particularly his emphasis on human pride and greed.

And yet this should not be taken to mean that Gandhi was naive or sentimental in this regard. Having contended for long years against the likes of General Jan Smuts in South Afrika he knew well the human tendency to assert its pride and vested interests at the interpersonal and collective levels. This is why Gandhi was adamant that the ethics of nonviolence does not require "meek submission to the will of the evil-doer...."[78] Instead, because he possessed a realistic view of human nature and the human inclination to both good and evil, Gandhi understood the necessity of the Satyagrahi putting the might of her whole soul against the will of evil-doers. So even as we pause to remember the dean of organized collective nonviolence fifty years after he was assassinated, I am left with questioning mind.

What can we make of this ethic of love and nonviolence

in a country and world where Machiavellianism and power politics reign supreme in every institution, including religious ones? Of what relevance is Gandhian ethics at a time when only select social crises tend to shock the moral sensibility of political, civic, business, educational and religious leaders? For example, I wonder why there is not literal public outrage over the phenomenon of massive intracommunity violence and murder among young Afrikan American males. What is to be made of the ethics of Satyagraha and Ahimsa in light of the many sacrifices made during the civil and human rights movements of the 1960s and where we are today in race relations? Is the Gandhian ideal little more than an "impossible possibility" in the ongoing struggle of Afrikan Americans and others to actualize the inherent right to be fully human and all that that entails in material life-chances?

Gandhi held that "everybody admits that sacrifice of self is infinitely superior to sacrifice of others."[79] But this is a troubling claim. There may be situations in which the morally superior move is to sacrifice others instead of one's self, or to sacrifice oppressors for the weak and systematically oppressed. I question in Gandhi's statement what sounds like a metaphysical claim. If one believes in the infinite inviolable worth of every person as Gandhi surely did, I don't see how the claim can be reasonably made that it is necessarily the morally superior stance to sacrifice one's own life, rather than to take the life of another. If I am morally obligated to respect humanity, whether in self or in others, always as an end and never as a means only, as Immanuel Kant contends in one form of his categorical imperative,[80] then I am obligated to protect and defend my own self as much as I am obligated to protect others. In addition, if I also happen to be a proponent of the Christian religion I must be concerned to protect the poor and the weak, or the hard living. Furthermore, in the case of systematically oppressed groups one cannot reasonably make the claim that it is necessarily the morally superior position for such groups to sacrifice themselves for others, especially for their oppressors.

There is no question that Gandhi's is a tough, demanding, and perhaps impossible ethic for most individuals and groups. And although Gandhi taught that thoroughgoing nonviolence must become one's life breath or a way of life, not even he was a literalist or a legalist. I alluded to this in the discussion on Ahimsa. Although the term literally means non-injury or nonviolence, Gandhi knew that all persons engage in some injury, violence, or death to other life forms. We seem to have little choice in this. However, we have considerable choice in the type or level of life we violate. And yet Gandhi insists that in any case we have to be honest and acknowledge that any injury to life forms - for whatever reason - is a violation of the ethics of Ahimsa. He himself admitted to this when confronted with the problem of monkeys destroying the crops on land he held in common with others. Gandhi wrote about his response to the crisis.

I believe in the sacredness of all life, and hence I regard it as a breach of Ahimsa to inflict any injury on the monkeys. But I do not hesitate to instigate and direct an attack on the monkeys in order to save the crops. I would like to avoid this evil. I can avoid it by leaving or breaking up the institution. I do not do so because I do not expect to be able to find a society where there will be no agriculture, and therefore no destruction of some life. In fear and trembling, in humility and penance, I therefore participate in the injury inflicted on the monkeys, hoping some day to find a way out.[81]

Gandhi held firm to the principle of Ahimsa and was adamant that it is the only reasonable way to live together in the world. But in the case of the monkeys we can see the element of situationism in his ethic. Gandhi knew that moral choice is frequently very complex and that despite our ethical principles persons have to live in and make choices in this world. The challenge is to avoid compromising one's highest principles as far as possible, while making the necessary adjustments in one's practices.

Although there appears to be an opening in Gandhi's ethic for the *moral exception,* it is crucial to remember that one who appeals to this bears the moral burden of proof. In addition, one must not come to such an appeal easily. But if one has to make the moral exception to the ethics of Satyagraha and Ahimsa she should be left with heaviness of heart and conscience. This means among other things, that she has to be honest about having made the exception; acknowledging, if necessary, that there is no way to square it with her presumption in favor of life, for example. Gandhi himself had occasion to experience this both during the monkey incident and when he did ambulance work during the Boer War, World War I, and the Zulu 'Rebellion' of Natal in 1906. And yet Gandhi was forthright in confessing that despite the fact that his was only ambulance work, it was still a contribution to the war effort, and therefore his action, no matter how well intended, was a violation of Ahimsa.[82] In other words, on reflection Gandhi admitted to not being able to square his decision with the non-injury principle. He initially did ambulance work because he reasoned that he was a citizen of the British Empire and benefited from its policies. Later he would say that he could never again support a country's war efforts, especially when his people were denied basic human and civic rights.[83]

The success of Gandhian nonviolence is not dependent on the level of development of the moral conscience of the opponent. And yet the non-purist may argue that it would seem that this must be an important consideration, especially for those who witness the Satyagrahi being attacked. That is, the on-lookers must have a fairly developed moral sense. Otherwise we must wonder about the effect that such attacks on nonviolent protesters will have on witnesses. What, for example, would be the meaning of the beatings sustained by the Satyagrahi if the moral sense of some of the on-lookers is not affected? Or, if they simply turn and walk away? If the on-lookers are morally gutless and unmoved by what they witness, it is conceivable that the attackers will simply beat the Satyagrahi to death. This in fact was the fate of a number of black, Jewish, and white protesters during the civil rights movement.

However, if the moral conscience of the on-lookers is sufficiently developed and sensitized it is at least conceivable that the attackers may begin to feel a sense of shame, knowing that witnesses to their behavior do not approve. If, in addition, the attackers have at least a modicum of moral sense they may not be able to cope with the shame and guilt enough to continue their attack. The optimum hope is that the attacker will be won over by the Satyagrahi.

At any rate, both Gandhi and King argued that nonviolence has a noble end, while violence inevitably leads to hatred, more violence, and bitterness. And yet I am reminded of what Reinhold Niebuhr said in 1935: "Non-resistance may shame an aggressor into goodness, but it may also prompt him to further aggression."[84] Indeed, in struggles led by Gandhi and King it was often the case that the meeting of hate with love intensified already existing evil and hatred. Love begot hate. Nonviolence begot violence and intensified the already existing violence. And so the question remains for us: What is the relevance of Gandhi's experiments in love?

But whatever the case, it seems to me that nonviolence can be a potent and effective weapon in social struggles only if those who see it in action are conscious of their own moral sense as well as the inherent worth of the persons being attacked. On the other hand, I observed earlier that thoroughgoing Gandhian nonviolence is a way of life, and therefore is much more than a strategy for social change. Consequently, even if nonviolence fails as a strategy this does not mean that it is completely ineffective in an ultimate sense. In this regard we may say that the moral effectiveness of Satyagraha is not dependent on the outcome of specific nonviolent campaigns, but on the faith and sense of commitment of proponents. That is, at bottom the ethics of Satyagraha and Ahimsa requires not success, but a vigilant, unshakable faith and determination to live the nonviolent way.

REFERENCES

1. See Jewelle Taylor Gibbs, ed., *Young, Black and Male in America: An Endangered Species* (New York: Auburn House, 1988).
2. Martin Luther King, Jr., "An Experiment in Love" in A *Testament of Hope: Essential Writings of Martin Luther King, Jr.,* edited by James M. Washington (New York: Harper, 1986), p. 17.
3. King, "My Trip to the Land of Gandhi" in A *Testament of Hope,* p. 26.
4. King, *Strength to Love* (New York: Harper & Row, 1963), p. 139.
5. King, *Stride Toward Freedom* (New York: Harper & Row, 1958), p. 97.
6. See John Ansbro, *Martin Luther King, Jr: The Making of a Mind* (Maryknoll, New York: Orbis, 1983), p. 3.
7. See David J. Garrow, *Bearing the Cross: Martin Luther King, Jr., and the Southern Christian Leadership Conference* (New York: William Morrow Company, 1986), p. 43. King himself wrote of this in his first book, Stride Toward Freedom (New York: Harper and Brothers, 1958), p. 96.
8. Ansbro, *Martin Luther King, Jr.: The Making of a Mind,* p. 251.
9. See Sudarshan Kapur, *Raising Up a Prophet: The African-American Encounter with Gandhi* (Boston: Beacon Press, 1992), p. 164.
10. King, "An Experiment in Love" in *A Testament of Hope* edited by Washington, p. 16.
11. Taylor Branch, *Parting the Waters: America in the King*

Years 1954-63 (New York: Simon and Schuster, 1988), pp. 250, 255.

12. See Coretta Scott King's discussion of the India visit in her book, *My Life With Martin Luther King, Jr.* Revised edition (New York: Henry Holt & Company, 1993), pp. 160-161. It is significant that while in New Delhi the Kings met and heard Vice-President Sarvepalli Radhakrishnan talk about his philosophy of life, an experience they thoroughly enjoyed (p. 162). King himself had studied the philosophy of personalism at Boston University. Radhakrishnan was also a Personalist. One scholar has said that his personalism "surpassed the personalists in his philosophy of spirit...," [George P. Conger, " Radhakrishnan's World" in *The Philosophy of Sarvepalli Radhakrishnan* edited by Paul Arthur Schilpp (New York: Tudor Publishing Company, 1952), p. 86]. Like King he emphasized the view of God as personal and respect for persons. Unlike King, Radhakrishnan did not name or declare himself a Personalist. "But this spiritual humanism permeates his thought so completely that he feels no necessity to advance a special plea for personalistic values. For they are implicit in the whole philosophy of the Upanisads and the Bhagavadgita" [Lawrence Hyde, " Radhakrishnan's Contributions to Universal Religion" in *The Philosophy of Sarvepalli Radhakrishnan* edited by Schilpp, p. 381. We get a good sense of his conception of God as personal in his essay, "The Spirit in Man" [Sarvepalli Radhakrishnan, " The Spirit in Man" in *Contemporary Indian Philosophy* edited by Radhakrishnan and J.H. Muirhead (London: George Allen & Unwin LTD, 1966) [1936], pp. 498-500]. Against Plato and Aristotle he likened his God to that of the Hebrews. "He is personal and active in history and interested in the changes and chances of this developing world" (p. 497). His is a God who communicates with persons. In addition, his God is both needed by and needs persons (p. 499), which is contrary to much of classical Greek philosophy. This conception of God is very similar to King's.

13. Coretta Scott King, *My Life With Martin Luther King, Jr.*, p. 164.

14. See Louis Fischer, *The Life of Mahatma Gandhi* (New York: Harper & Row, 1983) [1950], p. 128.

15. Mahatma Gandhi, *In Search of the Supreme* edited by V.B.

Kher (Ahmedabad: Navajivan Publishing House, 1961), p. 238.

16. *Ibid.,* pp. 237, 241.

17. *Ibid.,* p. 235

18. *Ibid.,* p. 241. See also Homer A. Jack, ed., *The Gandhi Reader: I* (New York: Grove Press, Inc., 1961). "Gandhi himself said that 'people describe me as a saint trying to be a politician, but the truth is the other way around'" (p. viii).

19. R.R. Diwakar, "The Relevance of Gandhi" in *Gandhi: His Relevance for Our Times* edited by G. Ramachandran and T.K. Mahadevan (Berkeley, California: World Without War Council, 1967), p. xiv.

20. Charles F. Andrews, *Mahatma Gandhi's Ideas* (New York: Macmillan, 1930), p. 143.

21. Homer A. Jack, ed., *The Gandhi Reader: I* (New York: Grove Press, Inc., 1961), p. ix.

22. Robert Ellsberg, ed., *Gandhi on Christianity* (Maryknoll, New York: Orbis, 1997) [1991], p. 29.

23. Jack, ed., *The Gandhi Reader: I,* p. 37.

24. Mohandas K. Gandhi, *Gandhi: An Autobiography, The Story of MyExperiments with Truth* (Boston: Beacon Press, 1957), p. 160.

25. Shriman Narayan, ed., *The Selected Works of Mahatma Gandhi* (Ahmedbad, India: Navajivan Publishing House, 1968), V:10-26.

26. Ellsberg, ed., *Gandhi on Christianity,* p. 19.

27. This would also be an accurate description of Martin Luther King, Jr. And, ironically, both deans of nonviolence were murdered; Gandhi as an old man of 78, and King as a young man of 39.

28. Andrews, *Mahatma Gandhi's Ideas,* p. 190.

29. Fischer, *The Life of Mahatma Gandhi,* p. 10.

30. Quoted in *Ibid.,* p. 10.

31. Narayan, ed., *The Selected Works of Mahatma Gandhi,* III:150.

32. Anthony J. Parel, ed., *Gandhi: Hind Swaraj and Other Writings* (Cambridge: Cambridge University Press, 1997), p. 93n.

33. Narayan, ed., *The Selected Works*, VI:181.
34. Reinhold Niebuhr, *Moral Man and Immoral Society* (New York: Scribner's, 1932), Chapter 9.
35. Gandhi, *An Autobiography*, p. 318.
36. Gandhi, *All Men are Brothers* (New York: Columbia University Press and UNESCO, 1958), pp.91-92
37. Niebuhr, *Moral Man and Immoral Society*, p. 243.
38. Gandhi, *An Autobiography*, p. 319.
39. Narayan, ed., *The Selected Works*, VI:179.
40. See Louis Fischer, *Gandhi: His Life and Message for the World* (New York: Mentor Books, 1954), p. 35.
41. Parel, ed., *Gandhi: Hind Swaraj and Other Writings*, p. 98.
42. *All Men are Brothers*, p. 99.
43. *Ibid*., pp. 92, 93, 94.
44. Kenneth Smith and Ira Zepp, Jr., *Search for the Beloved Community*(Valley Forge, Pennsylvania: Judson Press, 1974), p. 49.
45. Gandhi, *In Search of the Supreme* edited by V.B. Kher, p. 315.
46. Parel, ed., *Gandhi: Hind Swaraj and Other Writings*, p. 98.
47. Quoted in Fischer, *Gandhi: His Life and Message for the World*, p. 36.
48. *All Men are Brothers*, p. 80.
49. *Ibid*., p. 88.
50. See Fischer, *Gandhi: His Life and Message for the World*, p. 36.
51. *All Men are Brothers*, p. 93.
52. *Ibid*., p. 92.
53. *Ibid*., pp. 95-96.
54. Quoted in G. Bromley Oxnam, *Personalities in Social Reform* (New York: Abingdon Press, 1950), p. 132.
55. Mahadevan and Ramachandran, eds., *Gandhi: His Relevance for our Times*, p. 121.
56. Smith and Zepp, *Search for the Beloved Community*, p. 50.

57. Gandhi, *In Search of the Supreme* edited by V.B. Kher, p. 37.
58. *Ibid.*, p. 37.
59. *All Men are Brothers*, p. 78,
60. Gandhi, *An Autobiography*, p. 349.
61. Andrews, *Mahatma Gandhi's Ideas*, p. 138.
62. *All Men are Brothers*, p. 84.
63. Niebuhr, *Moral Man and Immoral Society*, pp. 240-241.
64. Fischer, *The Life of Mahatma Gandhi*, p. 115.
65. Andrews, *Mahatma Gandhi's Ideas*, p. 103.
66. *Ibid.*, p. 136.
67. Narayan, ed., *The Selected Works*, IV:218.
68. Gandhi, *Non-Violent Resistance* (New York: Schocken Books, 1961), p. 284.
69. *Ibid.*, p. 282.
70. *Ibid.*, p. 286.
71. *Ibid.*, p. 287.
72. Gandhi, *In Search of the Supreme* edited by V.B. Kher, p. 26.
73. *Ibid.*, p. 38.
74. Andrews, *Mahatma Gandhi's Ideas*, p. 142.
75. Narayan, ed., *The Selected Works*, VI:185.
76. *All Men are Brothers*, p. 84.
77. *Ibid.*, p. 48.
78. Narayan, ed., *The Selected Works*, VI:185.
79. *All Men are Brothers*, p. 81.
80. Immanuel Kant, *Groundwork of the Metaphysic of Morals* translated and analyzed by H.J. Paton (New York: Harper Torchbooks, 1964), pp. 95, 96.
81. Andrews, *Mahatma Gandhi's Ideas*, p. 141.
82. *Ibid.*, p. 140.
83. *Ibid.*, pp. 141-142.
84. Niebuhr, *An Interpretation of Christian Ethics* (New York: Seabury Press, 1979) [1935], p.28.

6

Gandhi's Satyagraha : A Pragmatic Linguistic Analysis

Not new to the world, but novel in form and content, the Great Mohandas K. Ghandi developed the concept and a surrounding philosophy on living in *Satyagraha,* which would change the notion of non-violence and transform the already existing idea *of passive resistance.* For Gandhi, there are only two ways of changing human social ills: i.e. either by violence or by nonviolence. He chose the latter as his essential remedy for India's ills, both internal and external. Anchored on truth, love, compassion, patience and suffering, the term was developed by Gandhi in 1906 while in South Africa to combat the traits of injustice and discrimination, influenced by the Christian reading, the Sermon on the Mount, as well as the following verse of the Gujarati poem, which had a profound impact on him as a child:

> For a bowl of water to give a goodly meal;
> For a kindly greeting bow thou down with zeal;
> For a simple penny pay thou back with gold;
> If thy life be rescued, life do not withhold.
> Thus the words and actions of the wise regard;
> Every little service tenfold they reward.
> But the truly noble know all men as one,
>
> And return with gladness good for evil done.

As such, *Satyagraha* evolved as a term that conveys truth and love in the fight against the untruth through a path of suffering, patience, compassion and understanding. It is the matchless weapon— *Satyagraha.*

Existing Meanings of Satyagraha

According to Diwakar, the word *Satyagraha,* of Sanscrit origin, is a compound word formed from *Satya,* which means "truth," and *Agraha,* meaning "holding fast," "adherence," or "insistence." As such, Diwakar observed, it has come to denote the meanings of clinging to truth, holding fast to truth, or insistence on truth. The term *Satya* itself, Diwakar noted, is derived from *Sat,* which means "being" or "that which exists." Thus, the word *Satya,* Diwakar suggested, has come to entail "that which is in accordance with *Sat* or being," that is "truth," therefore, that which is in accordance with truth (1948:1).

As Gandhi explained, "the term *Satyagraha* was coined by me in South Africa to express the force that the Indians there used for full eight years and it was coined in order to distinguish it from the movement then going on in the United Kingdom and South Africa under the name of Passive Resistance". For Diwakar, although he initially used the term *passive resistance,* Gandhi later "felt ashamed of using an English word, which was neither easily understood nor used as current coin by our people". He felt that the movement he had started was essentially different from that of passive resistance and, thus, deserved a different denomination, such as *Satyagraha.* The term *Satyagraha* was intended to express the essence and nature of the Indian struggle: namely, "Truth-Force," or the force born of truth and love or nonviolence (Diwakar 1948:2). In essence, following Mathews, *Satygraha* was to entail Truth-Force, Soul-Force, A Firm Grasp Upon Truth, Insistence on Truth or the Vindication of Truth, as the power of the soul, which fights for what is true in the search for justice, peace, and love.

In addition, according to Mathews, an important symbol used by Gandhi to describe *Satyagraha* was the coin: "one side being love" and "the other truth," thereby describing the two essential sides which form *Satyagraha* . At the same time, for Mathews, Gandhi also believed *Satyagraha* to be "indefinable" in its fullest, as it was conceived by him to be "a science in the making," an ever growing knowledge, which time could not grasp (Mathews 1989:67). As such, Mathews concluded, Gandhi often compared the concept to the sun, which "cannot be adequately described". Thus, this essay seeks to tease out the deeper meanings of *Satyagraha* by employing a pragmatic linguistic approach.

A pragmatic Linguistic Analysis

This section entails a pragmatic analysis of the requirements for a *Satyagrahi* delineated by Gandhi within a linguistic framework. Linguistic pragmatics has been generally defined by Stephen Levinson as "the study of language usage". The subject matter of this essay is pragmatics—an approach that is attributable to language philosopher Charles Morris, who sought to outline the general shape of a science of signs, or *Semiotics.* In its essence, pragmatics is the study of meaning from the point of view of language users, especially of the choices they make, the constraints they encounter in using language in social interactions, and the effects their uses of language have on other participants in an act of communication. The study of pragmatics can be divided into two major categories: (1) *Applied Pragmatics* deals with verbal interactions in such domains as medical interviews, language teaching, judicial sessions, etc., where problems of communication are vital; (2) *General Pragmatics* deals with the principles governing the communicative uses of language, especially as encountered in conversations.

What pragmaticists cover has become so enormous that to discuss all that goes under the rubric of pragmatics in dealing with a relatively short text (requirements for a *Satyagrahi)* is neither possible nor desirable. As such, this essay considers only the main topics in the Anglo-American linguistic tradition that builds directly, for the most part, on philosophical approaches to language of both logic and ordinary language variety. These topics include speech acts, deixis, presupposition, and implicature. A fifth topic is conversational structure, which is not dealt with in this essay simply because the text studied is not conversational.

The alternative approach is called the continental tradition. This approach is broader and includes much that is subsumed under the rubric of *Sociolinguistics*—a discipline that investigates the relationship between language and society.

The term linguistic framework as used here refers to a way of studying various aspects of human language and its interaction with other areas of human culture and behavior. This calls for collecting pertinent data concerning a range of linguistic phenomena, observing the patterns which underlie those phenomena, and expressing the observed regularities by means of certain linguistic rules.

By delineating the pragmatic features of the requirements, their philosophical symbolic meanings are teased out. According to Roger Cobb and Charles Elder, "a symbol is any object used by human beings to index meanings that are not inherent in, nor discernible from, the object itself" (1983:28). This is important because symbols, as some scholars have observed, are critical in promoting social integration, fostering legitimacy, inducing loyalty, gaining compliance, and providing citizens with security and hope.

Also, an examination of the requirements for a *Satyagrahi* text clearly shows that like other textual symbols, it also conveys not only surface contents, but a great deal of auxiliary contents as well. Thus, the major thesis in this essay is the following: Analyses of peace philosophies or other textual symbols that fail to account for pragmatic features risk ignoring relevant contents that may be central to the texts' meanings.

Consequently, this essay is also about the possibility

that significant *functional* explanations of textual symbols can be evaluated using linguistic features. The essence of an approach of this nature was captured by Stephen Levinson when he suggested the following:

> Most recent linguistic explanations have tended to be internal to linguistic theory: that is to say, some linguistic feature is explained by reference to other linguistic features, or to aspects of the theory itself. But there is another possible kind of explanation, often more powerful, in which some linguistic feature is motivated by principles outside the scope of linguistic theory.

Thus, by employing pragmatic approaches to analyze the requirements for a *Satyagrahi,* the ideas underlying its text can be illuminated. This is possible because in the study of linguistic texts, as in the study of physics, special instruments, formulae, and laboratories beyond the grasp of the uninitiated can be utilized. Because one trained in linguistics possesses analytical skills and tools, and concepts that permit insights into the nature of language in general, s/he is in a better position than other analysts to explain the formal linguistic structures which constitute cues as to how Gandhi's requirements for a *Satyagrahi* can be interpreted.

Thus, the major questions probed in this essay are the following: (1) What salient pragmatic features are imbedded in the text of the requirements for a *Satyagrahi?* (2) How can the delineated pragmatic features be explained? In exploring these questions, the systematic application of discovery procedures well known in linguistic pragmatics will help to uncover propositions that will illuminate the text examined for current readers.

The following are Gandhi's requirements for a *Satyagrahi* :

1. He must have a living faith in God.
2. He must believe in truth and non-violence as his

creed and, therefore, have faith in the inherent goodness of human nature which he expects to evoke by his truth and love expressed through his suffering.

3. He must be leading a chase life and be ready and willing for the sake of his cause to give up his life and his possessions.
4. He must be a habitual khaki-wearer and spinner.
5. He must be a teetotaler and be free from the use of other intoxicants.
6. He must carry out with a willing heart all the rules of discipline as may be laid down from time to time.
7. He should carry out the jail rules unless they are especially devised to hurt his self-respect.

Historical Context of Satyagraha

The major purpose of this subsection is to discuss the historical context within which *Satyagraha* was developed by Gandhi. It is anticipated that this context will provide some background information that will help to account for the types of pragmatic meanings embedded in the text. Before doing so, however, it makes sense to begin with a discussion of the essence of historical context.

According to David and Chava Nachmias (1981:87), the historical method involves the examination of related events occurring during the time the main event being studied took place. The strength of the historical method, as Babbie (1992:312) has pointed out, hinges on the fact that it is a qualitative approach employed to master many subtle details. The main sources for observation and analysis are historical records.

However, as Kaplan argued more than 30 years ago, "the historian does not provide us with a picture of the past, a representation of it 'as it really was' apart from any interpretations of his own; neither does any other scientist with respect to his subject matter". This is not to suggest, according to Kaplan, "that the historian must engage in the process of interpretation even to arrive at what are distinctively his data does not mean that his findings are doomed to subjectivity" (1964:361). Indeed, what the historian deals with is an affirmation about the event—an interpretation of an act as a certain act—that constitutes for the reader a historical fact.

In terms of textual analysis, Patterson suggested that the new interest in history stems from a polemic: "it derives its energy from a conviction that literary texts have always been, more or less, products of their historical, social, political, and economic environments and that they cannot be understood unless one attempts to re-situate them within those conditions". Thus, it is the historicist's job to interpret texts in light of their original contexts.

Also, Hume identified four aspects of the historicist's enterprise in interpreting literary texts. These four aspects are: (1) the collection of new facts and primary materials, (2) the contextual interpretation of facts, (3) the application of context to text, and (4) making contexts from texts. Going from text to context, according to Hume, "helps sensitize us to the original, the abnormal, the subversive".

Indeed, without the notion of *context,* there would be no theory of pragmatics. This is one reason pragmatics calls for some explicit characterization of the concept of context, despite the difficulty encompassed in such an activity. This truism is captured by Schiffrin when she posited that Discourse markers, contextualization cues, and sociolinguistic variables all have a contextual-izing function. The markers are clues to the local contexts of utterances, contextualization cues to the interpretive schemas within which communicative intent is situated, and sociolinguistic variables to the social and expressive meanings of self, other, and situation. But because discourse markers are functionally linked to these other devices, the study of all these devices together can provide an emic guideline to speakers' contextualization of language at several different levels at once.

For ethnomethodologists in particular, the analyzability of actions in context as a practical accomplishment is a must. As Garfinkel insisted, this must be the case because "not only does no concept of context-in-general exist, but every use of context without exception is itself essentially indexical". Ethnomethodologists are interested, therefore, less in he contribution to the conversational system made by the specific identities of the speakers and more in the contribution of immediate conversational context.

As Heritage stated, the significance of a speaker's communicative action is doubly contextual in both *context-shaped* and *context-renewing*. Furthermore, he suggested that while these aspects of context are traceable to Garfinkel's notions of indexical and reflexive characteristics of talk and action, they have also found some parallel expression in Goffman's more enthnographically-oriented studies.

For Goffman, context helps an analyst to rule out unintended meanings and suppress misunderstandings. And that the immediate surrounding could not have this power apart from the cultural competence of interpreters. In addition, he noted that the correct interpretation of any statement may have as one of its implications the saving of the interpreter from exposure as someone who presumes cultural and linguistic competence s/he does not possess.

This way of conceptualizing context can be thought of as a process whereby the native speaker of a given language produces contextually appropriate and internally coherent utterances—a process which involves a lot more than knowledge of the language system. Thus, the factors identified by a system's framework as contextual must be those factors that determine the native speaker's production and interpretation of utterances in actual activities of use.

Another notion of context in Goffman's work (even though he did not call it so) is a *physical* one: the role *of setting* in performance. According to Goffman, *setting* includes furniture, decor, physical layout, and other background items which provide the scenery and stage props for the spate of human action. *Setting* stays put, geographically speaking, so that those who use it as part of their performance cannot begin their act until they have brought themselves to the appropriate place and must end their performance upon their departure. Goffman's formulation of context is, indeed, pragmatic: It covers the identities of participants, the temporal and spatial parameters of speech events, the knowledge and metaknowledge, intentions and beliefs of the participants in those speech events. This makes context paramount in any analysis of meaning.

When Gandhi, as leader of the South African Indian Congress, a political party he formed in 1894, developed his philosophy of *Satyagraha* in South Africa in 1906, the country was in turmoil. The Bambatha Rebellion was underway in Natal. The Brtish also granted colonial self-government to the Transvaal during that year, followed by the giving of the same status to the Orange Free State the subsequent year. This led to the creation of the Union of South Africa comprising of the four White settler colonies (Cape, Natal, Orange Free State and the Transvaal) in 1910, with Whites having complete power.

As Thompson and Prior pointed out, the Natal government operated exclusively in the interest of the White community. The partisan tax laws coupled with the partisan administration led to the small but alarming Bambatha Rebellion by the Africans.

Magubane cited Edward Roux's characterization of the rebellion and the changeover from armed resistance to political struggle as follows:

> The Bambatha Rebellion in Natal in 1906 may very well be taken as the turning point between two periods

in the history of the black man in South Africa: The early period of tribal wars and fights against white invaders which ended in the loss of the country and the reduction of the Bantu to the status of an internal proletariat; and the second period, one of struggle for national liberation and democratic rights within the framework of present-day South Africa, where black and white intermingle in complex economic and political relationships. During the first period the Bantu fought as isolated tribes and on military lines. Though they did not meet the whites on equal terms, but opposed shield and assegai to the rifle and machine gun, at least they met them as members of independent tribes or nations having their own territory and military organization.

In essence, 1906 was a year of melancholy strain. While Gandhi was developing his philosophy of *Satyagraha,* most non-Whites in South Africa were far from ready to entertain a philosophy of passive resistance while they were being killed and oppressed by Whites. Even Indians were suffering from South African Prime Minister General Jan Smuts' discriminatory measures against them, forcing some Indian leaders to later join the Communists.

Deixis

In this subsection, the deixis embedded in the text of the requirements for a *Satyagrahi* are discussed. The word *deixis,* as Lyons pointed out, comes from a Greek word meaning "pointing" or "indicating" and "is now employed in linguistics to refer to the function of personal and demonstrative pronouns, of tense and of a variety of other grammatical and lexical features which relate utterances to the spatio-temporal co-ordinates of the act of utterance". Thus, as Levinson later observed, the single most obvious way in which the relationship between language and context is reflected in the structures of languages is through deixis. Essentially, according to Levinson, deixis deals with the ways in which languages encode or grammaticalize features of the *context of utterance* or *speech event* and, therefore, also deals with ways in which the interpretation of utterances hinges upon the analysis of that context of utterance). As Hoffman later stated, deictic or pointing words exist in all languages and are very useful for "referring" to objects around us.

Combining traditional and contemporary categorizations of deixis, Levinson has developed the following five categories within which they can be subsumed:

(1) *Person deixis* encodes the *role* of participants in a speech event in which the utterance inquestion is delivered—i.e. *first person* encodes the speaker's reference to her/himself, *second person* encodes the speaker's reference to one or more addresses, and *third person* encodes the reference of persons and entities which are neither speakers nor addresses of the utter ance in question.

(2) *Place or Space deixis* encodes spatial location *relative* to the location of the participants in the speech events—i.e. *proximal* encodes closeness to speaker, and *distal* encodes non-proximal or sometimes closeness to the addressee.

(3) *Time deixis* encodes temporal points and spans *relative* to the time at which an utterance was spoken, or a written message inscribed—this time is referred to as *coding time* or CT, which is distinct from *receiving time* or RT.

(4) *Discourse or Text deixis* encodes reference to portions of the unfolding discourse in which the utterance, which includes the text referring expression, is located.

(5) *Social deixis* encodes social distinctions that are relative to participants-roles, particularly as pects of the social relationship holding between speaker and addressee(s) or speaker and some referent.

System in deixis, deictic context, demonstrative and the definite articles, anaphoras and cataphoras are not discussed here. The interested reader can consult Bangura.

The following deixis were delineated after examining the text of the requirements for a *Satyagrahi:*

Type	*Deixis*
1. Deity or Supreme Being	God
2. Person	He
His	
Human	
Khaki-wearer	
Spinner	
Teetotaler	
3. Time	From time to time

Deity or Supreme Being, person, and time deixis exist in the text of the requirements for a *Satyagrahi.* Discourse or text, place or space, and social deixis are absent. It should be noted that the Deity or Supreme Being deictic category if lacking in both traditional and contemporary works in linguistics. Thus, I have added this new deictic category made possible by the text examined for this essay.

The Deity or Supreme Being deixis refers to God. The person deixis comprise of two third-person pronouns (he and his) and four nouns. The four nouns refer to *Homo sapiens* (human), a wearer of dust-colored cloth made of cotton (khaki-wearer), one who draws out and twists fiber into yarn or thread (spinner) and one who practices or advocates complete abstinence from alcoholic drinks (teetotaler). And the time deixis suggests a future time.

Indeed, in order to interpret the preceding deictic forms, contextual knowledge about the Third World was required. Thus, deixis is not reducible to matters of truth-conditional semantics.

Presuppositions

The rhetorical tactic of presupposition in political discourse is by now familiar to many linguists. A paradigm example is the reporter's query: "Did the President lie again about his reasons for going to war with Iraq?" Without explicitly making the assertion, the reporter implies that the President has indeed lied before about his reasons for going to war with Iraq based on the iterative 'again.' A less contentious presupposition can be suggested as well: that the President is a male in light of the pronoun 'his.' This example illustrates the fact that speakers or writers often express more than they assert. Their utterances or scripts convey not only their surface contents, but a great deal of auxiliary content as well.

In this subsection, the linguistic presuppositions in the requirements for a *Satyagrahi* are identified and analyzed. The concept presupposition is first defined.

The phenomenon of linguistic presupposition can be traced back to the philosophical writings of Gottlob Frege. He raised many of the issues that later became central to the discussion of presupposition. According to Frege, "If anything is asserted there is always an obvious presupposition *(voraussetzung)* that the simple or compound proper names used have a reference".

A later exchange between Bertrand Russell and Peter Strawson brought the notion of presupposition more fully into scholarly discourse. Russell, in his first essay on the subject (1905), argued that Frege's views were simply wrong. Struggling with the problem of how to account for the fact that sentences lacked proper referents, Russell came up with conclusions that were different from those of Frege.

Russell's analysis remained unchallenged until Strawson, in his 1950 essay, suggested a different approach. For Strawson, many of the puzzles in Russell's essay emerged from a failure to distinguish sentences from uses of sentences to make, for instance, statements that are true or false. Consider the following sentences:

(1) The President of the United States is a warmonger.

(2) The President of the United States is not a warmonger.

(3) There is one and only one President of the United States.

In his analysis of definite descriptions, Russell suggested that propositions of the form (1) entail presuppositions of the form (3). Strawson did not agree with this suggestion. Instead, Strawson pointed out that (2), the negation of (1), does not affect the truth conditions of (3). If the relation between (1) and (3) were one of entailment, then, by *modus ponens,* i.e. the inference $p > q$ and $\sim p$ to $\sim q$, (2) could not entail (3). One's linguistic intuitions tell her/him, however, that if *either* (1) or (2) is true, then (3) is also true. Strawson labeled the relation one of presupposition, which he formally designated as:

(4) Sentence S_1 logically presupposes sentence S_2 if the truth of S_2 is a precondition for the truth or falsity of S_1.

The practical approach for distinguishing presuppositions from entailments is the employment of the traditional *constancy under negation* rule. One sentence is said to presuppose another if and only if the sentence and its negation both require it to be true.

A detailed discussion of semantic presupposition and implications for logic, presuppositional defeasi-bility, the projection problem, and pragmatic presupposition is not presented here. For details on these aspects, the reader can refer to Bangura.

The following presuppositions are extracted from Gandhi's requirements for a *Satyagrahi:*

(1) One can have faith in God.

(2) One can believe in truth and nonviolence as a creed.

(3) One can have faith in the inherent goodness of nature.

(4) Truth and love can be expressed through suffering.

(5) One can live a chaste life.

(6) One can give up his life and possessions for his/her cause.

(7) One can be a habitual khaki-wearer and spinner.

(8) One can be a teetotaler and abstain from other intoxicants.

(9) One can obey all rules of discipline with a willing heart.

(10) One can obey jail rules not devised to hurt his/her self-respect.

Presuppositions (1), (2), (4), (6), (7), and (10) are triggered by the implicative predicates "must have," "must believe," "must be leading," "must be," "must carry out," and "should carry out." As Kartunnen pointed out, implicative predicates carry presuppositions that represent a necessary and sufficient condition for the truth of their complement sentences. An asserted main sentence with an implicative verb commits the writer/speaker to an implied presupposition which consists of a complement sentence as augmented by the tense and other modifiers of the main sentence.

Presuppositions (3), (5), (8), and (9) are triggered by the factive verbs "have," "be," and "devised." Factive verbs, according to Kiparski Kiparski, trigger the presuppositions of their clausal complements.

Indeed, the preceding presupposition triggers carry presuppositions of some necessary and sufficient conditions which determine whether the requirements for a *Satyagrahi* can be met. The main statements of the requirements can thus be looked upon as statements about whether the decisive conditions envisioned for a *Satyagrahi* can be fulfilled, and under what spatial and temporal circumstances.

This is good to know because these presupposition triggers indicate the sort of range of presupposi-tional phenomena Gandhi had for developing *Satyagraha.* This set of core phenomena will make it possible for the examination in future research of some further basic properties that Gandhi's presuppositions exhibit.

Implicatures

The notion of linguistic implicature does not have an extensive history like presupposition or many other topics in pragmatics. The idea of implicature can be traced back to Grice's theory of conversational implicature. This theory, according to Grice, is derived from a general principle of conversation called the *cooperative principle* plus a number of maxims which speakers will normally obey. Levinson, however, noted that there was considerable speculation within philosophy about the utility of the notion of pragmatic implication, and some proto-Gricean ideas appear in Fogelin.

The term implicature, as used by Grice, accounts for what a speaker (or a writer) can imply, suggest, or mean, as distinguished from what the speaker (or the writer) literally says (or writes). Linguistic implicatures, Grice suggested, are determined by "the conventional meaning of the words used".

Implicature is, therefore, an important unit of linguistic analysis for at least five reasons, following Levinson. First, the concept of implicature offers some significant functional explanations of linguistic facts because the sources of this concept can be shown to lie outside the organization of language, in some general principles for cooperative interaction. And yet the principles have a pervasive effect upon the structure of language. This makes implicature a paradigmatic example of the nature and power of pragmatic explanations of linguistic phenomena.

Second, implicature provides some explicit account of how it is possible to mean more than what is actually said or written. Put differently, the concept allows an analyst to identify more than what is literally expressed by the conventional sense of the linguistic expressions uttered or written.

Third, implicature seems likely to effect substantial simplifications in both the structure and the content of semantic descriptions. For the semanticist, the distinct senses of a word can be declared simply ambiguous, or it can be claimed that the meanings of words are, in general, vague and protean and are influenced by collocational environments.

Fourth, the notion of implicature seems to be essential when various basic facts about language are to be accounted for properly. For example, particles like *well* and *by the way* require some meaning specification in a theory of meaning just like other words in English; but when a linguist comes to consider what their meaning is, s/he will find her/himself referring to the pragmatic mechanisms that produce implicatures.

Finally, the principles that generate implicatures possess a very general explanatory power in the sense that a few basic principles provide explanations for a large array of apparently unrelated facts. Examples suggested and discussed by Levinson include why English has no lexical item *nall,* meaning 'not all,' why Aristotle got his logic wrong, 'Moore's paradox,' how obvious tautologies like *War is* war can convey any conceptual import, and how metaphors work and many other phenomena besides.

Grice suggested that the essential properties of implicatures are largely predictable. He isolated four characteristic properties that can be employed to test for implicatures. These characteristic properties are: (a) *cancellability* or *defeasibility,* (b) *non-detachability,* (c) *calculability,* and (d) *non-conventionality.* A possible fifth characteristic property of implicature can be referred to as "multiplicity"—that is, what Levinson referred to as "an expression with a single meaning (which) can give rise to different implicatures on different occasions, and indeed on any one occasion the set of associated implicatures may not be exactly determinable".

Existing in Gandhi's requirements for a *Satyagrahi*are the following implicatures:

(1) There is a God.

(2) Truth and nonviolence comprise a creed.

(3) Human nature is inherently good.

(4) Suffering is an expression of truth and love.

(5) A chaste life can be lived.

(6) Readiness and willingness are necessary to give up life and possessions for a cause.

(7) Khaki-wearing and spinning can be a habit.

(8) Teetotaling involves being free of all intoxicants.

(9) A willing heart is necessary to obey all of the rules of discipline.

(10) Jail rules can be devised to hurt one's self-pride.

These implicatures, as stated earlier, are triggered by the following implicative predicates: "must have," "must believe," "must be leading," "must be," "must carry out," and "should carry out." As also noted earlier, implicative predicates carry presuppositions that reflect a necessary and sufficient condition for the truth of their complement sentences. Furthermore, an asserted main sentence with an implicative verb commits the writer/speaker to an applied proposition which consists of a complement sentence as suggested by the tense and other modifiers of the main sentence.

In the preceding analysis, I have somehow limited the number of possible implicatures that can be delineated from the text. This is because the implications one can draw from some act are much broader than meaning in natural language. There is also a real danger based on the fact that a contradiction implies anything and everything. All self-contradictory concepts must have precisely the same meaning, namely everything. Unfortunately, the theory of implicature has not yet developed limits to prevent this.

Speech Acts

This subsection is about the speech acts in the text of the requirements for a *Satyagrahi*. First, a synopsis about the theory is presented. Second, the speech acts in the text are discussed.

Speech Act Theory postulates that the utterance of certain sentences, must, in special environments, be seen as the performance of an act, either direct or indirect. The notion of speech acts can be traced to the works of two major linguistic philosophers: J. L. Austin and J. R. Searle.

Austin observed that, while sentences can often be used to report state of affairs, the utterance of some sentences, in special cases, are to be treated as the performance of an act. Such sentences, suggested Austin, can be called *Performatives,* and the special circumstances required for their success, he referred to as *a set of felicity conditions.* By extension, Austin proposed that in uttering any sentence (a *Locutionary Act),* a speaker can be seen to have performed some act (an *Illocu-tionary Act).* Associated with each illocutionary act is the *Force* of the utterance that can be interpreted as a performative like "promise," "warn," etc. Austin also pointed out that, in uttering a sentence, a speaker also performs a *Perlocutionary Act,* which is described in terms of the effect the illocutionary act, at the particular time in use, has on the hearer.

Seven years later, Searle introduced a variation

between *direct* and *indirect* speech acts which depends on the recognition of the intended perlocutionary effect of an utterance on a given occasion. For Searle, indirect speech acts are cases in which one illocutionary act is performed indirectly by way of performing another. To support this proposition, he provided his now famous example, "Can you pass the salt?," and proposed two ways it can be interpreted: (1) it can be seen as a question about the hearer's *ability* to pass the salt; (2) it can be interpreted as a *request* for the action of passing the salt.

The use of Speech Act Theory in studying language phenomena is, thus, important because it provides an account of how some apparently formally unconnected statements go together in discourse to form a coherent sequence. However, there is a general problem with such an approach, and it has been pointed out by Levinson as follows: "If one looks even curiously at a transcribed record of a conversation, it becomes immediately clear that we do not know how to assign speech acts in a non-arbitrary way".

More concretely, Leech has pointed out two aspects of the problem. The first aspect is that of polysemy: i.e. some verbs are so versatile that they can fit both syntactically and semantically into more than one category. For instance, *advise, suggest,* and *tell* can either be classified as assertive or directive. Thus, according to Leech, our classification should not be so much a classification of verbs, but one of verb SENSES.

The second aspect, according to Leech, is that certain verbs, such as *greet* (which is simply followed by a direct object), do not take clausal complementizers, although semantically they must imply one. To solve this shortcoming, Leech suggested that the analyst could do what Searle suggested by stipulating that the syntactic frames that go with each verb category are 'deep structures' which may appear in surface structure in various disguises. Leech also suggested that the analyst can replace the 'deep structure' analysis by an analysis at the semantic representation level, where one is "no longer concerned with speech-act verbs, but rather with the speech-act PREDICATES which they realize, and where the reported utterance is represented by a metapropositional argument".

The problem with identifying speech acts should not necessarily lead the analyst to abandon their investigation. Rather, it should lead the analyst to recognize that the way speech acts are conventionally classified into discrete act-types such as 'request,' 'promise,' 'warn,' etc. may lead to an inappropriate view of what speakers do with utterances.

What solidifies this axiom (i.e. Speech Acts Theory), despite the fact that it had been traditionally subsumed under the rubric of *Theoretical Linguistics,* is the notion of *Sociolinguistics:* i.e. the desire to capture how languages are embedded in the surrounding frameworks of cultures and social institutions.

A detailed discussion of Austin and Searle's works, and how to do things with words is absent here. The interested reader can refer to Bangura.

An examination of Gandhi's requirements for a *Satyagrahi* makes is possible to tease out the following speech acts imbedded in them:

(1) He must have a living faith in God.

(2) He must believe in truth and nonviolence as his creed.

(3) He must have faith in the inherent goodness of human nature.

(4) He must expect to evoke truth and love through his suffering.

(5) He must live a chaste life.

(6) He must be ready and willing for the sake of his cause to give up his life and possessions.

(7) He must be a habitual khaki-wearer and spinner.

(8) He must be a teetotaler.

(9) He must be free from the use of other intoxicants.

(10) He must obey with a willing heart all the rules of discipline as may be laid down from time to time.

(11) He should obey the jail rules unless they are especially devised to hurt his self-respect.

Interestingly, all of the speech acts in the requirements for a *Stayagrahi* are commissives. These speech acts seek to get one to commit himself/herself to have faith in God, to believe in truth and nonviolence, to have faith in the inherent goodness of human nature, to evoke truth and love through suffering, to live a chaste life, to be willing to give up his/her life and possessions for the sake of his/her cause, to be a habitual khaki-wearer and spinner, to be a teetotaler, to be free of all intoxicants, to be willing to obey all rules of discipline, and to obey jail rules that are not devised to hurt his/her self-respect. These are triggered by the verbs "have," "believe," "expect,' "be," and "carry."

In essence, most of the speech act types are absent in the requirements for a *Satyagrahi*. There are no representatives (those that commit a speaker/writer to something being the case), no imperatives (those that attempt to get someone to do something, either modest or fierce), no expressives (those that express a psychological state), and no declaratives (those that alternate status or a condition by declaration).

Understanding the Pragmatic Linguistic Features in the Text

From the preceding analysis, at least three content categories can be delineated within which the pragmatic linguistic features can be subsumed: (1) *Satyagraha* as a moral truth, (2) *Satyagraha* as a peaceful weapon, and (3) forms and techniques of *Satyagraha*. Explanations of these pragmatic linguistic categories are important because any social scientific endeavor must seek to provide general explanations to "Why?" questions. In this case, why are the preceding linguistic categories evident in the text examined? When social scientists attempt to explain why a given phenomenon took place, they must provide a systematic and empirical analysis of these antecedent factors in the given situation that made possible the occurrence of that phenomenon.

Satyagraha as a Moral Truth

Early in his life, Gandhi became an opponent of injustice, oppression, and falsehood. His passion for truth was, thus, innate in him and this was what led him to the path of *Satyagraha*. In addition to being a peaceful idea and movement, *Satyagraha* also became part of the moral philosophy that guided and influenced the Mahatma's life. One thing that took deep root in Gandhi was, in his own words, "the conviction that morality is the basis of things and that truth is the substance of morality. Thus truth became my sole objective" (Diwakar 1948:11). Correspondingly, the power of truth, love and justice comprise the force that guides *Satyagraha*. In opposition to injustice and violence, *Satyagraha* calls for the use of love and truth to combat evil and solve the ills of the world. As such, it is an active movement that calls for the sacrifice and duty of the *Satyagrahis* to fight against violence, not through the use of sanguinary weapons, but through the weapons of truth, love and, essentially, nonviolence. As Gandhi once described it, *Satyagraha* "is essentially an active movement, much more active than the one involving the use of sanguinary weapons. Truth and non-violence are perhaps the [most active] weapons you have in the world," and "this internal weapon acts asleep or awake," for it is "not a negative but positive force" (Mathews 1989:68).

In relation to Satyagraha, there exists a variety of concepts which equate to this movement, such as civil disobedience, non-cooperation, civil resistance, nonviolent resistance or nonviolent non-cooperation, constructive program, truth and Ahimsa or nonviolence. In this light, Gandhi established a relationship between these terms by comparing Satyagraha to a tree from which the previous concepts emanate as its branches: "the whole tree is Satyagraha". More specifically, he compared it to a banyan tree with a multiple trunk and many branches. The tree is rooted in Truth or Absolute Reality, and its branches are the forms by which we search and find the one Truth and Reality. These are the outer manifestations of the inner search for Truth: i.e. the means by which we can seek the Truth and Ultimate Reality through nonviolence or Constructive Program. Together, they form the path that leads to Satyagraha.

Satyagraha as a Peaceful Weapon

The importance of *Satyagraha* hinges upon the fact that it is based on truth and love, and it was made to conquer ills such as injustice and violence. Consequently, it is also a weapon of justice and nonviolence. It fights through compassion and brings down the opponent with love rather than blood. The means of *Satyagraha* were made for this sole purpose, with the goal of instructing the opponent rather than inflicting pain, harm, or death on him/her. The use of violence will not serve to eradicate violence, but to make it greater. Thus, we must fight violence through greater means, more powerful and effective, and that will serve to spread our message and not contradict it. The search for truth, which is the main goal for the *Satyagrahi,* makes no room for violence, since the ultimate goal is *Satyagraha:* i.e. the use of Soul-Force, Truth-Force, or Love-Force to combat evil and create peace.

Therefore, the pursuit of truth entails no violence. Rather, it deals with the opponent, not by inflicting pain or hatred, but through the force of love and compassion. Since it is truth that guides him/her, truth must also be the ultimate end; and there is no violence, or hatred, or pain. Instead, the opponent is treated with respect and submission. The main task for the *Satyagrahi* is to attempt to overcome the opponent by making him/her realize the ill s/he has committed through patience and sympathy, even if it means undertaking severe suffering, pain, or even death. This is the way in which *Satyagraha* fights injustice. As the Mahatma urged,

> In the application of Satyagraha I discovered in the earliest stages that pursuit of truth did not admit of violence being inflicted on one's opponent but that he must be weaned from error by patience and sympathy. For what appears to be truth to one may appear to be error to the other. And patience means self-suffering. So the doctrine came to mean vindication of truth not by infliction of suffering on the opponent but on one's self".

Thus, truth is achieved through patience, sympathy and self-suffering, not through hatred, pain, violence, or death of the opponent. The duty of the *Satyagrahi* is to fight for the truth, and only with truth alone.

In essence, although it has been claimed to be the way of the weak, the path of *Satyagraha* has proven to be the task of the strong. Unlike those who engage in violence or hatred and resort to the use of sanguinary weapons, which act as covers or shields for their cowardice, those who follow the path of *Satyagraha* are stronger, both in body and mind, to fight through greater means which will cause them pain or even death. As Gandhi once said, "The path of truth is for the brave alone, never for a coward". As such, in order to instruct the opponent on his/her wrongdoing, the *Satyagrahi* must go as far as accepting death with the use of the only permissible weapons: love, patience, sympathy, and compassion. According to Gandhi, "*Satyagraha* used in direct action does not aim at appealing to reason. Rather, it attempts to reach the opponent's reason through the heart". The self-suffering on the part of the *Satyagrahi,* thus, has an educative effect on the opponent, calling attention to injustice as well as arousing public sentiment. Therefore, it does not appeal to reason directly but through the heart, with the force of the soul, truth and love, which are the only means to transform reason.

One of the basic assumptions of *Satyagraha* is the essential goodness of human nature. As such, the *Satyagrahi* "looks upon none as his enemy. Everyone is a friend, a fellow being, a brother". Therefore, the *Satyagrahi* should not attempt to injure the opponent but, rather, to destroy the evil without injuring the evildoer. Instead of physically resisting wrong, s/he "attempts to reach the heart of the wrongdoer" by suffering cheerfully. By suffering and assuring the opponent of his/her physical safety, the *Satyagrahi* causes his/her opponent to think about the wrong s/he has committed. Thus, his/her attack is on the opponent's mind, and s/he aims at curing evil at its source.

Another important aspect of *Satyagraha* is its relation with *Ahimsa,* nonviolence. As stated by Gandhi, "Ahimsa and Truth are my two lungs. I cannot live without them". Therefore, there is an intrinsic connection between both concepts; and as mentioned earlier, nonviolence is part of *Satyagraha* as one of its major branches. Consequently, *Satyagraha* and nonviolence, resistance, suffering, patience and compassion all go hand-in-hand in search for the ultimate truth, the path by which we oppose evil, wrong, and injustice through the power of love, mercy, and compassion, all done with the will of nonviolence and the skills of forgiveness. In this light, to Gandhi, evil must be turned into good, injustice must be fought with justice, hatred must be conquered with love, and untruth must be erased with the power of truth. From here arise his conceptualizations of truth and nonviolence, since the one leads to the other. Truth is to be achieved through nonviolence, and we can only resist violence thtough the force of truth. In Gandhi's words, "Resist not evil with evil, but resist evil with good at all costs. But at any rate, resist. Resistance is better than cowardly nonresistance"

(Diwakar 1948:26). Gandhi also added that we must insist on the strength of the *Satyagrahi* and oppose the weakness of the soldier.

Forms and Techniques of Satyagraha

As *Satyagraha* includes both purification and suffering, the forms *Satyagraha* might take would be based on these as well as on patience, service, and sacrifice. Due to the nature of *Satyagraha,* its essential elements—truth, compassion, love, suffering, duty, and patience—may be classified into three main stages: constructive, purificatory, and aggressive.

The constructive stage is that which deals with the organization and preparation for *Satyagraha.* At this stage, the task lies in preparing the people to participate through means such as the selection of clear issues, recruitment and mobilization, organization and training. For Gandhi, the interest lay not in the number of volunteers for *Satyagraha,* but in their quality. As such, he expected much from his volunteers and posed the list of requirements (analyzed for their pragmatic linguistic content earlier) by which they should abide.

The second stage, i.e. purification, includes techniques such as fasting, the practice of silence, *hartal* (the cessation of business out of respect, or for mourning, or as a protest), prayer meetings, vows, and pledges. Also included are other self-denying actions which illustrate the cleansing and purificatory forms of *Satyagraha.*

Following the completion of the constructive and purificatory stages, the *Satyagrahi* is then prepared to undertake the third stage—that of aggression—in which the attack on evil is effected through direct action, with techniques such as non-cooperation, civil disobedience, boycott, and other measures, even serving jail sentence. Any of these actions should be done with a full understanding of the consequences.

Conclusion

In sum, we can say that *Satyagraha,* the matchless weapon, is the means of the strong, the good-willed, and the full-hearted. It is the force of the Soul, the current of Love, the path of Truth, and the search for Reality. Its necessary skills of pain, suffering, and commitment make *Satyagraha* a movement of the strong and powerful, as it attempts to correct the world, not through inflicting equal pain, but through the overwhelming power of Love.

Indeed, as Gandhi once said, "Ruled by Love, the world goes on." He added: "If ill-will were the chief motive-force, the world would have been destroyed long ago," but "We are alive solely because of love". Thus, it is the power of Love alone that can save the world; and as conceived by Gandhi, the power of Love and Truth is capable of destroying the greatest evils. And it is this belief that made Gandhi's *Satyagraha* the movement it became. To Gandhi, Truth is the one Reality; and in order to achieve this Ultimate Truth, we can only fight with the weapons of Truth itself.

In the rest of this conclusion, I present a résumé of ideas which emerged during my preoccupation with this work. As always, in the application of academic ideas to vital documents such as symbolic texts, there is the very real possibility of the premature acceptance of untested concepts and theories. The analyst must, therefore, shoulder the responsibility of pointing out the limitations of current approaches (as is done in the preceding section) and to demonstrate the empirical basis for the working categories employed. It is for this reason that this essay surveyed many approaches in linguistic pragmatics.

The analysis in the preceding section shows that pragmatic analyses can be glossed as 'covert factors making the overt coherent.' Real-world factors determined the intralinguistic, grammatical choices of Gandhi, the author of *Satyagraha.* Social-world factors covertly determined their overt, intralinguistic grammars differently.

Since semantic representation should be able to identify tautologies, contradictions, anomalies and paraphrases, it must be able to compare *given* (overt, occurrent) bits with the rest of language, infinite resources which are covert, non-occurrent. This pairing task can appear simple at a categorical competence level, daunting at the boundaries of lexical, contextualized performance level.

Presupposition, for instance, can designate a state, process or action. These three possibilities correspond to some ambiguities in linguists' use of that expression. Presupposition may be coherently said to *inhere* in language viewed as a state, to *emerge* in language viewed as a process, or to be something languages cause when considered as actions. Questions about presupposition become relevant or unanswerable, depending on these points of view.

We can ask if a state is absolute or relative, inherent or resultant from a process or an action; or process, we can ask under what conditions they occur. We ask who is responsible for actions and effects of instruments. Questions that have been raised, therefore, have included (a) Who or what presupposes? (b) What is covert and overt? (c) What is to be said about overt expressions for which only overt incoherence can be found? Notice that "coherence" sidesteps vexing questions about "truth."

Distinguishing sense and reference involves different norms for determining synonymy and its consequences in semantic interpretation of truth-conditions. If existence (a basic concern in presuppositions) must be decided on empirical testability, differences about "truth" and "meaning" are predictable. While a normative solution to these questions is not obvious, some of the sources of confusion are. By examining the terms involved, and some assumptions of linguists considered in this essay, the danger of confusing a gloss with a translation can be pointed out, if not avoided. In this perplexing area, a short sketch can prepare only for caution, not sure interpretation.

In non-technical usage, the terms imply, infer, and entail are often used indiscriminately. Sometimes, it is clear that *(a)* the point of view shifts from viewing language as a state, process, or action; and *(b)* from viewing language as an Agent to that of an Instrument employed by an Agent. Once this stance has been identified, the status of presuppositions is still to be determined as coherent or incoherent within each metaphor. Distinctions commonly recognized involve norms such as (a) overt versus covert; (b) simultaneous versus successive, with the priorities based either on time, logic, psychologically explicit advertence and the like.

In general usage, a covert *Implication* can be distinguished from an overt *assertion* and an implicit *entailment* from an explicit *conclusion*. An *inference* is ambiguously contained in texts or made by people. Both *implicatures* and *inferences* can be inexplicit in textual or human terms, while a *deduction* is explicit in both. *Inference* can be a process or action appropriate to people who *infer,* while both texts and people can be ambiguously said to *imply*. A *deduction* can be an act or process, while deducibility is a state. All of these involve analogous (systematically ambiguous) notions *of necessity,* which involve a kind *of priority* or *simultaneity* (temporal, logical, natural). Usage is confused when the type of *necessity* or *priority* is inexplicit or undecidable.

Modern scientific statements made in the linguistic form 'If...then' can be referred to as implicatures. This *form* is a Constant. What might fill it? Variables. The constant formal relations are independent of the material (substantive) nature of variables filling them, so formal validity and truth are inextricably related, in that, given true premises and a valid form, a conclusion must be true.

Stated this way, a *system* is presented as a network of dependence (e.g., grammatical and phonological systems) and a *system of systems* (a meta-system per se) allows both for independent and interdependent relations between them. Presupposition currently looks particularly to the syntax of what is overtly asserted and covertly taken for granted in a true or false context. Linguistic pragmatic usage involves contexts where truth or falsity are not involved, but appropriateness is in question.

This is a point at which ambiguity necessarily arises. But ambiguity can be shown to be systematic, and a term like "presuppose" analogical, if its sense (and possible reference) can be established as clear in a defining environment and the differences calculated from the defining differences of other environments. The clearest logical instance is *existential presupposition;* less clear are grammatical, social, psychological, and other factors which are demanded, tolerated or excluded in semantic interpretation.

Assuming normal, unmarked, non-contrastive sentences which do not *assert* existence, a subject is taken as old information (so can be presupposed), a predicate as new (so normally asserted). Without a distinction of *sense* and *reference,* anomalies arise when the sole norm of truth and falsity is referential. Sentences consisting of words that have independent 'sense' allow at least a grammatical presupposition of "existence" identical in affirmation and negation, but if that is excluded referentially in the assertion, its negation must be logically 'true': if an assertion is 'false,' its negation must be 'true.'

Necessities of language can be distinguished from those of real-world conditions, and both from psychological constructs. Even scientific theories properly 'reside' in thought where their substantial condition is conceptual; both this abstracted status and the states of affairs to which they can be reduced are different from the conventions of language in which they are expressed. Logicians now employ the notion of "possible worlds," within which real-world incoherence (and truth or falsity defined in those terms) can be neutralized, so stressing the formality of their enterprise. It reminds one of the time when Nuclear Bombs only 'existed' in physicists' heads.

So, the first matter of *Satyagraha* we ought to consider is its dual nature: (a) as an aesthetic human experience, which not only gives pleasure but also teaches life in varying degrees of intensity (an individual re-creates what has been created by the author); and (2) as the object of study, or of our intellectual curiosity. One might well ask the professor of Peace Studies whether in his/her teaching, and even in his/her research, s/he recognizes the inseparable nature of these aspects *of Satyagraha.*

Satyagraha can no longer be considered merely an adventitious or decorative object in life or in culture; it must be seen rather as one of the deepest expressions of the ethos of a people. Professors of Peace Studies cannot ignore this reality: *Satyagraha* is *life,* readily available to the hearer/reader and full of humanizing tension. If *Satyagraha* is a transcendental aesthetic experience which not only is *present* in the 'then' and 'there' of the text and the feelings of the author but can also *be moving toward* the 'here' and 'now' of the hearer/reader, then, the Peace Studies student ought to be considered first of all as a *hearer/reader.* And in order to help him/her be a real hearer/reader—the best possible hearer/reader, we have to make him/her see that being such a hearer/reader comes near to being a writer: a writer or an author in the widest meaning of the word, but in a passive sense one who re-creates in his/her hearing/reading what was felt and intuited by the original, active author.

We might propose as a starting point that all studies of peaceful creeds, even on the most elementary levels, aim at the following objectives. First, we must stress the uniqueness of the creed-aesthetic experience, an act of creed per se; and recognize that to fail to enter into the imaginative creed of 'speaker/writer-hearer/reader' may be whatever else one wishes, but most certainly is not to come to grips with the essence of the creeds. To abstain from this aesthetic experience of being a 'participant' is, in the final analysis, not to study the creeds.

Second, we should give the hearer/reader such scholarly assistance (historical, philosophical, sociological, political, and linguistic contexts, etc.) as may be necessary to illustrate and help him/her understand and place the text in the 'then' and 'there' in which it was conceived. But all effort along these lines ought to be subordinate to the first one, the aesthetic purpose.

Finally, we should orient the hearer/reader of the creeds in the search for ethical implications which all works pose. The moral responsibility (or irresponsibility) of an author is inseparable from his/her aesthetic vision. In this way, the hearer/reader would examine the value of the text in a dual perspective—ethical and aesthetic—and new dimensions would be added to the traditional historical-philosophical analysis.

To study creeds in this way as a deeply-rooted manifestation of life would lead to a better understanding of the customs, the social institutions, and the individual historical events of institutions. The creeds would also provide an approach to the visual arts, whose deeper meanings often escape the eye of the uninitiated observer because of his/her tendency to isolate cultural phenomena from their context in order to judge them in the context of his/her own culture where these phenomena may have little or no meaning or a totally mistaken one.

We ought never to falsify the cultural reality (life, art, literature) which is the goal of the student's study. We would, thus, have to oppose all sorts of simplified, or supposedly simplified, texts and stress instead the methods which will achieve the best possible access to real life, language and philosophy.

The observations I have made in this conclusion are not directed at the discovery of any method or pedagogical panacea. I present them in complete modesty in the belief that what matters most is not the method but the professor. May my observations serve then, at best, as a starting point for that self-examination. Since teaching about peace and other academic phenomena is one to which many of us are deeply committed, I venture to address my colleagues in the profession with the hope that they will not only give serious consideration to my suggestions and perplexities, but also strive to suggest better solutions than those I have here proposed.

REFERENCES

Alston, W. P. 1964. *The Philosophy of Language.* Englewood Cliffs, New Jersey: Prentice-Hall. Austin, J. L. 1962. *How to do Things with Words.* New York, New York: Oxford University Press.

Babbie, E. 1992. *The Practice of Social Research* 6th ed. Belmont, California: Wadsworth Publishing Company.

Bangura, A. K. 2004. *Surah Al-Fatihah: A Linguistic Exploration of Its Meanings.* New York: Publishers Choice Press.

Bangura, A. K. 2002a. *Sojourner-Douglass College's Philosophy in Action: An African-Centered Creed.* San Jose, CA: Writers Club Press.

Bangura, A. K. 2002b. *The American University Alma Mater and Fight Song.* San Jose, CA: Writers Club Press.

Bangura, A. K. 2000. Divisive barbarity or national civilization: Linguistic presuppositions of the Sierra Leone National Anthem as a teaching tool for peaceful behavior. *International Journal of Sierra Leone Studies & Reviews* 1, 1:71-82.

Bangura, A. K. 1997. *The Presuppositions and Implicatures of the Founding Fathers.* Larchmont, New York: Cummings & Hathaway Publishers.

Bangura, A. K. 1996. *Political Presuppositions and Implicatures of the Most Popular African-American Hymns.* Commack, New York: Nova Science Publishers.

Bangura, A. K. and M. O. Thomas. 1998. *Bowie State University Alma Mater: Historical Context and Linguistic Presuppositions.* Washington, DC: The African Institution Publications.

Bartlett, F. C. 1932. *Remembering.* Cambridge, England:

Cambridge University Press. Bateson, G. 1972. *Steps to an Ecology of Mind.* New York, New York: Ballantine Books.

Benson, M. 1986. *Nelson Mandela: The Man and the Movement.* New York: W. W. Norton and Company.

Brown, G. 1977. *Listening to Spoken English.* London, England: Longman.

Brown, P. and S. C. Levinson. 1978/1987. *Politeness: Some Universals in language Usage.* Cambridge, England: Cambridge University Press.

Brown, G. and G. Yule. 1983. *Discourse Analysis.* Cambridge, England: Cambridge University Press. Carnap, R. 1942. *Introduction to Semantics.* Cambridge, Massachusetts: MIT Press.

Chafe, W. L. 1972. Discourse structure and human knowledge. In R. O. Freedle and J. B. carroll, eds. *Language Comprehension and the Acquisition of Knowledge.* Washington, DC: V. H. Winston.

Chafe, W. L. 1970. *Meaning and the Structue of Language.* Chicago, Illinois: Chicago University Press.

Charniak, E. *Towards a Model of Children's Story Comprehension.* Cambridge, Massachusetts: MIT Press, MIT Artificial Intelligence Laboratory Monographs, No. 226.

Chomsky, N. 1964. Current issues in linguistic theory. In J. Fodor and J. J. Katz, eds. *The Structure of Language.* Englewood Cliffs, New Jersey: Prentice-Hall.

Chomsky, N. 1959. On certain formal properties of grammar. *Information and Control* 2:137-167. Cleary, T. 1993. *The Essential Koran.* San Francisco, California: HarperSan Francisco.

Cobb, R. and C. Elder. 1976. Symbolic identification and political behavior. *American Politics Quarterly* 4.

Copi, I. and C. Cohen. 1994. *Introduction to Logic.* New York, New York: Macmillan Publishing Company.

Dahl, O. 1969. *Topic and Comment: A Study of Russian and Transformational Grammar.* Goteborge, Sweden: Slavica Gothoburgensia 4.

De Beaugrande, R. 1980. *Text Discourse and Process.* London, England: Longman.

Descrates, R. 1968 ed. *Philosophical Works* (in two volumes). E. S. Haldane and G. R. T. Ross (translators). Cambridge, England: The University Press.

Diwakar, R. R. 1948. *SATYAGRAHA: The Power of Truth.* Chicago, Illinois: Henry Regnery Company. Edelman, M. 1964. *The Symbolic Uses of Politics.* Urbana, Illinois: The University of Illinois Press. Elder, C. and R. Cobb. 1983. *The Political Uses of Symbols.* New York, New York: Longman.

Filmore, C. J. 1975. An alternative to checklist theories of meaning (proceedings of the first annual meeting of the Berkeley Linguistic Society, University of California).

Filmore, C. J. 1968. The case for case. In E. bach and R. Harms, eds. *Universals in Linguistic Theory.* New York, New York: Holt, Rinehart and Winston.

Fischer, L. 1962. *The Essential Gandhi: His Life, Works and Ideas.* New York: Vintage Books. Fogelin, R. 1967. *Evidence and Meaning.* New York, New York: Humanities Press.

Frege, G. 1892/1952. On sense and reference. In P. T. Geach and M. Black, eds. *Translations from the Philosophic Writings of Gottlob Frege.* Oxford, England: Blackwell.

Gandhi, M. K. 1961. *Non-Violent Resistance (Satygraha).* New York: Schocken Books. Garfinkel, H. 1967. *Studies in Ethnomethodology.* Cambridge, England: Polity Press.

Gazdar, G. 1979. *Pragmatics: Implicature, Presupposition and Logical Form.* New York, New York: Academic Press.

Givon, T. 1979. *On Understanding Grammar.* New York, New York: Academic Press. Goffman, E. 1974. *Frame Analysis.* New York, New York: Harper and Row.

Grice, H. P. 1981. Presupposition and conversational implicature. In P. Cole, ed. *Radical Pragmatics.* New York, New York: Academic Press.

Grice, H. P. 1978. Further notes on logic and conversation. In P. Cole, ed. *Syntax and Semantics 9: Pragmatics.* New York, New York: Academic Press.

Grice, H. P. 1975. Logic and conversation. In P. Cole and J. L.

Morgan eds. *Syntax and Semantics: vol. 3: Speech Acts.* New York, New York: Academic Press.

Grice, H. P. 1968. Utterer's meaning, sentence-meaning, and word-meaning. *Foundations of Language* 4:1-18.

Grice, H. P. 1957. Meaning. *Philosophical Review* lxvi:377-388.

Gunn, G. 1992. Interdisciplinary studies. In J. Gibaldi, ed. *Introduction to Scholarship in Modern Languages and Literatures.* New York, New York: The Modern Languages Association of America.

Harman, G. H. 1986/1989. *Change in View.* Cambridge, Massachusetts: MIT Press. Harman, G. H. 1968. Three levels of meaning. *The Journal of Philosophy* lxv:590-602. Heritage, J. 1984. *Garfinkel and Ethnomethodology.* Cambridge, England: Polity Press. Hofmann, Th. R. *Realms of Meaning.* London, England: Longman. Holmes, R. L. 1990. *Nonviolence in Theory and Practice.* Chicago, IL: Waveland Press.

Hume, R. D. 1992. Texts within contexts: Notes toward a historical method. *Philological Quarterly* 71:69-100.

Iyer, R. 1990. *The Essential Writings of Mahatma Gandhi.* Ahmedhabad, India: Oxford University Press.

Jones, E. 1964. The psychology of constitutional monarchy. In E. Jones, ed. *Essays in Applied Psycho-analysis.* London, Engand: The Hogart Press.

Kaplan, A. 1964. *The Conduct of Inquiry.* San Francisco, California: Chandler Publishing Company. Karttunen, L. 1973. Presuppositions of compound sentences. *Linguistic Inquiry* iv, 2:169-193. Karttunen, L. 1971. Implicative verbs. *Language* 47:340-358.

Kates, C. A. 1980. *Pragmatics and Semantics: An Empiricist Theory.* Ithaca, New York: Cornell University Press.

Katz, J. J. 1966. *The Philosophy of Language.* New York, New York: Harper and Row.

Katz, J. J. and J. Fodor. 1964. *The Structure of Language.* Englewood Cliffs, New Jersey: Prentice-Hall.

Kiparsky, P. and C. Kiparsky. 1971. Fact. In D. D. Steinberg and L. A. Jakobovits, eds. *Semantics.* Cambridge, England: Cambridge University Press.

Leech, G. N. 1983. *Principles of Pragmatics.* London, England: Longman.

Kintsch, W. 1974. *The Representation of Meaning in Memory.* Hillsdale, New Jersey: Lawrence Erl-baum Publishing Company.

Levinson, S. C. 1983. *Pragmatics.* Cambridge, England: Cambridge University Press. Lyons, J. 1977. *Semantics 1 & 2.* Cambridge, England: Cambridge University Press.

Magubane, B. M. 1979. *The Political Economy of Race and Class in South Africa.* New York: Monthly Review Press.

Mathews, J. K. 1989. *The Matchless Weapon: Satyagraha.* Bombay, India: Bharatiya Vidya Bhavan. Merelman, R. 1966. Learning and legitimacy. *American Political Science Review* 60.

Meyer, B. J. F. 1975. *The Organization of Prose and Its Effects on Meaning.* Amsterdam, Holland: North Holland Press.

Morris, C. W. 1946. *Signs, language, and Behavior.* Englewood Cliffs, New Jersey: Prentice-Hall. Morris, C. W. 1938. *Foundations of the Theory of Signs.* Chicago, Illinois: Chicago University Press.

Nachmias, D. and C. 1981. *Research Methods in the Social Sciences* 2nd ed. New York, New York: St. Martin's Press.

Patterson, A. 1992. Historical scholarship. In J. Gibaldi, ed. *Introduction to Scholarship in Modern Languages and Literatures.* New York, New York: The Modern Language Association of America.

Putnam, H. 1975. *Mind, Language and Reality* vo. 2. Cambridge, England: Cambridge University Press.

Pyarelal. 1950. *A Pilgrimage for Peace.* Ahmedhabad, India: Navajivan Publishing House.

Robinson, I. 1978. *The New Grammarians' Funeral: A Critique of Noam Chomsky's Linguistics.* New York, NY: Cambridge University Press.

Roux, E. 1965. *Time Longer than Rope: A History of The Black Man's Struggle for Freedom in South Africa.* Madison, WI: University of Wisconsin Press.

Russell, B. 1957. Mr. Strawson on referring. *Mind* 66. Russell, B. 1905. On denoting. *Mind* 14.

Schank, R. C. and R. Abelson. 1977. *Scripts, Plans, Goals and Understanding*. Hillsdale, New Jersey: Lawrence Erlbaum Publishing Company.

Schiffrin, D. 1987. Discovering the context of an utterance. *Linguistics* 25:11 -32. Searle, J. R. 1985. Indirect speech acts. *Language and Society* 14:58-82.

Searle, J. R. 1976. A classification of illocutionary acts. *Language and Society* 5:1-24. Searle, J. R. 1968. *Speech Acts.* New York, NY: Cambridge University Press. Sellars, W. 1954. Presupposing. *Philosophical Review*63:197-215.

Stalnaker, R. C. 1978. Assertion. In P. Cole, ed. *Syntax and Semantics 9: Pragmatics.* New York, New York: Academic Press.

Stalnaker, R. C. 1974. Pragmatic presuppositions. In M. K. Munitz and P. K. Unger, eds. *Semantics and Philosophy.* New York, New York: New York University Press.

Steinberg, D. D. and L. A. Jakobovits. 1971. *Semantics.* Cambridge, England: Cambridge University Press.

Strawson, P. F. 1952. *Introduction to Logical Theory.* London, England: Metheun. Strawson, P. F. 1950. On referring. *Mind* 59.

Taylor, C. 1971. Interpretation and the sciences of man. *Review of Metaphysics* 25:24. Van Dijk, T. A. 1977. *Text and Content.* London, England: Longman.

Wilson, D. and D. Sperber. 1981. On Grice's theory of conversation. In P. Werth, ed. *Conversation and Discourse.* London, England: Croom Helm.

Worff, B. L. 1956. *Language, Thought and Reality.* Cambridge, Massachusetts: MIT Press. Ziff, P. 1967. On H. P. Grice's account of meaning. Analysis xxviii:1-8.

7

The Making of the National Movement: 1870s—1947

The Emergence of Nationalism

The above-mentioned developments led the people to ask a crucial question: what is this country of India and for whom is it meant? The answer that gradually emerged was: India was the people of India - *all the people* irrespective of class, colour, caste, creed, language, or gender. And the country, its resources and systems, were meant for all of them. With this answer came the awareness that the British were exercising control over the resources of India and the lives of its people, and until this control was ended India could not be for Indians.

This consciousness began to be clearly stated by the political associations formed after 1850, especially those that came into being in the 1870s and 1880s. Most of these were led by English-educated professionals such as lawyers. The more important ones were the Poona Sarvajanik Sabha, the Indian Association, the Madras Mahajan Sabha, the Bombay Presidency Association, and of course the Indian National Congress.

Note the name, "Poona Sarvajanik Sabha". The literal meaning of *"sarvajanik"* is "of or for all the people" *(sarva* = all + *janik* = of the people). Though many of these associations functioned in specific parts of the country, their goals were stated as the goals of all the people of India, not those of any one region, community or class. They worked with the idea that the people should be sovereign - a modern consciousness and a key feature of nationalism. In other words, they believed that the Indian people should be empowered to take decisions regarding their affairs.

The dissatisfaction with British rule intensified in the 1870s and 1880s. The Arms Act was passed in 1878, disallowing Indians from possessing arms. In the same year the Vernacular Press Act was also enacted in an effort to silence those who were critical of the government. The Act allowed the government to confiscate the assets of newspapers including their printing presses if the newspapers published anything that was found "objectionable". In 1883, there was a furore over the attempt by the government to introduce the Ilbert Bill. The bill provided for the trial of British or European persons by Indians, and sought equality between British and Indian judges in the country. But when white opposition forced the government to withdraw the bill, Indians were enraged. The event highlighted the racial attitudes of the British in India.

The need for an all-India organisation of educated Indians had been felt since 1880, but the Ilbert Bill controversy deepened this desire. The Indian National Congress was established when 72 delegates from all over the country met at Bombay in December 1885. The early leadership - Dadabhai Naoroji, Pherozeshah Mehta, Badruddin Tyabji, W.C. Bonnerji, Surendranath Banerji, Romesh Chandra Dutt, S. Subramania Iyer, among others - was largely from Bombay and Calcutta. Naoroji, a businessman and publicist settled in London, and for a time member of the British Parliament, guided the younger nationalists. A retired British official, A.O. Hume, also played a part in bringing Indians from the various regions together.

A Nation in the Making

It has often been said that the Congress in the first twenty years was "moderate" in its objectives and methods.

During this period it demanded a greater voice for Indians in the government and in administration. It wanted the Legislative Councils to be made more representative, given more power, and introduced in provinces where none existed. It demanded that Indians be placed in high positions in the government. For this purpose it called for civil service examinations to be held in India as well, not just in London.

The demand for Indianisation of the administration was part of a movement against racisim, since most important jobs at the time were monopolised by white officials, and the British generally assumed that Indians could not be given positions of responsibility. Since British officers were sending a major part of their large salaries home, Indianisation, it was hoped, would also reduce the drain of wealth to England. Other demands included the separation of the judiciary from the executive, the repeal of the Arms Act and the freedom of speech and expression.

The early Congress also raised a number of economic issues. It declared that British rule had led to poverty and famines: increase in the land revenue had impoverished peasants and zamindars, and exports of grains to Europe had created food shortages. The Congress demanded reduction of revenue, cut in military expenditure, and more funds for irrigation. It passed many resolutions on the salt tax, treatment of Indian labourers abroad, and the sufferings of forest dwellers - caused by an interfering forest administration. All this shows that despite being a body of the educated elite, the Congress did not talk only on behalf of professional groups, zamindars or industrialists.

The Moderate leaders wanted to develop public awareness about the unjust nature of British rule. They published newspapers, wrote articles, and showed how British rule was leading to the economic ruin of the country. They criticised British rule in their speeches and sent representatives to different parts of the country to mobilise public opinion. They felt that the British had respect for the ideals of freedom and justice, and so they would accept the just demands of Indians. What was necessary, therefore, was to express these demands, and make the government aware of the feelings of Indians.

Freedom is our Birthright

By the 1890s many Indians began to raise questions about the political style of the Congress. In Bengal, Maharashtra and Punjab, leaders such as Bepin Chandra Pal, Bal Gangadhar Tilak and Lala Lajpat Rai were beginning to explore more radical objectives and methods. They criticised the Moderates for their "politics of prayers", and emphasised the importance of self-reliance and constructive work. They argued that people must rely on their own strength, not on the "good" intentions of the government; people must fight for *swaraj*. Tilak raised the slogan, "Freedom is my birthright and I shall have it!"

In 1905 Viceroy Curzon partitioned Bengal. At that time Bengal was the biggest province of British India and included Bihar and parts of Orissa. The British argued for dividing Bengal for reasons of administrative convenience. But what did "administrative convenience" mean? Whose "convenience" did it represent? Clearly, it was closely tied to the interests of British officials and businessmen. Even so, instead of removing the non-Bengali areas from the province, the government separated East Bengal and merged it with Assam. Perhaps the main British motives were to curtail the influence of Bengali politicians and to split the Bengali people.

The partition of Bengal infuriated people all over India. All sections of the Congress - the Moderates and the Radicals, as they may be called - opposed it. Large public meetings and demonstrations were organised and novel methods of mass protest developed. The struggle that unfolded came to be known as the Swadeshi movement, strongest in Bengal but with echoes elsewhere too - in deltaic Andhra for instance, it was known as the Vandemataram Movement.

The Swadeshi movement sought to oppose British rule and encourage the ideas of self-help, *swadeshi* enterprise, national education, and use of Indian languages. To fight for *swaraj,* the radicals advocated mass mobilisation and boycott of British institutions and goods. Some individuals also began to suggest that "revolutionary violence" would be necessary to overthrow British rule.

The opening decades of the twentieth century were marked by other developments as well. A group of Muslim landlords and nawabs formed the All India Muslim League at Dacca in 1906. The League supported the partition of Bengal. It desired separate electorates for Muslims, a demand conceded by the government in 1909. Some seats in the councils were now reserved for Muslims who would be elected by Muslim voters. This tempted politicians to gather a following by distributing favours to their own religious groups.

Meanwhile, the Congress split in 1907. The Moderates were opposed to the use of boycott. They felt that it involved the use of force. After the split the Congress came to be dominated by the Moderates with Tilak's followers functioning from outside. The two groups reunited in December 1915. Next year the Congress and the Muslim League signed the historic Lucknow Pact and decided to work together for representative government in the country.

The Growth of Mass Nationalism

After 1919 the struggle against British rule gradually became a mass movement, involving peasants, tribals, students and women in large numbers and occasionally factory workers as well. Certain business groups too began to actively support the Congress in the 1920s. Why was this so?

The First World War altered the economic and political situation in India. It led to a huge rise in the defence expenditure of the Government of India. The government in turn increased taxes on individual incomes and business profits. Increased military expenditure and the demands for war supplies led to a sharp rise in prices which created great difficulties for the common people. On the other hand, business groups reaped fabulous profits from the war. As you have seen (Chapter 7), the war created a demand for industrial goods (jute bags, cloth, rails) and caused a decline of imports from other countries into India. So

Indian industries expanded during the war, and Indian business groups began to demand greater opportunities for development.

The war also lead the British to expand their army. Villages were pressurised to supply soldiers for an alien cause. A large number of soldiers were sent to serve abroad. Many returned after the war with an understanding of the ways in which imperialist powers were exploiting the peoples of Asia and Africa and with a desire to oppose colonial rule in India.

Furthermore, in 1917 there was a revolution in Russia. News about peasants' and workers' struggles and ideas of socialism circulated widely, inspiring Indian nationalists.

The Advent of Mahatma Gandhi

It is in these circumstances that Mahatma Gandhi emerged as a mass leader. As you may know, Gandhiji, aged 46, arrived in India in 1915 from South Africa. Having led Indians in that country in non-violent marches against racist restrictions, he was already a respected leader, known internationally. His South African campaigns had brought him in contact with various types of Indians: Hindus, Muslims, Parsis and Christians; Gujaratis, Tamils and north Indians; and upper-class merchants, lawyers and workers.

Mahatma Gandhi spent his first year in India travelling throughout the country, understanding the people, their needs and the overall situation. His earliest interventions were in local movements in Champaran, Kheda and Ahmedabad where he came into contact with Rajendra

Prasad and Vallabhbhai Patel. In Ahmedabad he led a successful millworkers' strike in 1918.

Let us now focus in some detail on the movements organised between 1919 and 1922.

The Rowlatt Satyagraha

In 1919 Gandhiji gave a call for a *satyagraha* against the Rowlatt Act that the British had just passed. The Act curbed fundamental rights such as the freedom of expression and strengthened police powers. Mahatma Gandhi, Mohammad Ali Jinnah and others felt that the government had no right to restrict people's basic freedoms. They criticised the Act as "devilish" and tyrannical. Gandhiji asked the Indian people to observe 6 April 1919 as a day of non-violent opposition to this Act, as a day of "humiliation and prayer" and *hartal* (strike). *Satyagraha Sabhas* were set up to launch the movement.

The Rowlatt Satyagraha turned out to be the first all-India struggle against the British government although it was largely restricted to cities. In April 1919 there were a number of demonstrations and *hartals* in the country and the government used brutal measures to suppress them. The Jallianwala Bagh atrocities, inflicted by General Dyer in Amritsar on Baisakhi day (13 April), were a part of this repression. On learning about the massacre, Rabindranath Tagore expressed the pain and anger of the country by renouncing his knighthood.

During the Rowlatt Satyagraha the participants tried to ensure that Hindus and Muslims were united in the fight against British rule. This was also the call of Mahatma Gandhi who always saw India as a land of *all* the people who lived in the country - Hindus, Muslims and those of other religions. He was keen that Hindus and Muslims support each other in any just cause.

Khilafat Agitation and the Non-Cooperation

The Khilafat issue was one such cause. In 1920 the

British imposed a harsh treaty on the Turkish Sultan or Khalifa. People were furious about this as they had been about the Jallianwala massacre. Also, Indian Muslims were keen that the Khalifa be allowed to retain control over Muslim sacred places in the erstwhile Ottoman Empire. The leaders of the Khilafat agitation, Mohammad Ali and Shaukat Ali, now wished to initiate a full-fledged Non-Cooperation Movement. Gandhiji supported their call and urged the Congress to campaign against "Punjab wrongs" (Jallianwala massacre), the Khilafat wrong and demand *swaraj*.

The Non-Cooperation Movement gained momentum through 1921-22. Thousands of students left government-controlled schools and colleges. Many lawyers such as Motilal Nehru, C.R. Das, C. Rajagopalachari and Asaf Ali gave up their practices. British titles were surrendered and legislatures boycotted. People lit public bonfires of foreign cloth. The imports of foreign cloth fell drastically between 1920 and 1922. But all this was merely the tip of the iceberg. Large parts of the country were on the brink of a formidable revolt.

People's Initiatives

In many cases people resisted British rule non-violently. In others, different classes and groups, interpreting Gandhiji's call in their own manner, protested in ways that were not in accordance with his ideas. In either case, people linked their movements to local grievances. Let us look at a few examples.

In Kheda, Gujarat, Patidar peasants organised non-violent campaigns against the high land revenue demand of the British. In coastal Andhra and interior Tamil Nadu, liquor shops were picketed. In the Guntur district of Andhra Pradesh, tribals and poor peasants staged a number of "forest *satyagrahas*", sometimes sending their cattle into forests without paying grazing fee. They were protesting because the colonial state had restricted their use of forest resources in various ways. They believed that Gandhiji would get their taxes reduced and have the forest regulations abolished. In many forest villages, peasants proclaimed *swaraj* and believed that "Gandhi Raj" was about to be established.

In Sind (now in Pakistan), Muslim traders and peasants were very enthusiastic about the Khilafat call. In Bengal too, the Khilafat-Non-Cooperation alliance gave enormous communal unity and strength to the national movement.

In Punjab, the Akali agitation of the Sikhs sought to remove corrupt *mahants* - supported by the British -from their gurdwaras. This movement got closely identified with the Non-Cooperation Movement. In Assam, tea garden labourers, shouting *"Gandhi Maharaj ki Jai"*, demanded a big increase in their wages. They left the British-owned plantations amidst declarations that they were following Gandhiji's wish. Interestingly, in the Assamese Vaishnava songs of the period the reference to Krishna was substituted by "Gandhi Raja".

The People's Mahatma

We can see from the above that sometimes people thought of Gandhiji as a kind of messiah, as someone who could help them overcome their misery and poverty. Gandhiji wished to build class unity, not class conflict, yet peasants could imagine that he would help them in their fight against zamindars, and agricultural labourers believed he would provide them land. At times, ordinary people credited Gandhiji with their *own* achievements. For instance, at the end of a powerful movement, peasants of Pratapgarh in the United Provinces (now Uttar Pradesh) managed to stop illegal eviction of tenants; but they felt it was Gandhiji who had won this demand for them. At other times, using Gandhiji's name, tribals and peasants undertook actions that did not conform to Gandhian ideals.

The following is an extract from a CID report on the kisan movement in Allahabad district, January 1921:

The currency which Mr. Gandhi's name has acquired

even in the remotest villages is astonishing. No one seems to know quite who or what he is, but it is an accepted fact that what he says is so, and what he orders must be done. He is a Mahatma or *sadhu,* a Pundit, a Brahmin who lives at Allahabad, even a *deota* ... the real power of his name is to be traced back to the idea that it was he who got *bedakhli* [illegal eviction] stopped in Pratapgarh ... as a general rule, Gandhi is not thought of as being antagonistic to Government, but only to the *zamindars* ... We are for Gandhiji and the Sarkar.

The Happenings of 1922-1929

Mahatma Gandhi, as you know, was against violent movements. He abruptly called off the Non-Cooperation Movement when in February 1922 a crowd of peasants set fire to a police station in Chauri Chaura. Twenty-two policemen were killed on that day. The peasants were provoked because the police had fired on their peaceful demonstration.

Once the Non-Cooperation movement was over, Gandhiji's followers stressed that the Congress must undertake constructive work in the rural areas. Other leaders such as Chitta Ranj an Das and Motilal Nehru argued that the party should fight elections to the councils and enter them in order to influence government policies. Through sincere social work in villages in the mid-1920s, the Gandhians were able to extend their support base. This proved to be very useful in launching the Civil Disobedience movement in 1930.

Two important developments of the mid-1920s were the formation of the Rashtriya Swayamsevak Sangh (RSS), a Hindu organisation, and the Communist Party of India. These parties have held very different ideas about the kind of country India should be. Find out about the ideas with the help of your teacher. The revolutionary nationalist Bhagat Singh too was active in this period.

The decade closed with the Congress resolving to fight

for *Purna Swaraj* (complete independence) in 1929 under the presidentship of Jawaharlal Nehru. Consequently, "Independence Day" was observed on 26 January 1930 all over the country.

Revolutionary nationalists such as Bhagat Singh and his comrades wanted to fight colonial rule and the rich exploiting classes through a revolution of workers and peasants. For this purpose they founded the Hindustan Socialist Republican Association (HSRA) in 1928 at Ferozeshah Kotla in Delhi. Members of the HSRA assassinated Saunders, a police officer who had led a lathi-charge that caused the death of Lala Lajpat Rai.

Along with his fellow nationalist B.K. Dutt, he threw a bomb in the Central Legislative Assembly on 8 April 1 929. The aim, as their leaflet explained, was not to kill but, "to make the deaf hear", to remind the foreign government of its callous exploitation. Bhagat Singh was tried and executed at the age of 23.

The March to Dandi

Purna Swaraj would never come on its own. It had to be fought for. In 1930, Gandhiji declared that he would lead a march to break the salt law. According to this law, the state had a monopoly on the manufacture and sale of salt. Mahatma Gandhi along with other nationalists reasoned that it was sinful to tax salt since it is such an essential item of our food. The Salt March related the general desire of freedom to a specific grievance shared by everybody, and thus did not divide the rich and the poor.

Gandhiji and his followers marched for over 240 miles from Sabarmati to the coastal town of Dandi where they broke the government law by gathering natural salt found on the seashore, and boiling sea water to produce salt.

Women in the Freedom Struggle

Women from diverse backgrounds participated in the national movement. Young and old, single and married, they came from rural and urban areas, from both conservative and liberal homes. Their involvement was significant for the freedom struggle, for the women's movement, and for themselves personally.

Both British officials and Indian nationalists felt that women's participation gave the national struggle an immense force. Participation in the freedom movement brought women out of their homes. It gave them a place in the professions, in the governance of India, and it could pave the way for equality with men.

What such participation meant for women is best recounted by them. Ambabai of Karnataka had been married at age twelve. Widowed at sixteen, she picketed foreign cloth and liquor shops in Udipi. She was arrested, served a sentence and was rearrested. Between prison terms she made speeches, taught spinning, and organised *prabhat pheris*. Ambabai regarded these as the happiest days of her life because they gave it a new purpose and commitment.

Women, however, had to fight for their right to participate in the movement. During the Salt Satyagraha, for instance, even Mahatma Gandhi was initially opposed to women's participation. Sarojini Naidu had to persuade him to allow women to join the movement.

Peasants, tribals and women participated in large numbers. A business federation published a pamphlet on the salt issue. The government tried to crush the movement through brutal action against peaceful *satyagrahis*. Thousands were sent to jail.

The combined struggles of the Indian people bore fruit when the Government of India Act of 1935 prescribed provincial autonomy and the government announced elections to the provincial legislatures in 1937. The Congress formed governments in 7 out of 11 provinces.

In September 1939, after two years of Congress rule in the provinces, the Second World War broke out. Critical of

Hitler, Congress leaders were ready to support the British war effort. But in return they wanted that India be granted independence after the war.

The British refused to concede the demand. The Congress ministries resigned in protest.

Quit India and Later

Mahatma Gandhi decided to initiate a new phase of movement against the British in the middle of the Second World War. The British must quit India immediately, he told them. To the people he said, "do or die" in your effort to fight the British - but you must fight non-violently. Gandhiji and other leaders were jailed at once but the movement spread. It specially attracted peasants and the youth who gave up their studies to join it. Communications and symbols of state authority were attacked all over the country. In many areas the people set up their own governments.

The first response of the British was severe repression. By the end of 1943 over 90,000 people were arrested, and around 1,000 killed in police firing. In many areas orders were given to machine-gun crowds from airplanes. The rebellion, however, ultimately brought the Raj to its knees.

Towards Independence and Partition

Meanwhile, in 1940 the Muslim League had moved a resolution demanding "Independent States" for Muslims in the north-western and eastern areas of the country. The resolution did not mention partition or Pakistan. Why did the League ask for an autonomous arrangement for the Muslims of the subcontinent?

From the late 1930s, the League began viewing the Muslims as a separate "nation" from the Hindus. In developing this notion it may have been influenced by the history of tension between some Hindu and Muslim groups in the 1920s and 1930s. More importantly, the provincial elections of 1937 seemed to have convinced the League that Muslims were a minority, and they would always have to play second fiddle in any democratic structure. It feared that Muslims may even go unrepresented. The Congress's rejection of the League's desire to form a joint Congress-League government in the United Provinces in 1937 also annoyed the League.

The Congress's failure to mobilise the Muslim masses in the 1930s allowed the League to widen its social support. It sought to enlarge its support in the early 1940s when most Congress leaders were in jail. At the end of the war in 1945, the British opened negotiations between the Congress, the League and themselves for the independence of India. The talks failed because the League saw itself as the sole spokesperson of India's Muslims. The Congress could not accept this claim since a large number of Muslims still supported it.

Elections to the provinces were again held in 1946. The Congress did well in the "General" constituencies but the League's success in the seats reserved for Muslims was spectacular. It persisted with its demand for "Pakistan". In March 1946 the British cabinet sent a three-member mission to Delhi to examine this demand and to suggest a suitable political framework for a free India. This mission suggested that India should remain united and constitute itself as a loose confederation with some autonomy for Muslim-majority areas. But it could not get the Congress and the Muslim League to agree to specific details of the proposal. Partition now became more or less inevitable.

After the failure of the Cabinet Mission, the Muslim League decided on mass agitation for winning its Pakistan demand. It announced 16 August 1946 as "Direct Action Day". On this day riots broke out in Calcutta, lasting several days and resulting in the death of thousands of people. By March 1947 violence spread to different parts of northern India.

Many hundred thousand people were killed and numerous women had to face untold brutalities during the

Partition. Millions of people were forced to flee their homes. Torn asunder from their homelands, they were reduced to being refugees in alien lands. Partition also meant that India changed, many of its cities changed, and a new country - Pakistan - was born. So, the joy of our country's independence from British rule came mixed with the pain and violence of Partition.

8

Mahatma Gandhi and the Politics of Nonviolence

This view of Gandhi's contributions has lent credibility to the principle of nonviolence in the fights against injustice around the world since then.

But the Indian revolt against British rule was anything but nonviolent. Gandhi's tactical ideas, moreover, had serious limitations as a guide to struggle. Movements that began under Gandhi's sponsorship often ended in premature retreats or escalated into physical confrontations. And the final ouster of the British in 1947 can't be counted as a victory for Gandhi's methods, since India's independence came as the movement was shoving Gandhi and his nonviolent philosophy to the political margins.

Gandhi, nevertheless, did make major contributions to the movement. Most crucial was his success in leading masses of people into struggle against British rule—something he did better than any other Indian leader. But while Gandhi's leadership was the spark for some major struggles, it was not their cause. The struggles arose from real, deep grievances against British rule, and the masses, once mobilized, showed repeatedly that they were willing to adopt militant tactics when nonviolent ones didn't work.

To understand the grievances and the struggles they inspired, we have to look at the background of British colonial rule.

India must be Bled

To the British conquerors, India was a source of profits and a base for military operations—using Indian troops—from Africa to Indonesia. From the early stages of conquest in the late eighteenth century, the British began setting up taxation to finance their presence and to send money home.[3] As early as 1765, when the British East India Company first took over the northeastern region known as Bengal, the company also set up monopolies on common necessities like salt.[4]

These monopolies bred resentment and rebellion in the next two centuries. But the British innovation that brought misery to millions was the imposition of market relations—the cash economy—in agriculture.

The first step in introducing cash relations was to tax all the land. As the British replaced the crumbling Mughal empire, they took over and greatly expanded the Mughal system of land-revenue, which had been based on local tax collectors known as *zamindars*. In Bengal, the British nearly doubled the Mughals' rate of land taxation over the course of three decades.[5] They pressed on with the increases even as an estimated one-third of the Bengali population died from famine in 1770-71. Lord Charles Cornwallis, Bengal's next governor-general, noted that large areas rich farmland had reverted to jungle because peasants had abandoned it.[6]

Ultimately, Cornwallis crafted a deal with the *zamindars* to stabilize Bengali agriculture and to guarantee steady revenue. The deal, struck in 1793 and known as the "Permanent Settlement," specified that land taxes in Bengal and neighboring Bihar would stop increasing and that *zamindars* would be allowed to help themselves to 10 percent of the revenues.

In most places outside the Permanent Settlement, and especially in the South, the British instituted direct taxation.[7] Around the southeast coastal city of Madras—a region first officially absorbed by the British in 1801—the initial tax rate was 45 percent of the produce of the soil. In later decades the British reduced the rate to a still-ruinous maximum of 33 percent.[8]

Peasants throughout British-ruled India now needed to sell a major portion of their produce on the market to raise cash to pay the taxes. By I860, this market began to spread throughout British India, facilitated by a new railway system whose first tracks were laid in 1853 to connect the western port city of Bombay to inland towns.[9] The railways carried cotton, food grains, and indigo to ships that were ultimately bound for Britain and other markets.[10] The Suez Canal, completed in 1869 and directly controlled by the British after 1875, connected the Red Sea to the Mediterranean and greatly sped up the flow of goods.

The new connections to the world market had a profound effect on the villages. Social power shifted decisively to the moneyed classes, including *zamindars* and moneylenders— often the same people—who, backed by British legal guarantees of their property rights, began to buy up large tracts of land. Ownership allowed them to charge rent to peasant cultivators on top of the taxes they extracted.[11]

Dispossessed peasants became agricultural day laborers, a class that grew from almost nothing in 1852 to 18 percent of the rural population in 1872.[12] By the mid-twentieth century, agricultural proletarians—those who owned no land, or so little land that they had to work for others to survive—made up half of the rural population.[13]

A similar mass confiscation of agricultural wealth had occurred in England in the previous two centuries, a process that Marx had dubbed the "primitive [i.e., initial] accumulation of capital." But dispossessed Indian peasants could not seek out industrial jobs as English peasants had. England's head start in industry was allowing it to flood the Indian market with factory goods, and these imports began to crush India's skilled handicraft industries, including metalworking and—especially—cloth production.[14]

The result was to trap the peasants into rural misery and to further expand the rural proletariat with unemployed spinners and weavers.

British rule thus marked a dramatic setback in the material welfare of most Indians. Before conquest, India suffered an average of one major famine every 50 years, but famines or scarcity gripped some part of India for 20 out of the 49 years in the period 1860-1908.[15] The reserves that peasants formerly held to tide themselves over through periods of low rainfall were now routinely being sold to pay rent, debts, and taxes—and shipped out by rail to be consumed overseas. The railroads also ensured widespread uniformity in market prices. As a result, grain shortages in one region caused prices to rise everywhere, thus thrusting the pain of local crop failures onto all of India's poor.

Since the famines' immediate cause was the peasants' financial ruin, these catastrophes only served to speed up the concentration of land in the hands of the rich. What's more, the British let tens of millions die by refusing to ease up on revenue collections or to return the revenue to the peasants in the form of famine relief. This murderous policy arose partly from a fanatical attachment to *laissez-faire* market economics—and partly from the fear that poor Indians would start to demand relief even when there weren't famines.[16]

Lord Robert Salisbury, British Secretary of State for India and one of the architects of the *laissez-faire* approach to famines, summed up British aims in this period by declaring that "India must be bled."[17] Karl Marx put some numbers to it:

> What the English take from them annually in the form of rent, dividends for railways useless to the Hindoos, pensions for military and civil servicemen, for Afghanistan and other wars, etc. etc.—what they take from them *without any equivalent* and *quite apart* from what they appropriate to themselves annually *within* India, speaking only of the *value of the commodities* the

Indians have *gratuitously* and annually to send over to England, it amounts to *more than the total sum of income of the 60 millions of agricultural and industrial laborers of India! This is Process, with a vengeance.*[18]

Resistance before Gandhi

Indians did not merely accept this situation. The history of the British *raj* (that is, British rule) is marked by different forms of resistance, including local uprisings of peasants and "tribal" groups.

Up until 1857, however, no movement connected local grievances into an all-India effort to expel the British. Indians were divided from each other by caste, class, religion, language, and region. At the time, the only all-India force that could stand up to the British were the soldiers—known as *sepoys*—in the army. When the *sepoys* rebelled in 1857 against racial and religious abuse, they sparked and linked up to peasant rebellions in north, central, and western India.[19]

The revolt was nearly national in scope, but it was not nationalist in consciousness. The revolt's demands were to expel the British and to return power to local princes—the only legitimate authority the rebels could conceive.[20]

The rebellion broke down in the face of British repression. As a spontaneous uprising, it lacked planning and coordination. What's more, the nearer the movement got to the goals of "local control," the weaker and more divided it was bound to become against British terror.

Thus, although the Sepoy Mutiny was anti-imperial, it was backward-looking. The classes and the consciousness that could carry a truly nationalist movement in the future were only in embryonic stages at the time.

In the wake of the mutiny, the British government took over direct rule of India, replacing the British East India Company's administration. From then on, viceroys ruled in the name of the British crown, and Queen Victoria promised that Indians would receive—eventually—the same rights as other British subjects.

In the following decades, nationalist politicians arose from the new middle class of Indian lawyers and civil servants that was growing under the British *raj*. To the extent that this class existed in 1857, its members stood aside from the Sepoy Mutiny. They saw their own future connected to modernization, and thus would sooner strive for acceptance as equals in the *raj* than put their fate back into the hands of the princes.

But the nationalist middle class was motivated by more than ambition. In the first place, they saw that the racism that held them back professionally fell even more brutally on other Indians:

> For the less fortunate, racism took cruder forms of kicks and blows and shooting "accidents" as the "sahib" disciplined his *punkha* coolie [whose duty was to fan the "sahib" with a palmyra leaf—*a. punkha]* or bagged a native by mistake [while hunting]... No less than 81 shooting "accidents" were recorded in the years between 1880 and 1900. White-dominated courts regularly awarded ridiculously light sentences for such incidents, and a glance at contemporary Indian journals or private papers immediately reveals how important such things were for the rise of nationalism.[21]

The middle class could also see the poverty inflicted by British rule—in contrast to the prosperity of England, where many Indian lawyers and civil servants went to school. Many of the students became attracted to ideas of nationalists such as Dadabhai Naoroji (1825—1917), who was living in England and is best known for the "drain of wealth" theory of Indian poverty—the anti-imperialist complement to Salisbury's "India must be bled."

In 1885, many of these former students founded the Indian National Congress to press the interests of Indians under the British *raj*.[22]

Congress' methods in its first decades were confined mostly to petitioning the administration behind closed doors. Even as some nationalists became radicalized enough to demand *swaraj* (home rule), Congress remained an elite affair—a yearly conference dominated by lawyers and professionals. Although Congress became known for increasingly radical speeches, it did not have real roots in other classes—or much concrete achievement to show for itself. In fact, it barely existed between its annual conferences.

One spur to Congress' radicalization was the growth of a tradition of populism within the middle class, which began as urban nationalists responded to outbreaks of peasant resistance to British oppression. These inter-class alliances began to form intermittently even in the years before the foundation of Congress. As early as 1859—60, when Bengali indigo cultivators rose up to resist their virtual enserfment to their landlords (who were primarily British), Calcutta's middle class sprang into action to support the struggle. The Indigo Revolt thus united Hindu and Muslim peasants with Hindu city-dwellers, who took up the peasants' cause in mass meetings, newspaper columns, and law courts.[23]

By the late 1890s, populists progressed from supporting roles in peasant movements to positions of direct leadership within them. One such leader in Congress was Bal Gangadhar Tilak (1856-1920), who led peasants in the province of Maharashtra in a successful revenue strike during a famine in 1896.[24] In the course of such agitation, Tilak earned the nickname "Lokamanya"—beloved of the people.

The turn to mass agitation reflected a growing impatience with the "mendicant" (begging) methods of the older Congress generation, who became known as "Moderates" after the turn of the twentieth century. Tilak's "Extremist" wing of Congress distinguished itself by its demand for immediate *swaraj*—as opposed to gradual Indianization of the regime—and by its injection of Hindu revivalism into politics. Although the Extremists' main target was the British, some, including Tilak, also supported provocative anti-Islamic campaigns, such as those against the slaughter of cows.[25]

In their use of religious identification as a mobilizing force in politics—a practice known in India as "communalism"— the Extremists were building on a trend that had caught hold within the middle class in the previous decades. To understand why communalism arose, and to understand why it played a role for a period (roughly 1895-1920) as the most militant expression of resistance to British rule, it is important to recall that Congress' middle-class constituency represented the only section of India's population that was at all Anglicized or secular. Congress spoke English as it pursued its course of making pleas to the British, whose society was evidently superior to India's in scientific knowledge, military prowess, and productive power. And Britain's liberal political principles were attractive, too, even though the British refused, in practice, to apply them in the colonies. The goal of many Congress members was simply to get the British to live up to these principles and thus to extend the benefits of British freedom and prosperity to India. In the process, many became more British than the British in their dress, their speech, their constitutional legalism, and their secular approach to politics.

At the same time, within the same middle class, a realization was growing that the *raj* was not living up to its promises and that, by its nature, it could not. Extremists took the "drain of wealth" theory, originated by the Moderates, as the key to understanding why the *raj* would never treat Indians as equals. As Tilak said in a 1907 speech:

> *Pax Britannica* has been established in this country in order that a foreign government may exploit the country.... It was an unhappy circumstance that [this] was not realized sooner. We believed in the benevolent intentions of the government, but in politics there is no

benevolence. Benevolence is used to sugar-coat the declarations of self-interest But soon a

change came over us. English education, growing poverty, and better familiarity with our rulers, opened our eyes...especially [those of] the venerable leader [Naoroji, who was] the first to tell us that the drain from the country was ruining it. He went...to England and spent 25 years of his life in trying to convince the English people of the injustice that is being done to us. He worked very hard.

He has come here at the age of 82 to tell us that he is bitterly disappointed.[26]

Tilak went on to note that the British would be unable to rule without the collaboration of the middle class, including Congress members, who were pacified by their illusions in British intentions. Congress, it seemed, was living up to the words of British historian Thomas Macauley, who, as an administrator for the British East India Company in the 1830s, had written of the need to cultivate a class who may be interpreters between us and the millions whom we govern; a class of persons, Indian in blood and color, but English in taste, in opinions, in morals, and in intellect.'

Fired by the realization of Congress' unwitting complicity in propping up British rule, the Extremists pioneered the tactics of "passive resistance" (non-cooperation) that Gandhi would take up later—boycott of British goods and institutions, nonpayment of taxes, etc.

But this turn in tactics also required the Extremists to make a decisive shift away from the elite style of politics that focused on appeals to the British—toward the populist style that consistently sought out new allies among ordinary Indians. In this task of making anti-British connections with peasants and workers—or with as-yet unpoliticized sections of the middle class—English words and manners could only get in the way. The Extremists thus used vernacular languages and indigenous symbolism in their agitation, including appeals to local heroes, to regional history and myths—and to religious solidarity. Tilak was a sincere Hindu, but admitted that his real reason for using religion in politics was opportunistic; it was effective in motivating people.[28] Others were genuine Hindu fanatics, including a generation of anti-British terrorists who formed a "revolutionary" flank of assassins and bombers outside Congress in the period from 1900-20.

However effective Hindu-based nationalism was in some mobilizations, it alienated ordinary Muslims and left them out of the movement. What's more, it provided an opening for reactionary well-to-do Muslims to pose as defenders of Muslim interests and to forge an alliance with the *raj*. In 1906, Lord Minto, viceroy of India, received a delegation of Muslim nobles and landholders and gave them what they came for: an assurance that the administration would recognize them as the voice of India's Muslims, who made up 20 to 25 percent of the population. The two parties struck the deal, of course, without consulting most Muslims, who, as peasants, were exploited by both the landholders and the British state. The delegation promptly founded the Muslim League.[29]

The meaning of the meeting with Minto, said a British official with a bit of optimistic exaggeration, was "nothing less than the pulling back of 62 million of people from joining the ranks of the seditious opposition."[30]

The British willingly granted the Muslim League its main demands: reserved positions for Muslims in government jobs and separate Muslim electorates to choose representatives in any elected councils. The demand for affirmative action reflected an underrepresentation of Muslims in government service, but not because Muslims were relatively more "backward" or oppressed than Hindus. In fact, Muslims were scattered through all classes—though unevenly in different regions— and, by 1921, had higher overall literacy rates than Hindus.[31] The Muslims' lag in getting government jobs arose from the fact that Muslim population was concentrated in inland areas, while the pattern of British conquest had been to control the coastal areas for decades before they moved inland. Despite their presence in all classes, Muslims were weakest in the industrial bourgeoisie, so the relative political power of landowners was greater among Muslims than among Hindus.[32]

Within Congress, Muslims and other minorities (including the Zoroastrians known as Parsis) worked harmoniously with Hindus. In fact, Muhammad Ali Jinnah (1875-1948), who later led the Muslim League's drive for a separate Pakistan, married a Parsi in his early years—and served as Tilak's defense counsel in a show trial in 1908.

The trial, which took place in Bombay, also marked a new breakthrough in connecting the official national movement to popular struggle. In the wake of terrorist attacks on British officials in Bengal, Tilak had written an article declaring that, while he did not advocate terrorism, he understood that the ultimate cause of the attacks was British oppression. The British convicted him of treason for publishing the article, and workers in Bombay struck in protest. They mounted a six-day strike, one day for each year of the Lokamanya's sentence. The strike affected 76 of Bombay's 85 textile mills and a railway workshop.[33]

The strike marked the emergence of the working class as a force in politics. In a contemporary article on political struggles around the world, Russian revolutionary V.I. Lenin noted the strike and wrote:

> In India, too, the proletariat has already developed to conscious political mass struggle—and that being the case, the Russian-style British regime in India is doomed!... The class-conscious European worker now has comrades in Asia, and their number will grow by leaps and bounds.[34]

Only at this time was India's trend toward de-industrialization beginning to turn around, with the appearance of major Indian-owned enterprises. By 1921, the working class in industry and on big plantations would reach 2.7 million—with a potential to exercise disproportionate influence in a country of 300 million.[35]

Just as important was the growth of the Indian bourgeoisie, segments of which became solidly nationalist as they chafed under British control of currencies and tariffs.

Practically every class had grievances against British rule: lower and middle peasants, workers, the professional middle class, and the bourgeoisie. It was a matter of time before enough of these sections of society would unite to throw the British out. The real question was which sections would coalesce into an alliance to lead the rest—and with what ideas about the shape of post-independence India.

Gandhi, more than anyone else, would pull together the leading alliance of forces. His political vision put a stamp on the direction of the movement at crucial turns. Ultimately, though, social forces stronger than Gandhi's personality were to shape the outcome.

Gandhi's Approach to Politics

Mohandas K. Gandhi was born in 1869 in the Indian province of Gujarat. His family was in the commercial *bania* caste that produced, along with the Brahmins, much of the middle class. As a young man, he went to England to receive legal training. He would later abandon his profession, however, and adopt the lifestyle and dress of the Hindu peasantry—thus going several steps beyond the Congress Extremists in their stylistic identification with India's common folk.

The intensity of his religious convictions did not come from orthodox training in childhood but from adult studies that he began as a political activist in South Africa. Upon his return to India from England, he had a rough start as a lawyer and accepted an offer in 1893 to work on a commercial case in South Africa. He ended up staying, with brief returns to India and Britain, for more than 20 years.[36]

In South Africa, racism was even more intense than in India, and Gandhi became an advocate and leader of the Indian immigrant population. Struggles for Indian rights escalated over his stay in South Africa, and Gandhi's political development paralleled the course of nationalist debates back in India. He began as a loyalist of the empire, dressed in a three-piece suit, demanding that South Africa's Indian population be accorded the full rights of British subjects—even though the starting point of many Indians in South Africa was the near-slave status of indentured servants. In the course of struggle, Gandhi ultimately concluded that something was systematically wrong with British society and adopted the cultural trappings of traditional India.[37]

Gandhi taught himself skills that would make him unique upon his return to India, including how to overcome caste, class, and religious divisions to build a base for dramatic mass actions. Unlike the Congress Extremists, Gandhi was a strenuous advocate of interreligious unity and scrupulously avoided using his Hindu identification to channel people's anger in the direction of Muslims or other minorities. And, far from being unworldly, Gandhi also learned the fundraising and accounting skills necessary to sustaining mass politics.[38]

Gandhi's religious and political development were intertwined. In the writings of Leo Tolstoy, with whom he corresponded, and the writings of social theorist Robert Ruskin, Gandhi found a philosophy that—along with an idiosyncratic reading of Hindu scripture—diagnosed modern oppression as the product of industrialism and proposed nonviolent political action as a cure.[39]

Gandhi believed, in one historian's words:

> The search for truth was the goal of human life, and as no one could ever be sure of having attained the ultimate truth, use of violence to enforce one's own necessarily partial understanding of it was sinful.[40]

By 1907 he had worked out the basic strategy of nonviolent resistance, which he called *satyagraha* ("the path of truth"). It consisted of training a disciplined core of volunteer *(satyagrahis)* who helped to lead mass marches and mass violations of specific laws that resulted in intentional mass arrests.[41] Three *satyagraha* campaigns in the next seven years, along with a growing body of articles and pamphlets, made him famous in India even before he returned.

Although the aims and methods of *satyagraha* resembled those of passive resistance, Gandhi insisted that the two tactics differed "as the North pole from the South." Advocates of passive resistance such as Tilak adopted nonviolence as a policy— not as a principle—to avoid retribution from the overwhelming force of the British.[42] But *satyagraha* was far from being a means to avoid suffering. *Satyagrahis* actually aimed to make a show of inflicting suffering on themselves in order to demonstrate their seriousness and patience in resisting injustice.[43]

While still in South Africa, Gandhi wrote about India in his 1909 pamphlet, "Hind Swaraj" (Indian Self-Rule), and targeted what he thought was the real enemy, industrial civilization:

> It would be folly to assume that an Indian Rockefeller would be better than the American Rockefelle India's salvation consists in unlearning what she has learnt during the past 50 years or so. The railways, telegraphs, hospitals, lawyers, doctors and such like have all to go, and the so-called upper class have to learn to live consciously and religiously and deliberately the simple life of a peasant.[44]

This vision of Indian society going backwards in time was unrealistic, of course, especially given the new growth of an Indian working class and bourgeoisie, and it found little real support among the leading elements of the national movement—Indian intellectuals and industrialists.

It was Utopian particularly in upholding the idea that the "so-called upper class" would willingly give up its privileged position to live like peasants. Far from this scenario, the Indian upper class increasingly wanted the British out of the way precisely to become the new "Indian Rockefellers."

Although Gandhi's anti-industrial vision had little appeal for India's rising urban classes, it struck a chord among India's larger masses—especially the poor peasants and unemployed weavers and spinners—who had been crushed by their connection to Britain's industrial system.

Gandhi was to put the anti-modern current of his thought into practice through the village social workers who organized self-help among the rural poor.[45] Although this "constructive work" made little real headway against poverty, it was later to create mass support for the Congress Party—and mass bases from which to launch future campaigns.[46]

The appeal of Gandhi's strategy was two-fold. It appealed to masses of villagers because it was a collective way to resist, to rise above all the state's violence and show the dignity of their cause. It also appealed to the wealthy merchants, landlords, and small-holding peasants because it offered the hope of getting rid of the British while not threatening to destroy their property or endanger their economic and social position. To those who had something to lose from unrestrained social revolt, *satyagraha* promised to bring the benefits of mass mobilization—already evident from mass campaigns led by the Extremists—while maintaining the strictest possible control over the movement.[47]

India's New Mass Leader

Gandhi returned to India and joined the Indian National Congress in the midst of the First World War. The war was bringing an economic and political crisis for the British, and space opened up for Indian textile bosses to get a greater share of the home market.[48] A growing section of them was impatient with British control of the market, and many became fervent supporters of the nationalist movement.[40]

They were particularly drawn to Gandhi's promises of a nonviolent removal of British rule. Through Gandhi's appeal, Congress began to receive funding from some of India's richest industrialists, including the textile magnate Ambalal Sarabhai of Gujarat and the Calcutta-based G.D. Birla, who headed India's second-largest industrial group. They became Gandhi's regular consultants throughout his political career.[50]

For ordinary people in India, the war also awoke new aspirations. Indian soldiers fought for the British in a war they had no stake in and returned home wanting to be treated as equals. As Eqbal Ahmad described the situation,

> On the battlefield they were every day recognizing that they were equals, but they were also experiencing patterns of racial discrimination. Therefore they came back from World War I burning with anger. They and their relatives gave the push to the nationalist movement.[51]

The Russian Revolution of 1917 had a radicalizing impact on oppressed people throughout the world, and India was no exception. Wrote one historian:

> In the post-war years—what is repeatedly evident is a combination of multiplying grievances with new moods of strength or hope: the classic historical formula for a potentially revolutionary situation.[52]

The aftermath of the Russian Revolution thus saw growing militancy among workers and peasants that erupted into massive struggles. Gandhi tried to play the role of mediator and acted as a restraint on the movement.

In 1918, a dispute broke out at a textile factory in Ahmed-abad when the owner, Gandhi's friend Ambalal Sarabhai, tried to end a system of bonuses that he had introduced during an outbreak of plague. Sarabhai's sister

Anusya was a Gandhian disciple who had set up night schools for mill workers. Gandhi intervened to convince the workers to drop their demand for a 50 percent wage hike down to 35 percent and forbade militant picketing in favor of his own—successful—hunger strike. The district magistrate's report on the strike claimed that Gandhi undertook his fast after being "stung by.. .taunts" from workers who "assailed him for being a friend of the mill-owners, riding in their motorcars and eating sumptuously with them, while the weavers were starving."[53]

He advocated a labor philosophy of peaceful arbitration of disputes and argued that bosses should act as "trustees" for the workers. This message of class collaboration cloaked in the language of nonviolence would be Gandhi's continued approach as the class struggle intensified. His position on strikes was clear:

> In India we want no political strikes We must gain control over all the unruly and disturbing elements... We seek not to destroy capital or capitalists, but to regulate the relations between capital and labor. We want to harness capital to our side. It would be folly to encourage sympathetic strikes.[54]

This was an unfortunate position, since the power of the strike, in factories, on plantations, and on the railroads, could economically cripple the British in India—and permit workers to pose a concrete alternative to the exploitation over which the British presided.

The potential exploded in 1919. Mass agitation against repressive British legislation, the Rowlatt Act, which sought to extend wartime "anti-terrorist" restrictions on civil rights, coincided with a strike wave by mill workers.

Gandhi's launched the first all-India *satyagraha* in order to further stir up people's anger against the Rowlatt restrictions and to channel it in a nonviolent direction. But weeks into the campaign—with only fragments of a national activist network in place—fewer than a thousand

Indians had signed up nationwide to be official *satyagrahis.* To broaden participation, Gandhi added a call for a nationwide work stoppage, but called it for a Sunday so as to minimize its impact on businesses.[5 5]

Gandhi and the local leaders who responded to his call made special efforts to unite Hindus and Muslims in the campaign. In early April, they succeeded in putting together massive united demonstrations in most major cities. The British were particularly alarmed to see the breakdown of divisions they had worked so hard to maintain. When Muslims joined a Hindu festival in the Pubjabi city of Amritsar, for example— and then drank from the same cups with Hindus—the authorities became terribly frightened.[56]

The Punjab, in fact, was the site of the movement's greatest upsurge. Punjab's administrator, Michael O'Dwyer, fanned the flames when he prevented Gandhi from entering the province. Gandhi's arrest enraged Punjabis and deprived O'Dwyer of the mediating services of the one man who might have kept the movement from escalating.

In Amritsar, British police cracked down by arresting the movement's main leaders—one Hindu and one Muslim. When a crowd gathered to protest the arrests, the British open fire, killing twelve. In response to the shootings, the crowd looted buildings associated with the British and killed five Britons, including some civilians. In defiance of a British ban on future assemblies, the remaining leadership planned a mass rally for the following Sunday.

When news of the repression in Amritsar reached the city of Lahore just thirty miles away, peaceful demonstrations escalated into clashes with police. Factory and railway workers struck, and the British withdrew their forces from the city. A mass rally elected a People's Committee that ran the city for four days. The key event of the Lahore upsurge was the entry of tens of thousands of Muslim workers and artisans into the movement, which had been started by the mostly-Hindu middle class. The British enlisted "respectable" Muslim landholders to persuade the Muslim workers to quit the movement, but the workers were unmoved by their "social superiors."[57]

Then the big crackdown began in Amritsar. The Sunday, April 13, rally brought thousands to an walled-in park area known as Jallianwala Bagh, where more thousands—unaware of the ban on meetings—had arrived from out of town for a Sikh festival. General Reginald Dyer, on the authority of O'Dwyer, brought his soldiers to break up the crowd of 20,000 by force. Without issuing a warning, Dyer instructed his troops to fire into the thickest parts of the crowd, not to disperse it but, as he testified later, to produce a "moral effect" throughout the whole Punjab.[58]

Back in Lahore, the middle-class leaders of the People's Committee were trying to call off the strikes and rebellion— against vehement objections from workers— when the British attacked under a province-wide martial law decree.[59]

The official casualty count at Jallianwala Bagh was 379 dead and 1,200 wounded, but Indian accounts speak of two or three times that number. In the following weeks of martial law terror, the British massacred many hundreds more Punjabis, tortured and flogged others—and generally reimposed their authority in the most humiliating ways they could dream up.[60]

Forces Realign, and Gandhi's Star rises

The year's events effectively wiped out the old sources of division between Congress Extremists and Moderates. Extremists such as Tilak (who was to die in 1920) already supported Gandhi's leadership before 1919 and helped him to put together the national agitational network that Congress needed.[61] For their own part, many Moderates took up the demand for immediate *swaraj* as British repression disgusted and radicalized them. Most now backed a populist agitational course for Congress, as long as Gandhi's leadership promised to keep the movement within acceptable bounds.

The British re-thought their approach as well. From late 1919 onward, they would centralize their response to Congress' agitation so that men like O'Dwyer...would no longer be permitted to stoke the fires of nationalism through brutal repressions of popular will British policy was [thereafter] characterized by restraint and coercion in finely balanced proportions. The objectives of this policy were threefold: first, to bring to the surface different strands of opinion which had rallied around Gandhi; secondly, to drive a wedge between moderates and extremists; and thirdly, to strike down the extremists the moment they had lost the goodwill of moderate opinion.[62]

Gandhi was only too ready to hang the militants (and later, the leftists) out to dry—something he did with numbing frequency for the next 28 years.[63] He began in the aftermath of the Rowlatt agitation itself. Five days after the Jallianwala Bagh massacre, Gandhi called off the movement. He declared that he had committed a "Himalayan blunder" in calling for mass civil disobedience without enough organizational and ideological control over the movement,[6 4] thus suggesting that British repression was simply a response to the movement's lack of self-discipline. He condemned the violence that had broken out on both sides, though it was far from equal. In the Punjab, for example, every account places Indian deaths well over 1,200 and British deaths under 10.

Gandhi was quite calculating in offering his leadership as an alternative to radicalism. At the beginning of 1919, he wrote to a Congress Moderate to try to draw him into the Rowlatt agitation:

> The growing generation will not be satisfied with petitions... *Satyagraha* is the only way, it seems to me, to stop terrorism.[64]

At the end of the Rowlatt agitation, in which mass social revolt replaced terrorism as India's most important radical trend, Gandhi recommended himself to the British authorities as an acceptable bargaining partner—and as an ally against the left. As the British continued to press martial law terror upon the Punjab, Gandhi wrote to the viceroy June 8:

The awful experience of the past two months and a half have shown me that there is nothing save *satyagraha,* of which civil disobedience is an integral part, that can possibly save India from Bolshevism and even a worse fate.

Gandhi could play his unique mediating role only because his leadership served as a lens to focus the explosive discontent of ordinary Indians—which, by the end of the war, had become overripe for expression. By the early 1920s it was clear that Gandhi brought two elements to the anti-imperial struggle that had been missing since the Sepoy Mutiny. His political skills, plans, and charisma drew a mass base into the first all-India struggles since 1857, and the struggles themselves connected popular grievances against *aspects* of British rule to the final goal of *ending* British rule. Gandhi's success made him into the Congress Party's preeminent—and indispensible— leader.

In the course of these struggles, Gandhi remolded Congress from an organization of intermittently-active nationalist clerks and lawyers into a genuine mass party. Although to the mass of peasants he was known as *zMahatma* (a "great soul" or holy man), Gandhi was also a shrewd political organizer and infighter. In 1920, he insisted on reorganizing Congress into a hierarchy of committees built up from the villages to the district level, reworking provincial committees on a linguistic basis, and creating a 15-member Working Committee as an ongoing executive to oversee the whole party's work.[67]

To make sure that his own voice came through in national politics without relying on the commercial press—as he had been forced to do during the Rowlatt agitation[6]

[8]—Gandhi took over the editorship of the Ahmedabad weekly, *Young India,* in October of 1919.[69]

Despite Gandhi's extensive preparations, however, the next mass campaign, the Non-Cooperation Movement of 1921—22, also unleashed forces beyond Gandhi's control. Millions were inspired by Gandhi's call to win "*swaraj* in one year," and many resorted to methods that he did not approve.

As he toured the countryside in 1921, Gandhi's repeated the slogan that peasants must "turn *zamindars* into friends."[7 c] When peasants in Assam's tea plantations revolted in May, Gandhi and Congress were downright hostile. Some of the strikes hit plantations owned by Congress members, who did everything possible to stop the revolt, which continued into December.[71] He made it clear that he deprecated all attempts to create discord between landlords and tenants and advised all the tenants to suffer rather than fight, for they had to join forces against the most powerful *za-mindar,* namely the Government.[72]

He went so far as to reassure the landlords that, I shall be no party to dispossessing propertied classes of their private property without just cause. My objective is to reach your hearts and convert you so that you may hold all your private property in trust for your tenants and use it primarily for their welfare. But supposing that there is an attempt unjustly to deprive you of your property, you will find me fighting on your side.

Peasants, who were becoming increasingly radical, felt betrayed. In one village, the same people who had showered him with garlands later refused him food.

The largest uprising to occur during the Non-Cooperation Movement was in Malabar on India's southwest coast, an area now included in the state of Kerala. In the revolt, tens of thousands of peasants known as Moplahs rose up against the power of the landlords—and of the British. Following years of tenants' rights agitation, the revolt began in August, 1921, after a police raid on a mosque. The rebels, following "radical leaders preaching an egalitarian millennium,"[74] attacked official buildings and landlords' houses—and drove the British from some areas for several months.

Repression of the revolt was more severe than at Jallianwala Bagh. Official figures cite 2,337 rebels killed and 45,404 taken prisoner. But no Congress leader defended the rebels at any point. Instead Gandhi condemned this class revolt as an outbreak of communal hatred, since the Moplahs were predominantly Muslim peasants resisting landlords who were mostly Hindu. Religious bigotry did play a role in some aspects of the revolt, but the Moplahs pointedly left thousands of Hindu peasants unmolested—and arrested Muslim nobles when they needed to. Some Hindus were indeed forcibly converted to Islam, but the highest estimate (from a Hindu communal association) claimed only 2,500 forced conversions out of the 400,000 Hindus who resided in rebel-controlled territory.[75]

Finally, in 1922, Gandhi abruptly called off the movement nationwide when a crowd in Chauri Chaura responded to police beatings and gunfire by killing 22 cops. Even when a court sentenced 172 Indians to death for their act of retaliation, the Congress Party—which was full of lawyers experienced in using trials to expose British oppression—did not raise a finger to defend them. The only recorded protests were from an emigre Communist journal and the Executive Committee of the Communist International. Ultimately, 19 of the 172 were hanged, and the rest were deported.[76]

The fact that Gandhi could call not one but two all-India movements in four years—and then call off the second one when it got too militant for his taste—shows how crucial he had become to the national movement. It also exposes the lack of an alternative revolutionary leadership in the potentially revolutionary situation of 1919-22.[77]

The postwar movement transformed Indian nationality from an idea in the minds of Westernized lawyers into a real historical force. The involvement of workers and peasants on a mass scale also meant that the national movement would bring Indian social relations into question. As a result, politics polarized in the 1920s into the three trends that still dominate Indian politics today—a nationalist center, the religious right, and the secular left—whose positions on the national movement arose from their answers to the emerging "social question."

The new right organized along communal lines. Hindu communalists now shrank back from being the most militant anti-British force, a role that they had been able to play only as long as Hindu peasants and workers did not stir and begin to pose their own demands—thus upsetting traditional relations of caste subordination. The new right's leadership, both Muslim and Hindu, was made up social conservatives who were so frightened by the mobilization of workers and peasants that they recoiled from the mainstream of the national movement. To this day, although their professed enemies are those who belong to a different religion, communal organizations actually serve to discipline lower-caste and lower-class Indians to the authority of elite members of their own religion. As one study argues about the Hindu right,

> Organized Hindutva ["Hinduness"] emerges right from the beginning as an upper caste reaction to efforts at self-assertion by downtrodden groups within the Hindu fold The RSS [Rashtriya Swayamsevak Sangh—a Hindu fascist group founded in 1925], from its inception down to today, has been overwhelmingly middle class Brahmin or Bania in composition, drawn together on the basis of a fear psychosis directed against other social groups: Muslims, most overtly, but by implication also lower caste Hindus.[7] [8]

This modern form of street-thug communalism—which now targeted a rival religious group rather than the British as the main enemy—brought about a split in the older generation of Hindu nationalists. Some who favored broad popular struggle against the British, such as Tilak, cast their lot with Gandhi when he agitated on the basis of inter-religious unity.

But others who had been yesterday's "revolutionaries" became the most vociferous communalists. One, Vinayak Damodar Savarkar (1883-1966), began by collaborating with Tilak in a 1905 boycott campaign before he moved on to lead a seemingly more radical group in London (1906—10) that succeeded in assassinating a British official. Finally in the mid-1920s, after years in prison, Savarkar took up the leadership of the Hindu Mahasabha, a reactionary high-caste political party that spawned the RSS.[79] The thread connecting Savarkar's days of "revolutionary terrorism" to his days as the prime ideologue of *Hindutva* was his reliance on the actions of an elite— and a corresponding mistrust of mass action from below.[80]

In the 1920s, the Muslim right developed some urban street-thug groups that mirrored the RSS. But the main organization of the Muslim right, the Muslim League, was not built on the RSS's middle class basis. The League had begun as a trend dominated by big landowners. Following the Non-Cooperation Movement, the League withdrew from an alliance it had formed with Congress in 1916—and began to take a growing fraction of the middle class with it, including Muhammad Ali Jinnah. An anglophile with an aristocratic manner, Jinnah refused to back Congress' agitational turn in 1919, and he harbored a grudge against Gandhi for eclipsing his own star in the galaxy of Congress leaders. From these tactical and personal differences—not from religious conviction—Jinnah first withdrew from politics and then later used the Muslim League as a vehicle to promote his leadership.[81]

The League's political focus was on electoral campaigns for British-sponsored (and, initially, powerless) representative councils. But the League lacked a mass base and fared poorly in elections—losing to Congress for 20 years even in races for seats reserved for Muslims.[82] Like Congress, the Muslim League favored Indianization of the regime, but was willing to tolerate a slower pace than Congress because they foreswore the method that could speed up the process—mass agitation. And until the late 1930s, the League did not call for a separate Pakistan.

The nationalist center was by far the strongest organized political trend in India. This broad grouping formed the mainstream of the Congress Party, ranging from Gandhi on the right to reformist socialists on the left. This force regrouped in the 1920s from its failure to win "*swaraj* in one year" and relaxed its tactical stance of "non-cooperation." By the second half of the decade, the party gave up its boycott of British-sponsored councils and began to use them as a platform to advocate further concessions.

The party combined its "parliamentary" activity with Gandhian "constructive work" in the countryside (i.e., nationalist base-building). At the same time, it still wielded the threat of further mass action to push the pace of reform. Although this mixed bag of tactics actually reflected debates among different trends in Congress, together the tactics formed a fairly coherent strategy of winning political independence gradually through an "escalating series of compromises."[8] ~

This reformist approach required occasional use of mass action that focused on the national question while keeping the social question as far in the background as possible. For this strategy, Gandhi's leadership was crucial, for only he stood a chance of directing the mass struggles—from above—toward acceptable targets.

This kind of mass organizing would have to legitimate and strengthen existing indigenous authorities while attempting to bridge the divisions that the British had fostered among Indians. Gandhi's solution was to approach Indian nationality the way that earlier nationalists (and the British) had seen it—as a "composite" of separate communities in which people's first loyalty was religious—even though caste, class and regional ties were at least as strong as religious ones.[8 4] As a result, Gandhi tended to approach mass organizing as a task of convincing established local figures to lead their co-religionists into struggle.

The more or less conscious aim of this strategy was to undermine the class independence of the urban and rural proletariat, but its unintended effect was to give strength to communalism. Like the institution of separate electorates for different religious groups, Gandhian politics promoted a form of political power that was founded on a religious base. Thus, despite his avowed commitment to Hindu-Muslim unity, Gandhi's top-down methods helped to strengthen the communal organizations that took the initiative when nationalist action ebbed.[85] Just when nationalist agitation had raised and then disappointed people's hopes, communal organizations were thus ready to step in and direct people's bitterness toward scapegoats.

Congress showed its tolerance for communalism by allowing its members to belong to the RSS, the Hindu Mahasabha or the Muslim League until a Congress resolution in 1934 finally forbade such dual memberships. By then, however, Gandhi s solicitude toward the Hindu right had even alienated Congress party leaders such as Mohamed Ali (1895-1931). Ali began as a staunch Gandhi ally in 1919—22 and became Congress Party president in 1923. By 1930, however, he denounced Gandhi as the tool of the Hindu Mahasabha—an organization that cared more for cattle than for Muslims.[86]

As the postwar upsurge sparked the emergence of the right and the consolidation of the nationalist center, it also provided the opportunity to build a genuine Indian left for the first time. Embracing the self-activity of workers and peasants, the left could offer an anticolonial strategy that put the social question at the front of the anti-British movement—with the promise of building durable Hindu-Muslim unity on the basis of common class interests.

From its foundation in 1925, the Communist Party of India (CPI) refused to admit anyone who belonged to a communal organization[87]—and the party was an effective antidote to communal divisions in the places where it grew. The CPI had the most success in organizing unions like the Girni Kam-gar Union, which was strongest in Bombay. By 1929 the CPI had helped form 42 elected workers' committees in the textile mills following its success in leading a 1928 industry-wide strike for higher wages.[88] Communists were gaining influence among railway workers and oil workers as well.

By 1930, however, the labor movement and the Communist Party were being beaten back. Fierce repression from the British, along with the disastrous twists and turns of the CP's strategy, combined to weaken the only real alternative to com-munaiism and bourgeois nationalism. In 1928, the CPI adopted Stalin's policy of attacking relatively left Congress leaders. As a result, the CPI removed itself—and, tragically, removed most workers—from the next wave of nationalist struggle, the Civil Disobedience Movement of 1930—31.[89]

At the same time, the British crackdown removed the left's most important leaders from the scene. In 1929, the year that Congress itself declared its gc ıl of complete independence from Britain i

Thirtyone persons including practically all important communist and left-inclined trade-union leaders were arrested in different parts of the country and brought to Meerut to stand trial for entering "into a conspiracy to deprive the King [of England] of the sovereignty of British India."[90]

The trial dragged on until 1933, when long sentences were imposed. Then the CP itself was banned in 1934. Although Congress' new rising star, future prime minister Jawaharlal Nehru (1889—1964) had responded to the mass movement by moving to the left—and personally espoused socialism in his 1930 presidential address to Congress—the party did nothing to take up the defense of the Meerut "conspirators" during the movements of the early 1930s. At a Bombay "labor meeting" in 1931, Communists heckled Gandhi for ignoring the Meerut defendants (and for his compromising stance toward the British), but Congress continued to withhold support from the imprisoned leftists. The CPI was unable to reconstruct a functioning all-India leadership until the late 1930s.[91]

The CP's later support of Stalinist Russia in the Second World War, and thus, of the British war effort, would also remove them from biggest nationalist upsurge of the following decade, the Quit India Movement of 1942.

Despite the way that the CPI's policy kept shifting in response to Stalin's directives, the party's class-unity position remained a significant scounterweight to communal division in the countryside—where "the failure of Congress leaders to espouse agrarian radicalism even in Depression conditions, encouraged Muslim peasant movements to develop increasingly on separatist lines."[92]

Leading and Limiting the Struggle

Despite his skills and the powerful influence of his personality, Gandhi kept igniting forces that got beyond his control. The basic pattern could be seen again in the Civil Disobedience Movements of the early 1930s, which began with the famous campaign to violate the British salt monopoly. Gandhi chose this hated monopoly as a symbolic target to unite Indians on a nationalist basis while minimizing the risk that the movement would move on to pose class demands.

But the salt *satyagraha* escalated quickly. Mass marches to the coast to break the British salt monopoly led to mass arrests. News of Gandhi's own arrest sparked a strike by textile workers in Maharashtra who attacked police outposts, law courts and other official buildings.

The struggles repeatedly threw up the question of physical force in cases where the answer meant the difference between advance and retreat—and where retreat often meant dire consequences, including the loss of livelihood. In the Central Provinces, a *satyagraha* to violate restrictions on the use of forests escalated into attacks on the police pickets that had been set up to guard the forests—followed by mass illegal cutting of firewood. And throughout the country, peasants devastated by the Great Depression refused to pay their land taxes—and then put up physical resistance when police came to seize their property.[93]

Gandhi's refusal to endorse selective use of physical force also virtually ruled out strikes as a method of struggle. As one Bombay mill owner remarked about strikes in 1929, "peaceful picketing does not really exist," since the point of picketing is to prevent scab workers from getting into the mill.[94] Gandhi recommended that dissatisfied workers quit their jobs and look for other work rather than strike in a situation where they might have to confront scabs.[95]

Despite Gandhi's efforts, however, class divisions could not be smoothed over, and Gandhi's campaigns would continually move beyond the boundaries he tried to impose. This was because, in order to build up a mass base, he would deliberately tap into people's real grievances, which inevitably had a class aspect.

When those he mobilized met with repression, they felt justified in using any means necessary to get what they felt they deserved. What's more, civil disobedience campaigns led their participants to draw natural conclusions about resisting *all* unjust laws, such as those laws that defended the landlords' rights to crushing rents.

Gandhi, who in 1930 had promised a "fight to the finish" for Indian self-rule, wound up the massive Civil Disobedience Movement of 1930-31 after extracting only token concessions—disappointing even close collaborators like Nehru, who remarked in T.S. Eliot's words, "This is the way the world ends/Not with a bang but a whimper."[96]

Then, in May 1933, when Gandhi abruptly suspended a second Civil Disobedience Movement that he had begun the year before, his party comrades were furious. Said Nehru:

> After so much sacrifice and brave endeavor, was our movement to tail off into something insignificant? I felt angry with him [Gandhi] at his religious and sentimental approach to a political question and his frequent references to God in connection with it.[97]

Subhas Chandra Bose (1897—1945), a Congress militant, was scathing about Gandhis retreat:

> Today our condition is analogous to that of an army that has suddenly surrendered to the enemy in the midst of a protracted and strenuous campaign. And the surrender has taken place, not because the nation demanded it, not because the national army rose in revolt against its leaders and refused to fight...but either because the commander in chief was exhausted as a result of repeated fasting or because his mind and judgment were clouded owing to subjective causes which it is impossible for an outsider to understand.[98]

Independence, Partition and Communal Bloodbath

A combination of factors pushed the British to finally accept that they could no longer hold India. Some factors operated outside India, including broad pressures to decolonize—both from national movements and from the U.S., which had demanded that Britain open its colonial markets to postwar American penetration in return for its lend-lease military support.[99]

It was clear that the empire was crumbling. Japanese forces had swept through British colonies in Asia with little difficulty, showing Indians that the mighty British could be defeated. For their part, when the British lost their other possessions in Asia, they also lost their main incentive for maintaining an army based in India. And inside India, Gandhi launched the Quit India Movement in 1942, which became the biggest revolt since 1857.[100]

After the war, when Britain was negotiating terms of departure with Congress and the Muslim League, the revolt continued without Congress sponsorship. In 1946, nearly 2 million workers, more than half of the working class, went on strike. They earned the condemnation even of Nehru on the Congress left, who saw himself as the main leader of an independent India and did not want to inherit an undisciplined workforce.[101]

The most spectacular episode of the postwar upsurge was the Royal Indian Navy mutiny of *1946,* which, like the mutiny of 1857, was founded on Hindu-Muslim unity. In response to the mutiny, the CP called sympathy strikes that drew out 300,000 in Bombay. Gandhi and Congress condemned the mutiny and the strikes.[102]

In general, mass politics after the war was a patchwork of united class revolt and its opposite—communal bloodletting. Because the CP could not fill the vacuum of leadership left behind when Congress left the field of popular action, upsurges of united struggle were to alternate with gruesome communal violence—spurred on by both the Hindu right and the Muslim League. The one all-India mass action that the League ever called before independence, a "Day of Action" in August 1946 demanding the separation of Pakistan, precipitated murderous riots in Bengal that spread to other provinces.

In Bengal's capital, Calcutta, the riots killed 4,000 and injured 10,000 in just four days. Although the police favored the Muslims against the Hindus, the Muslims got the worst of it.[103]

The riots that followed the League's "Day of Action" pushed Congress Party negotiators to accept Partition.[104] The party was not prepared to support the only real alternative— class struggle on an increasingly leftist basis. In this way, the refusal to polarize the struggle along class lines virtually guaranteed a bloodbath along communal lines. The British themselves became eager for Congress to take over, since they realized that an Indian government could more easily put down the wave of strikes and mutinies than they themselves could.[105]

For its part, the Muslim League needed the expiring British *raj* to approve the Partition *before* independence, since the League was unlikely to win the partition of key provinces (including Bengal and the Punjab) through a post-independence referendum.[106] The League's members had always depended on the state to protect their property rights and their political clout,[107] so it's no surprise that they would seek help from the departing rulers to create a friendly state of their own. The late-developing Muslim bourgeoisie also looked forward to freeing itself from competition with India's more-established Hindu-owned businesses.[108]

The Muslim League's political ascendancy remained founded on a weak popular basis. The League finally won some provincial elections in 1946 when votes split along communal lines, but this victory came from an extremely narrow electorate; only the richest 10 percent were allowed to vote.[109] Later, in 1954, the League was to be tossed out of office in East Pakistan's first election based on universal suffrage, and the League would not provide political stability even where it was strongest, in West Pakistan.[110] In contrast, Congress was the top vote-getter in all-India elections for the first 30 years after independence.

Sumit Sarkar describes the immediate consequences of the Partition agreement:

> For far too many Muslims in India and Hindus in Pakistan, freedom-with-partition meant or came to mean a cruel choice between the threat of sudden violence and squeezing of employment and economic opportunities, or a forcible tearing out of age-old roots to join the stream of refugees.[111]

In 1947, millions celebrated the independence that they had won through decades of struggle. But the year was also marked by a holocaust of violence and ethnic cleansing that accompanied Partition. Estimates of the numbers killed and displaced vary from less than a half-million to "nearly a million" killed and from 10 to 22 million displaced.[112] Thousands of corpses littered the streets of cities like Calcutta and Delhi. There are descriptions of train cars arriving full only of dead people.[113]

Gandhi, now in his late seventies, personally journeyed to areas where communal violence had broken out and did his best to persuade people to stop, walking barefoot through the riot-torn slums and threatening "to fast unto death."[114] His moral authority was able to stop the violence sometimes, but when he left, all the social and political forces that led people to see another religious group as their main enemy were still in place.

Gandhi was disgusted with the opportunism he saw in Congress, and up to his death he displayed a principled anti-communalism. While riots raged in the Punjab, Gandhi told a leader of the Muslim League:

> I want to fight it out with my life. I would not allow the Muslims to crawl on the streets in India. They must walk with self-respect.[115]

Gandhi died for upholding Muslim equality, assassinated in 1948 by a Hindu fascist. The killer, Nathuram Godse, had been trained as an organizer in the RSS in the 1930s.[116] It is appalling to note that, as we first wrote these lines in September 2000, president Clinton (whose insistence on sanctions against Iraq killed more than half a million children) dedicated a statue of Gandhi in Washington, D.C.—assisted by India's prime minister, Atal Behari Vajpayee, who belongs to the RSS.

The Muslim population that remains in India is worse off than before Partition. Muslims now make up just 15 percent of the population and are disproportionately represented in poorer classes, are shut out of plum jobs by discrimination, and are targeted for communal terror by the Hindu right.[117]

Moral Force and Class Forces

Gandhi s principle of nonviolence, whose moral force propelled several mass movements forward in their initial phases, repeatedly held back the struggles at key moments. The outcome of these struggles was that the privileged groups in town and country had been able to successfully detach attainment of political independence from radical social change. The British had gone, but the bureaucracy and police they had built up continued with little change, and could prove as oppressive and ruthless as before (or even more perhaps at times).[118]

Gandhi never promoted the class forces that could have helped him in his final struggle to unite Hindus and Muslims. Only class struggle from below could have achieved what Gandhi s purely moral mission attempted.

The movement didn't have to turn out in such a mess. Potentially revolutionary situations existed in the periods 1919-22 and 1946-47, but no mass party with revolutionary goals had been forged to steer the movements to victory.

In the post—Second World War movement, the same social forces that had overthrown the Russian Tsar in 1917 were at the center of the upsurge—the industrial working class, along with peasants and workers in uniform. But in India's case, the country's only mass party saved the British from being overthrown by taking power "peacefully" themselves—at the price of leaving the class rebellion to be consumed in the fires of communalism.

Different alignments of class forces were possible, since most classes opposed British rule. The independence movement would have produced a different outcome if industrial workers and the agricultural proletariat had been able to form a revolutionary socialist party—and drawn the middle class and smallholding peasants behind their leadership. Instead, Gandhi's party reversed these relations, with the bourgeoisie included in the leadership with the middle classes of town and country.

Gandhi's life was history's longest experiment in nonviolent political action. The result of the experiment is fairly clear: An exploitative class structure cannot be broken without violence somewhere along the way. Property rights, defended by state violence, have never yielded to the peaceful pressure of the exploited class. Put in other terms, no exploiting class has ever left the stage of history without being pushed.

But moral force is, in fact, necessary to help draw together even a socialist movement. In some ways, our methods must indeed foreshadow a society that is more humane than the current one. Carpet-bombing civilian targets, showering thousands of anti-personnel weapons into rice paddies, or inflicting a starvation blockade upon an entire population, to take three examples, have been characteristic tactics of bourgeois war. Indeed, their use is a good reason to overthrow the bourgeois order. Conversely, it's hard to conceive of them as tactical options in a movement that aims at the liberation of ordinary people.

Moral force alone, however, cannot win a struggle against a class whose interests are inherently antagonistic to ours. Violence has to be part of the movement's arsenal. In a society founded on a violent class antagonism, our political aim cannot be like Gandhi's—to win over the whole of society. We must learn, instead, to draw the right battle lines.

REFERENCES

1. Martin Luther King Jr., "The Current Crisis in Race Relations," in *A* Testament of Mope: The Essential Writings and Speeches of Martin Luther King, Jr.,James M. Washington, ed. (United Kingdom: HarperCollins Publishers Ltd., 1986), p. 86.

2. Quoted from <http://www.engagedpage.com/gandhi.html> as of Septem ber 18, 2000.

3. Sam Ashman, "Indian: Imperialism, Partition and Resistance," *International Socialism* 77, Winter 1997, p. 82.

4. Anthony Read and David Fisher, *India's Long Road to Independence* (New York: WW Norton, 1997), p. 227.
5. Bipan Chandra, Mridula Mukherjee, Aditya Mukherjee, KN. Panikkar, and Sucheta Mahajan, *India's Struggle for Independence* (Calcutta: Penguin Books, 1989), p. 42.
6. Romesh C. Dutt, "Paper on the Indian Land Question," in *Speeches and Papers on Indian Questions, 1901 and 1902* (Calcutta: Elm Press, 1902), pp. 2-4.
7. Ashman, p. 82. See also Sumit Sarkar, *Modern India: 1885—1947*(Macmillan India Limited, 1983), pp. 32-33.
8. Romesh C. Dutt, "The economic causes of India's famines," in *Speeches and Papers,* pp. 38-39.
9. R.C. Majumdar and PN. Chopra, *Main Currents of Indian History* (New Delhi: Sterling Publishers, 1994), p. 224.
10. B.M. Bhatia, *Famines in India* (Delhi: Konark Publishers Pvt. Ltd., 1991), p. 16.
11. Bhatia, pp. 18-20.
12. Bhatia, p. 18.
13. Barrington Moore Jr., *Social Origins of Dictatorship and Democracy: Lord and Peasant in the Making of the Modern World* (Boston: Beacon Press, 1966), p. 368.
14. Sarkar, pp. 28-30.
15. Bhatia, p. 8.
16. For an appropriately hair-raising account of the British response to the famines they had helped to cause, see the chapters about India in Mike Davis, *Late Vktorian Holocausts: El Nitw Famines and the Making of the Third World* (New York: Verso, 2001), pp. 25-59 and 141-75.
17. Quoted in Dadabhai Naoroji, "India Must Be Bled," in *100 Best Pre-Independence Speeches 1870-1947,* ed. by H.D. Sharma (New Delhi, Harper Collins Publishers India, 1998).
18. Karl Marx, letter to N.F. Danielson, February 19, 1881, in *Karl Marx Frederick Engels Collected Works,* Vol. 46 (New York: International Publishers, 1992).
19. Ashman, pp. 83-84.

20. R.C. Majumdar and PN. Chopra, *Main Currents of Indian History* (New Delhi: Sterling Publishers, 1994), pp. 149-50.
21. Sarkar, p. 22.
22. Sarkar, p. 88.
23. Bipan Chandra, Mridula Mukherjee, Aditya Mukherjee, K.N. Panikkar, and Sucheta Mahajan, *India's Struggle for Independence* (Calcutta: Penguin Books, 1989), pp. 50-53.
24. Davis, p. 148.
25. Sarkar, p. 60.
26. Bal Gangadhar Tilak, "Not by petitions alone," January 2, 1907 address in Calcutta immediately after the Extremists' expulsion from the Indian National Congress, quoted in *Sources of Indian Tradition,* vol. 2, Stephen Hay, ed. (New Delhi: Penguin Books India, 1992), p. 144.
27. Quoted in Hay, ed., p. 31.
28. Prakash Chandra, *History of the Indian National Movement* (NewDelhi: Vikas Publishing House, 1997), p. 218.
29. Anthony Read and David Fisher, *The Proudest Day: India's Long Road to Independence (Nzw York:* WW Norton), pp. 91-93.
30. Read and Fisher, p. 93.
31. P. Hardy *Muslims in British India* (Oxford: Oxford University Press, 1972), cited in Tariq Ali, *Can Pakistan Survive?* (London: Penguin Books, 1983), p. 29.
32. Achin Vanaik, *The Painful Transition: Bourgeois Democracy in India,* (New York: Verso, 1990), p. 75.
33. Sarkar, p. 134.
34. V.I. Lenin, "Inflammable material in world politics," in *V.I. Lenin: Collected Works,* vol. 15 (Moscow: Progress Publishers, 1973), pp 184-85.
35. Sarkar, p. 174.
36. Judith Brown, *Gandhi: Prisoner of Mope* (New Haven: Yale University Press, 1989), p. 28.
37. For a succinct look at the evolution of Gandhi's political views during his South Africa years, see PH.M. van den

Dungen, "Gandhi in 1919: loyalist or rebel?" in Ravinder Kumar, ed., *Essays on Gandhian Politics: The Rowlatt Satyagraha of1919*'(London: Oxford University Press, 1971), pp. 43-63.

38. Brown, pp. 46-48.

39. Brown, pp. 78-81.

40. Sarkar, p. 179. See also Gandhi's oral testimony to the Hunter Committee investigating government massacres in 1919, reprinted in *Young India 1919-22* (New York: B.W Huebsch, 1924), pp. 16-45, esp. pp. 17-18 and 34-36.

41. Sarkar, p. 179.

42. Prakash Chandra, p. 218.

43. M.K. Gandhi, "The satyagraha movement," written statement to the Hunter Committee, serialized in *Young India* beginning November 5, 1919, reprinted in *Younglndia 1919-22,* pp. 11-16.

44. Quoted in Sarkar, p. 180.

45. Sarkar, p. 181.

46. Sarkar, p. 230.

47. Sarkar, p. 180.

48. Sarkar, p. 171.

49. Ashman, p. 90.

50. Alec Kahn. "Gandhi—hero or humbug? How nonviolence failed in India" (Australia: International Socialists, 1982), p. 2.

51. Eqbal Ahmad, *Confronting Empire: Interviews with David Barsamian* (Cam bridge, Massachusetts: South End Press, 2000), p. 8

52. Sarkar, p. 169.

53. Sarkar, p. 186.

54. Quoted in Sarkar, p. 208.

55. H.F. Owen, "Organizing for the Rowlatt satyagraha of 1919," in Ravinder Kumar, ed., p. 81.

56. Sarkar, p. 190.

57. Ravinder Kumar, "The Rowlatt Satyagraha in Lahore," in Kumar, ed., pp. 291-92.

58. Derek Sayer, "British reaction of the Amritsar massacre 1919—1920," in Jallianwala Bagh, Commemoration Volume and "Amritsar and Our Duty to *India,"* Gurharan Singh, Parm Bakshish Singh, Devinder Kumar Verma, and Raj Krishnan Ghai, eds. (Patiala, India: Publication Bureau, Punjabi University, 1994), p. 35.

59. Ravinder Kumar, "The Rowlatt Satyagraha in Lahore," p. 292—93.

60. For detailed accounts of the Amritsar movement and British repression in the Punjab, see the articles in *JaEianwala Bagh.* For the definitive account of the 1919 movement in Lahore—explaining the interplay of caste, class, and religious forces—see Ravinder Kumar's "The Rowlatt Satyagraha in La hore."

61. See Owen, pp. 68-74.

62. Ravinder Kumar, "Introduction" to *The Rowlatt Satyagraha,* p. 8.

63. Aside from the half-dozen cases noted in the text of this article, we should note one other significant instance where Gandhi allowed British repression to fall on the militant wing of the movement without making a peep—the Cawnpore Conspiracy Case of 1924, which led to long prison terms for four communists. See Irfan Habib, "The Left and the National Movement," in *Indian People in the Struggle for Freedom* (New Delhi: Safdar Hashmi Memorial Trust, 1998), p. 106.

64. Sarkar, p. 194.

65. Sarkar, p. 188.

66. Quoted in Satya M. Rai, "Jallianwala Bagh tragedy—its impact on the political awakening and thinking in India,' in *Jallianwala Bagh,* p. 135.

67. Sarkar, pp. 197-198.

68. Owen, p. 77.

69. M.K. Gandhi, "To the subscribers and readers," *Younglndia,* October 8, 1919, in *Younglndia 1919-22,* pp. 1-

3.

70. Sarkar, p. 210. See also M.K. Gandhi, "To the peasants of the United Provinces," *Young India,* March 9, 1921, reprinted in *Younglndia 1919-1922,* pp. 741-44.

71. Sarkar, 217-18.

72. Siddharth Dube, *In The Land Of Poverty: Memoirs of an Indian Family 1947-1997,* (New York: Zed Books, 1998), p. 36.

73. Dube, p. 55.

74. Sarkar, p. 216.

75. Details of the Moplah Revolt come from Sarkar, pp. 216-17 and Tariq Ali, pp. 23-26.

76. Sarkar, pp. 224-225.

77. Sarkar, pp. 225-226.

78. Tapan Basu, Pradip Datta, Sumit Sarkar, Tanika Sarkar and Sambuddha Sen, *Khaki Shorts and Saffron Flags* (New Delhi: Orient Longman, 1993), pp. 16-17.

79. Hay pp. 289-90.

80. Not every Indian terrorist followed a rightward trajectory. In the 1920s, a new generation of militants arose when the movement of 1919—22 dissipated without winning independence. Some, including the most famous terrorist of this generation, Bhagat Singh, became socialists. By the time of his 1931 execution, Singh had foresworn individual terror and advocated mass militance—a movement of self-emancipation by India's exploited. See *India's Struggle for Independence,* pp. 247—59.

81. Tariq Ali, p. 27.

82. Sarkar, p. 426.

83. Vanaik, p. 74.

84. See Ravinder Kumar, "Introduction," pp. 12-15 and *Khaki Shorts,* pp. 6-7.

85. *Khaki Shorts,* p. 22.

86. Hay, 195—204. For the details and context of Congress' concessions to the Mahasabha, see Sarkar, pp. 262—63.

87. Habib, p. 107.
88. Sarkar, p. 270-71.
89. Sarkar, p. 297.
90. Habib, p. 108.
91. Habib, pp. 108-110.
92. See Sarkar, pp. 302, 323, 354, and 364.
93. Sarkar, pp. 286-96.
94. Sarkar, p. 280.
95. M.K. Gandhi, "Strikes," *Young India,* February 16, 1921, .reprinted in *Younglndia 1919-1922,* pp. 736-41.
96. Jawaharlal Nehru, *An Autobiography* (New Delhi: Jawaharlal Nehru Memorial Fund, 1996), p. 259. First published 1936.
97. Quoted in Majumdar and Chopra, p. 197.
98. Subhas Chandra Bose, "The Fickle Leader," in *100 GreatestPre-Independence Speeches.*
99. Sarkar, p. 386 and Gabriel Kolko, *The Politics of War: The World and United States Foreign Policy* (New York: Pantheon Books, 1968), pp. 249 and 286.
100. Sarkar, p. 391.
101. Sarkar, p. 429.
102. Sarkar, pp. 323-25.
103. For accounts of the Calcutta riot and its spread, see Sarkar, pp. 432—37 and Read and Fisher, pp. 394-96.
104. Sarkar, p. 436.
105. Sarkar, p. 431.
106. Tariq Ali, p. 34.
107. Tariq Ali, p. 29.
108. Sarkar, p. 409.
109. Sarkar, p. 426-27.
110. Sarkar, p. 428.
111. Sarkar, pp. 452-53.

112. The higher estimate of deaths—and the lower estimate of displaced persons—is from Tariq Ali, pp. 155-56. The low figure for deaths and the high figure for displacement come from Ahmad, p. 13.

113. Ashman, p. 97.

114. Sarkar, p. 437.

115. Quoted in Sarkar, p. 437.

116. *Khaki Shorts,* pp. 23-24.

117. Pranav Jani and Ganesh Lai, "Behind Hindu Nationalism," *International Socialist Review,* Fall 1999, p. 70.

118. Sarkar, p. 453.

9

Gandhi's Writings in Harijan

Gandhi's social and political ideas remain a significant milestone in India's freedom struggle and its aftermath. Although these ideas were constructed during Gandhi's encounter with colonialism, they appear to be transcenden-tal both in connotation and application. What this suggests is the civilizational relevance of Gandhi's ideas in post-colonial societies 'where political power shifted from the colonial ruler without radically altering the social context in which colonialism flourished. While confronting the British government politically, Gandhi also launched crusades against socially crip-pling practices, which had been justified in the name of religion. Gandhism was not merely a political ideology,, but one with social and political aims. The basic model that Gandhi provided in Hind Swaraj remained a constant referent to his later writings in Harijan. There is a difference, however, because Hind Swaraj was written after the South African experiment of satyagraha, whereas many of his articles on pertinent themes in Harijan were written after he had become the supreme leader of the Indian national move-ment. These articles in Harijan were less philosophical and tended to be commentaries on the contemporary issues relating to the national movement and the evolution of India as an independent political entity after independ-ence. The aim of this chapter is twofold: first, it deals with rive different issues of contemporary relevance that Gandhi dealt with in Harijan and second, it contains a selective number of excerpts from Gandhi's own writ-ings in Harijan on these themes to lend the entire text an original flavour. Not only will this section acquaint the readers with Gandhi's prose and style, it will also bring in 'the thematic' focus of Gandhism in conjunction with its 'problematic'. These selective texts are very useful in understanding Gandhi's social and political ideas in the context of an incipient but independent nationalist thought confronting colonialism. This will also enable us to undertake a critical analysis of the nationalist thought, which was hardly derivative and yet had its roots in the discourse of colonialism.

Why Harijan?

Harijan, the mouthpiece of the Servants of Utouchable Society, was a weekly, usually published on Saturdays. It made ics appearance in 1933 and con-tinued publication almost uninterruptedly even after 1947. R.V. Shastri/ the founder-editor, held this responsibility while it was published from Poona. One of the reasons contributing to its emergence was as a defence of the 1932 Poona Pact in which Gandhi forced the Congress to accept the reservation of stats for the 'untouchables' even within the quota of CASCC Hindus as suggested by the 1932 Communal Award. Gandlii began writing in Harijan with arguments in favour of the arrangement as the only solution to avoid 'a caste war at 'a historical juncture' when he believed that the nationalist movement should nor lose sight of its principal goal. As a regular contributor — except when tie was incarcerated — Gandhi com-mented on the major socio-economic and political issues in lucid language. Unlike the Hind Swaraj, which had articulated his vision of a good society, his contributions in Harijan are varied and dwell on chemes which he might not have deal with in detail elsewhere. Since the weekly was popular and read by millions, of Indians., the Mahatma, on occasions, preferred to be polemical to establish an argument defending the Harijan cause. After one year of its publication, Gandhi stated its purpose very unambiguously by saying:

> It devotes itself solely to the Harijan cause. Even so it eschews all matters which may be calculated to bring it in conflict with the Government. It eschews politics altogether. These limitations were [obvious] because of the [context] in which it is working. [Given its focus, it will] draw only those men and women who are interested in the campaign against untouchability and who would help the cau:e even if it is only to the extent of subscribing to the paper and thus helping the only paper that is solely devoted to the cause of anti-untouchability and is the mouthpiece of che Harijan Sevak Sangh.

So Harijan provided a forum where Gandhi interacted which his colleagues and contemporaries over issues affecting the anti-British political movement in particular and the nation in general.

Apart from long pieces by Gandhi, a regular section in Harijan was the 'Question Box', where Gandhi responded co questions on various issues of contemporary relevance. Questions were generally structured around what Gandhi had written in the weekly and elsewhere. Since the Question Box ensured a. dialogue with those seeking to grapple with his views, the Mahatma was always favourably disposed towards the section. Harijan was significant in another respect, as the forum where Gandhi generally dealt with the criticism of his published views. While defending his arguments concerning 'the untouchables' and the reservation scheme, as enunciated in the 1932 Poona Pact, Gandhi, for instance, confronted Ambedkar, who declined to publish his views in Harijan simply because it was tilted in favour of caste Hindus." Not only was Ambedkar critical of the inherent castist tendencies of the weekly, he was unhappy which the term harijan being used to identify the untouchables. By designating the untouchables as hart jam, Gandhi sought, as Ambcdkar argued, to shift our attention from the curse of untouchability. The new name, he added:

has not elevated them in the eyes of the Hindus. The new name has become completely identified with the subject matter of the old. Every-body knows that Harijans are simply no other than the old untouch-ables. The new name [therefore] provides no escape to the Untouchables from the curse of untoiichabiltry.

A believer in the caste system, Gandhi attributed the articulation of untouchability to the distinction between high and low that has crept into Hinduism and is corroding it'." Despite being critical of untouchability as it was practised in Hinduism, he was in favour of 'unrouchability of a healthy kind [since] it is a rule of sanitation'. He therefore emphatically declared,

> the moment untouchability [in its present form} goes, [the] caste system itself will be purified, that is to say, according to my dream, it will resolve into the true varnadharma, the four divisions of society, each complementary of the other and none inferior or superior to the other, each is necessary for the whole body of Hinduism as any other.

Apart from the Gandhi-Ambedkar debate on this issue, Harijan also published the views of Rabindranath Tagore, which ran counter to those of Gandhi, especially after the 1932 Poona Pact. Reducing the seats of the caste Hindus both in the central and provincial legislatures in order to accommodate the 'Depressed Classes', the Pact, Tagore lamented, will be a source of perpetual communal jealousy leading to a constant disturbance of peace and fatal break in the spirit of mutual cooperation in [Bengal]'. Gandhi addressed the points raised by Tagore regarding the alleged injustice to Bengal since no representatives from Bengal participated in the delibera-tions. Articulating the difference with Tagore as an outcome of the dif-ference in their viewpoints, Gandhi did not seem to be persuaded, though this exchange of views adds hitherto unknown dimensions to the debare on untouchability in which

Ambedkar has so far been identified as the only nationalist figure opposing Gandhi in this regard.

This chapter seeks to organize Gandhi's views,, as published in Harijan, in terms of a number of themes, which are as important today as they were then in unravelling the dynamics of a transitional society like India, harijan is a reconfirmarion of a particular point of view that the Mahatma began espousing in systematic manner in the Hind Swaraj. These themes also Laid the foundation of a political theory which informed what later came to be identified as 'Gandhism'. As a practitioner if what he preached, Gandhi's comments on these themes are very helpful in grasping the context, which underwent dramatic changes in the wake of colonial rule. Gandhi's intervention is useful in another respect. His views in chew key themes contributed to a substantial text, one which lends itself to the study of comparative political thought. Seeking tu integrate what was worth salvaging in modern civilisation which in the framework of Indian civilization, Gandhi went beyond the conventional approach to 'nationalist' thought, where the so-tailed Indian vision ms always uncritically glorified, to champion 'a sectarian' political thought.

Prosperity of Harijan

The disease of untouchability is fairly old in our society. It generated social hatred and discriminatory feeling of high and low, and as a result of it latter category suffered for centuries in the hands of the former. Time and again, ceaseless efforts were made by social reformers to alleviate the status of downtrodden and bring them to a level by which they could breathe and subsist with some confidence in the society. This was, however, a most complex problem, the complete or satisfactory solution of which could not be evolved in spite of efforts by prominent personalities including social reformers, educationists and political leaders of our society. For example, Buddha, Mahavira, Kabir, Nanak, Dayanand and others played their social and religious role at one time or the other. Besides numerous socio-religious reform movements had deep linkage with the cause of the untouchables who were labelled as a serious stigma on the fair name of Hinduism.

The idea of social discrimination dawned on Gandhi in South Africa where he engaged himself against the discriminatory attitude of the South African government against Indians. The problem was akin to that of untouchability as the migrants were treated as inferior to the local population which enjoyed numerous basic rights legally denied to Indians. As a young man, Gandhi began to realize how much hellish was their life which had weakened their social and moral fabric essential for the growth of physical and economic faculties of human beings. In India, too, he was confronted with this problem when he came back to his motherland in 1915, during the second year of the First World War.

For him the reconstruction of the life of the nation was of utmost significance. This could be achieved by alleviating the social status of the untouchables. He always called untouchability as a cruel and inhuman institution. It violated human dignity. He did not believe that the imperial ambitions of Britain were alone responsible for our slavery, but it was the neglect of our national duty which was primarily responsible for it. A reformed India, he stated, would be a free India.

Untouchability in its extreme form always caused him so much pain, because he considered himself to be a Hindu of Hindus saturated with the spirit of Hinduism. As he always regarded it as an exerescence in Hinduism, he had even no hesitation in renouncing Hinduism itself. To remove untouchability was a penancea that caste Hindus owed to Hinduism and to themselves. Thus the purification required was not of untouchables, but of the so-called superior castes.

In fact, untouchability in India, as the race and colour problems in the West, rested upon the idea of the superiority of one section of people over another on account of their birth. A Brahman might be as poor as the untouchable, but he was not ill-treated by our society on that account. The Mahatma called these so-called religious sanctions as a serious stigma on the fair name of a society which have deep-rooted culture and historical traditions to support its identity.

Gandhi called Harijans as men of God and always kept in view their social plight which he endeavoured to uplift by devising schemes for a change in their status.

"Harijan means 'a man of God'. All the religions of the world describe God pre-eminently as the Friend of the friendless. Help of the helpless and Protector of the weak. The rest of the world apart, in India who can be more friendless; helpless or weaker than the forty millions or more Hindus of India who are classified as 'untouchable'? It, therefore, any body of people can be fitly described as men of God, they are surely these helpless, friendless, and despised people. I have always adopted Harijan as the name signifying 'untouchables'. Not that the change of name brings about any change of status, but one may at least be spared the use of a term which is itself one of reproach. When caste Hindus have of their own inner conviction and, therefore, voluntarily, got rid of the present-day untouchability, we shall all be called Harijans; for, according to my humble opinion, caste Hindus will then have found favor, with God and may therefore, be fitly described as His men."

Gandhi never reconciled himself to untouchability. According to him, 'untouchablity is an excrescene', 'I have never been able to reconcile myself to untouchability. I have always regarded it as an excrescence in Hinduism. It is true that it has been handed down to us from generations, but so are many evil practices even to this day. I should be ashamed to think that dedication of girls to virtual prostitution was a part of Hinduism. Yet it is practised by Hindus in many parts of India. I consider it positive irreligion to sacrifice goats to Kali and do not consider it a part of Hinduism. Hinduism is a growth of ages. The very name Hinduism, was given to the religion of the people of Hindustan by foreigners. There was, no doubt, at one time sacrifice of animals offered in the name of religion. But it is not religion, much less is it Hindu religion. And so also it seems to me, that when cow-protection became an article of faith with our ancestors, those who persisted in eating beef were excommunicated. The civil strife must have been fierce. Social boycott was applied not only to the recalcitrants, but their sins were visited upon their children also. The practice which had probably its origin in good intentions hardened into usage and even verses crept in our sacred books giving the practice a permanence wholly undeserved and still less justified, Whether my theory is correct or not, untouchability is repugnant to reason and to the instinct of mercy, pity or love. A religion that establishes the worship of the cow cannot possibly countenance or warrant a cruel and inhuman boycott of human beings. And I should be content to be torn to pieces rather than disown the suppressed classes. Hindus will certainly never deserve freedom, nor get it if they allow their noble religion to be disgraced by the retention of the taint of untouchability. And as I love Hinduism dearer than life itself, the taint has become for me an intolerable burden. Let us not deny God by denying to a fifth of our race the right of association on an equal footing.'

Gandhi claimed that he was a Sanatanist. For him Vedas were indefinable as God and Hinduism. The reverent reading greatly strengthened his faith in the Gita. To further elaborate his point of view, he opined :

'I have letters, some of them angrily worded, from those who style themselves Sanatanists. For them untouchability is the essence of Hinduism. Some of them regard me as a renegade. Some others consider that I have imbibed notions against untouchability and the life from

Christianity and Islam. Some again quote scriptures in defence of untouchability. To these I have promised a reply through my public statements. I would venture, therefore, to tell these correspondents that I claim myself to be a Sanatanist. Their definition of a Sanatanist is obviously different from mine. For me Sanatana Dharma is vital faith handed down from generations belonging even to pre-histoic period and based upon the Vedas and the writings that followed them. For me the Vedas are as indefinable as God and Hinduism. It would be only partially true to say that the Vedas are the four books which one finds in print. These books are themselves the remnants of discourses left by unknown seers. Those of later generations added to these original treasures according to their lights. There then arose a great and lofty-minded man, the composer of the Gita. He gave to the Hindu world a synthesis of Hindu religion, at once deeply philosophical and yet easily to be understood by any unsophisticated seeker. It is the one open book to every Hindu who will care to study it, and if all the other scriptures were reduced to ashes, the seven hundred verses of this imperishable booklet are quite enough to tell one what Hinduism is and how one can live up to it. And I claim to be a Sanatanist because for forty years I have been seeking literally to live up to the teachings of that book. Whatever is contrary to its main theme I reject as Un-Hindu. It excludes no faith and no teacher. It gives me great joy to be able to say that I have studied the

Bible, the Koran, the Zend-Avesta and the other scriptures of the world with the same reverence that I have given to the Gita. This reverent reading has strengthened my faith in the Gita. They have broadened my outlook and, therefore, my Hinduism. Lives of Zoroaster, Jesus and Mahommed as I have understood them have illumined many a passage in the Gita. What, therefore, these Sanatanist friends have hurled against me as a* taunt has been to me a source of consolation. I take pride in calling myself a Hindu, because I find the term broad enough not merely to tolerate but to assimilate the teachings of prophets from all the four corners of the earth. I find no warrant for untouchability in this Book of Life. On the Contrary it compels me, by an appeal to my reason and a more penetrating appeal to my heart, in language that has a magnetic touch about it, to believe that all life is one and that it is through God and must return to Him. According to the Sanatana Dharma taught by that venerable Mother, life does not consist in outward rites and ceremonial, but it consists in the uttermost inward purification and merging oneself, body, soul and mind, in the divine essence. I have gone to the masses in their millions with this message of the Gita burnt into my life, and they have listened to me, I am quite sure, not for any political wisdom or for eloquence, but because they have instinctively recognized me as one of them, as one belonging to their faith. As days have gone by, my belief has grown stronger and stronger that I could not be wrong in claiming to belong to Sanatana Dharma, and if God wills it, He will let me seal that claim with my death.'[3]

Time and again Gandhi pleaded for the temple-entry for the Harijans. He did this exercise through his consistent writing in *Young India* and the *Harijans*. He also practised it through numerous public meetings as well as by living amongst them. He opined that temple entry was the one spiritual act that would constitute the message of freedom to the untouchables and assured them that they were not outcastes before God.

Gandhi stated that there should be perfect freedom for Harijans to enter ordinary temples and ordinary schools and to use common wells. He also recommended erection of model schools and model temples specially designed for the convenience of untouchables.

"In the beginning of the movement as I had conceived it on my return from South Africa in 1915,1 had thought that it was wholly inconsistent with the movement for removing untouchability to build separate temples or schools for them. But experience taught me that the movement could not proceed upon strict logic, and that we Hindus had so much suppressed a third of ourselves that even after the articulate Hindus had with one voice declared for removal. The suppressed brethren would for a long time need the helping hand in a variety of ways. After the theoretical, lip-removal of untouchability, if no special effort was made, the vast bulk of them would not readily take advantage of the removal and the ignorant mass would not tolerate them especially when the latter would be naturally clumsy in their department or pardonably forward in the enjoyment of long withhold freedom. I am therefore convinced that the two things will have to go hand in hand—perfect freedom to enter ordinary temples and ordinary schools and to use common wells, at the same time as erection of model schools and model temples specially designed for the convenience of 'untouchables' but open to the others subject always to priority for 'untouchables'. It was along this line of reasoning that I suggested in the brief note for the *Calcutta Municipal Gazette that* the Municipalities could foster removal of untouchability by erecting temples and model schools for the suppressed classes side by side with the attempt to have the existing temples thrown open to these countrymen of ours. My note may therefore on no account be taken as an excuse for condoning prohibition against entry into temples etc."[4]

This movement against untochability has been daily gathering strength. It was in last September that leading Hindus, claiming to represent the whole of Hindu India, met together and unanimously passed a resolution, condemning untouchability and pledging themselves to abolish it by law, if possible even during the existing regime, and, failing that, when India had a Parliament of her own.

Among the marks of untonchability to be removed was the prohibition against temple-entry by Harijans. In the course of the struggle, it was discovered that the British

Courts in India had recognized this evil custom, so much so that certain acts done by 'untouchables' as such came to be offence under the British India Penal Code. Thus, the entry by an 'untouchable' into a Hindu temple would be punishable as a crime under theI.P.C.

Before, therefore, the movement of temple-entry can make headway, it has become imperative to have this anomaly removed. It is for this purpose that Shri Ranga Iyer has given notice of two bills to be introduced in the Central Legislature.

With due regard to the Sanatanists, it is difficult to understand the cry of 'religion in danger'. Under neither bill will a single temple be opened against the will of the majority of temple-goers in question. The second bill expressly says so. The first bill takes up a neutral attitude. It does not help a Harijan to force his way into a temple. The reformers do not seek to compel the opponents to their will. They desire, by the fairest means possible, to convert the majority or the minority, as the case may be, to their view of untouchability.

It is said that the Harijans themselves do not want temple entry and that they want only betterment of their economic and political condition. The reformer, too, wants the latter, but he believes that this betterment will be much quicker brought about, if religious equality is attained. The reformer denies that the Harijan do not want temple-entry. But it may be that they are so disgusted with Caste Hindus and Hindu religion itself as to want nothing from them. They may in sullen discontent choose to remain outside the religious pale. Any pedance on the part of caste Hindus may be too late.

Nevertheless, the caste Hindus who recognize that untouchability is a blot on Hinduism have to atone for the sin of untouchability. Whether, therefore, Harijans desire temple-entry or not, caste Hindus have to open their temples to Harijans, precisely on the same terms as to other Hindus. For a caste Hindu with any sense of honour, temple prohibition is a continuous breach of the pledge taken at the Bombay meeting of September last. Those, who gave their word to the world and to God that they would have the temples opened for the Harijans, have to sacrifice their all, if need be, for redeeming the pledge. Temple-entry is the one spiritual act that would constitute the message of freedom to the 'untouchables' and assure them that they are not outcastes before God.'[5]

Several correspondents have taken me to task for advocating temple-entry for Harijans without emphasizing the necessity of temple reform. There is no doubt that temple reform is necessary. But, here, again, there is need for caution. Some of them think that it is possible to replace all the existing temples with new ones. I do not share that view. All temples will never be alike. They will always vary, as they have done in the past, with the varying human needs. What the reformer should be concerned with is a radical change more in the inward spirit than in the outward form. If the first is changed, the second will take care of itself. If the first remains unchanged, the second, no matter how radically changed, will be like a whited sculpture. A mausoleum, however beautiful, is a tomb and not a mosque, and a bare plot of consecrated ground may be a real Temple of God.

Therefore the first desideratum is the priest. My ideal priest must be a man of God. He must be a true servant of the people. He should have the qualifications of a guide, friend and philosopher to those among whom he is officiating. He must be a whole-timer with the least possible needs and personal ties. He should be versed in the Shastras. His whole concern will be to look after the welfare of his people. I have not drawn a fanciful picture. It is almost true to life. It is based on the recollections of my childhood. The priest I am recalling was looked upon by the prince and the people. They flocked round him for advice and guidance in the time of their need.

If the sceptic says such a priest is hard to find now-a-days, he would be partly right. But I would ask the reformer to wait for building the temple of his ideal till he finds his priest.

Meanwhile let him cultivate in himself the virtues he will have in the priest of his imagination. Let him expect these from the priests of existing temples. In other words, by his gentle and correct conduct, let him infect his immediate surroundings with the need of the times and let him have faith that his thought, surcharged with his own correct conduct, will act more powerfully than the mightiest dynamo. Let him not be impatient to see the result in a day. A thought may take years of conduct to evolve the requisite power. What are years or generations in the life of a great reformer? The existing temples can become real Houses of God today, if the worshippers will insist on the priests conforming to the ideal presented by me.[4]

On the temple-entry Bill introduced by C.S. Ranga Iyer on 24 March 1933, the Mahatma commented thus :

'It is sad to think that the anti-untouchability measure has been hung up for one year by the Legislative Assembly and that the amendment to hung it up received the support of the Government. But the reformers may not rest till untouchability is blotted out of the Statute Boo. Meanwhile, the process of having temples opened by consent of trustees and temple-goers and the general propaganda in favour of opening temples should continue.

But I observe that a Harijan Conference at Agra has passed the following resolution :

> This Jatav Conference .... considers that the methods and system of work of the movement is not satisfactory. Harijan movement lays stress on the temple-entry problem more than on economic and educational problems. The former . . . will produce slave mentality .... Hence . . . great emphasis must be laid on the educational and economic aspect of the progress. Inter-

caste marriage and inter-dining must be on the programme of the movement....

Trie economic and educational uplit is no doubt an essential part of true repentance by caste Hindus. It is a test of the sincerity *oi* their professions. But the uplift will not be complete without the throwing open of temples. The throwing open of temples will be an admission of the religious equality of Harijans. It will be the surest sign of their ceasing to be the outcastes of Hinduism, which they are today.

It is beside the point that tens of thousands of Harijans do not want to enter temples. If it were properly probed, the fact would be found to be quite otherwise. Thousands of Harijans do want to enter temples. Only they have been so accustomed *to* the prohibition that the very hope of entering temples had dried up in them. They believe that admission to temples on a part with the other Hindus in an impossibility.

But whether Harijans desire the consolation of temple-entry or not, whether, if temples are thrown open to them, they will make use of them or not, caste Hindus have to perform their simple duty. They have to open their temples for Harijans to offer worship in, precisely on the same terms as for themselves. A debtor is not absolved from the duty of payment because his creditor does not care for the payment, or has forgotten the debt altogether.

And when temples are thrown open to Harijans, schools, wells and many similar facilities will be automatically open to Harijans. It is surely easy enough to realize that untouchability may subsist side by side with economic uplift. Many Ezhawas in Travancore and Namashudras in Bengal possess decent fortunes and are yet treated as pariahs of society. The bar sinister is all the more galling to them by reason of their flourishing condition. Dr. Ambedkar suffers from the curse in spite of his high educational attainments and his superior economic condition. He is naturally more sensitive to the insult of untouchability. But the reproach will be automatically removed, immediately caste Hindus proclaim the banishment of untouchability by admitting Harijans to their temples on terms of absolute equality with themselves. It will not then become necessary for any Harijan individually to go to temples, if he does not desire to do so. The declaration of the opening of temples will cover him with the rest. It will be like the abolition of slavery. It will be a vast and glorious step in the much needed and overdue purification of Hinduism.

Temple-entry permission, to be of use, has naturally to be a voluntary act on the part of Hindus. It has to be, therefore, a genuine change of heart in the caste Hindus. Legislation is nevertheless necessary because of the fact that in law the entry of Harijans into caste Hindu temples is said to be prohibited. Legislation will constitute the seal of approval of the vast mass of Hindus. I personally should not want that legislation in the teeth of universal caste Hindu opposition. My own belief is * that caste Hindus as a whole do not oppose temple-entry by Harijans. I should abide by the result of an honestly conducted referendum. Anyway, let the reformers realize that, whatever happens in the Legislature at Delhi, the movement for temple-entry and the necessary legislation must continue.

There are other things in the resolution quoted above which call for explanation or criticism. This must be postponed for a future issue of the *Harijan.*

The conversion of untouchable to Islam or Christianity was criticised by Gandhi. He favoured religious bonds as it was a "matter of the heart. Others should not take advantage of the helplessness of untouchables.

> "A remedy suggested to 'untouchables' is rejection of Hinduism and wholesale conversion to Islam or Christianity. And if a change of religion could be justified for wordly betterment, I would advise it without hesitation. But religion is a matter of the heart.

> No physical inconvenience can warrant abandonment of one's own religion. If the inhuman treatment of the Panchamas were a part of Hinduism, its rejection would be a paramount duty both for them and for those like me who would not make a fetish even of religion and condone every evil in its sacred name. But I believe that untouchability is no part of Hinduism. It is rather its excrescence to be removed by every effort, And there is quite an army of Hindu reformers who have set their heart upon ridding Hinduism of this blot. Conversion, therefore, I hold, is no remedy whatsoever.
>
> "Those who use the threat (of conversion) do not, in my humble opinion, know the meaning of religion. Religion is a matter of life and death. A man does not change religion as he changes his garments. He takes it with him beyond the grave. Nor does a man profess religion to oblige others. He professes a religion because he cannot do otherwise. A faithful husband loves his wife as he would love no other women. Even her faithlessness would not wean him from his faith. The bond is more than blood relationship. So is the religious bond if it is worth anything. It is a matter of the heart. An 'untouchable' who loves his Hinduism in the face of persecution at the hands of those Hindus who arrogate to themselves a superior status is a better Hindu than the self-styled superior Hindu, who by the very act of claming superiority denies his Hinduism. Therefore, those who threaten to renounce Hinduism are in my opinion betraying their faith."[8]

If, afflicted by the persecution and losing hope of ever receiving help from the other Savarna Hindus, the poor Harijans seek the shelter of Christianity, we may not be surprised. And our grief is worse than useless if we cannot turn it into powerful energy. Conversion under the stress of physical discomfort is no spiritual conversion. But we may not grumble if Harijans change their faith in order to better their material conditions and to secure protection from persecution.

What we need deplore is the cause of conversion. Let us realize and own that Savarna Hindus are the cause. Will they listen to this advice? Conversions are but one small result of the disease. Remove the cause, and the conversion will cease, as also many worse results.

Men who threaten to leave their religion, because some other men, pretending to be of the same faith as they, prevent them from entering temples, have little religion about them. Such men cannot be said to be actuated by the religious spirit. Temples are houses of worship. They are for all who believe in them. Religious persecution is not a thing of today. It is as ancient as religion itself. It tries and purifies the persecuted who prove themselves staunch in their faith. If Harijans can patiently bear persecution, they are bound to come triumphant in the end.

But the threat to desert the faith they have uncomplainingly professed from time immemorial, if their right of temple-entry is not recognized, puts them out of court. Sanatanists probably do not care if Harijans leave the Hindu fold. Reformers will be nonplussed if they have no case to fight for. Fortunately, there are tens of thousands of Harijans whose faith remains unshakable in spite of persecution.

Religion is an essentially personal matter. It is one between oneself and one's God. It should never be made a matter of bargain.'[9]

The apathy of the high-caste Hindus worried him much. He, however, dealt with them as best he could. During his discussion with Harijans, at Ahmedabad, he opined, 'This is a movement for the purification of Hinduism. Think what contribution you can make to it. If you bestir yourselves, if you shed you unclean habits, if you reform your way of living, irrespective of what the high-caste Hindus do, I assure you their superiority of birth will automatically disappear. Superiority consists in clean and pure living and I assure you that in spite of your unclean occupations you can live cleaner and purer lives than the rest of us. Yours is a service without which the community cannot do. I want you to be conscious of the dignity of your profession, to learn to practise it in a clean manner and I am sure you will be able to dictate your terms. Depend on yourselves, stand on your own legs and work your own salvation.'

Gandhi believed that the so called caste Hindus had a personal obligation to fulfil towards the Harijans which they must do unconditionally and it was to be their atonement. 'Whether in this world or the next, it is for each one to free oneself from bondage by one's own effort. Harijans should not look upon themselves as lowly, weak or crippled.'

Time and again, Gandhi asked the Harijans to magnify their own faults so that they appeared to be as big as mountains and then make constant efforts to overcome them. In it lay the key to obtaining the rights which they wanted. 'Never believe that since others have the same faults we need not mind our own. No matter what others do, it is your *dharma* to overcome the failings which you find in yourselves . . .. You will not be able, at the behest of others, to overcome what you yourselves do not look upon as failings. Hence, it should suffice to say that you should shake off whatever faults you can find in yourselves'.

In the process of regeneration of the nation, Gandhi wages an incessant and systematic war. 'If we are children of the same god how can there be any rank among us.' For him, there was only one *varnain* India, the *Sudras*. Indeed the *Sudrasare* those who serve. He wished that all the Hindus voluntarily call themselves *Sudras*.

He was critical of any person who would claim superiority over fellow-men. In his opinion there was no such thing as inherited or acquired superiority. He was happy and felt satisfied to call himself a scavenger, a spinner, a weaver and a labourer. He wrote in the *Hanrijan,* 'I have intentionally described myself as a *bhangi*. In man made social ladder I want to be at the bottom.'

He indeed was much pained to see the appalling plight of untouchables in various regions of the country. Its eradication greatly agitated his mind and he devised ways and means, from time to time, through his speeches and writings. He wrote in *Navajivan,* 'By passing resolutions and talking about their problem we have raised hopes in them. It was absolutely necessary to do this. It was necessary also that hopes should be raised in them and to tell those *antyaja* friend that what has happened should be sufficient answer to them. Another answer can be that they lay the entire burden on me. I can understand the sting in their words. They accuse me of being satisfied with the more or less that I do myself and of being gullible enough to be taken in by others who only befoul me. However, if I do something, there are others who may be doing less but still they do it.

"Untouchability is an attitude of the rrind, not a concrete object. To eradicate it, therefore, is not as easy as to persuade pupils to leave schools. No agitation, therefore, like the one with regard to schools can be suggested in respect of untouchability. A change of heart is necessary for this reform, as it is for receipting the principle of non-violence. The movement, therefore, can only be carried on along the same line as that for non-violence. Just as the extent to which the latter has been accepted by the people can be measured from the occasional incidents of violence which occur, so can progress in the removal of untouchability be measured from occasional evidence of its survival. No rule of arithmetic can be applied to judge this. You cannot work out as an arithmetical exercise, 'if so many Hindus have mixed with so many untouchables within such a period of time, what time will it take for all the crores of Hindus to mix with all the millions of untouchable?'—and ascertain the progress from the answer. But we get a measure of the progress from incidents which occur from time to time. The issue was first discussed as a principle in the Gujarat Vidyapith. As a result, the principle of admitting *Antyaja* pupils in its schools was accepted even at the risk of putting its very existence in danger, and some members who had tendered their resignations on this issue were allowed to leave the Vidyapith. If, again, the existence of an institution like the Dakshinamurti Bhavan is in serious danger today, the reason is the same. The teachers who are the very soul of the Bhavan are fighting a life-and-death struggle there to get the principle accepted. I cannot claim credit for either of these two results. I would have been defeated if the majority of the members of the Vidyapith had opposed me. But, on the contrary, they themselves believed in the principle independently of my view. In the holy fight which is being waged in the Dakshinamurti Bhavan, I cannot claim to have a hand even as an individual member. It was because of this issue that several proffered donations to the Tilak Swaraj Fund were withheld, but the managers of the Fund did dot care for the loss. *Antyajas* have freely attended hundreds of public meetings in Gujarat and elsewhere. The All-India Congress Committee has sanctioned an expenditure of more than Rs. 50,000 for *Antyaja* welfare activities at various places.

This amount excludes the money already spent by the Provincial Committees. Non-co-operators have thus been working all over India and independently of party considerations. In every province, enthusiastic young men of character have been, with the utmost sincerity of purpose, sacrificing their all in the service of *Antyajas*. This is the first time that in every constituency, *Antyaja* brothers have been elected delegates though they had expressed no such desire.

"This is for the satisfaction of the authors of the latter and other *Antyaja* friends like them who feel disappointed. But, while we may draw their attention to such a movement having spread we must admit at the same time that there is some truth in their complaint. Many persons simply make a show of mixing (with *Antyajas)* in order to hoodwink others, and are not sincere about the matter. Mixing with them in this spirit will yield bitter fruit. The practice of untouchability is against *dharma* and its disappearance will bear fruit only if the prejudice is shed from the heart. The campaign against it is not "a political move so that we may do just enough to throw dust in people's eyes. Nor is the movement undertaken in order to please or bribe *Antyajas.* Our only object is to satisfy our own conscience; our very conception of this evil is that, as long as Hindu society does not rid itself of it, it will continue to block our path invisibly, if not visibly, and will prevent our success in winning *swaraj.* The consequences of karma are hard to comprehend; its law admits of no exception. We always reap, visibly or invisibly, the fruits of our good and bad deeds, of our sins and virtuous acts.

"There is not a shred of doubt in my mind that so long as we have not cleansed our hearts of this evil and have not accepted the path of non-violence, so long as Hindus and Muslims have not become sincerely united, we shall not be free. Our progress in all these three fields is impossible to measure by any visible yard stick. Till we succeed in regard to all three we shall not get *Swaraj* and when we get it, we shall have succeeded in them. So long as Hindu society turns deaf ear to the six crores of *Antyajas* crying for justice at our doors, we shall not get *Swaraj* never.

"But even if caste Hindus wash off their sins, will *Antyajas* ascend to heaven in consequence. For that, they themselves should strive. They should give up drinking, refuse to eat leftovers, stop eating meat and, though for the sake of service, engaged in the most uncleanly work, remain clean and worship God. All this is for them to attend to. Others cannot do it for them. To banish hunger from among them, they have the spinning-wheel and the handloom at their service. Thousands of *Antyajas* have taken them up and prospered. The *Swedeshi* movement is such that it feeds and strengthens all the limbs and I, for one, am certain that it is *Swedish* which will, in time, end our abject poverty."

In his analysis of the religious *Satyagraha* there could be no room for aggressiveness, demonstrativeness and any kind of show. Those who happened to participate in it must have equal respect and regard for the religious convictions and susceptibilities of those who professed a different faith from theirs.

The slightest narrowness in their outlook, attitude and behaviour was likely to be reflected, magnified multi-fold in the opponent. To elaborate his point of view, he mentioned the qualities of a true *Satyagrahi.* This was explained by him in the context of the *Vykom satyagraha* about which he showed much concerned and time and again, he tendered a word of advice to the workers participating in it.'. . a *Satyagrahi* cannot go to law for a personal wrong. He sets out with the idea of suffering persecution . . . the *satyagrahi* seeks to convert his opponent by sheer force of character and suffering. The purer he is and the more he suffers, the quicker the progress. He must therefore resign himself to being excommunicated, debarred from the family privileges and deprived of his share in the family property. He must not only bear such hardships cheerfully but he must actively love his persecutors .... The *satyagrahi* . . . does not seek to carry out his reform by a system of punishments, but by penance, self-purification and suffering.

Undoubtedly Gandhi showed much concern about the *Vykom Satyagraha* undertaken in 1924-25 in order to obtain permission for 'untouchables' and 'unapproachable' to use certain roads round about the temple at *Vykom* in Travancore. In Travancore the *Satyagrahis* did not attack a whole system, but they fought sacerdotal prejudice. The Travancore State came in by a side door as it were. Indeed the *Vykom Satyagraha* had attracted a wide public attention. Though restricted to a small area, it presented so many problems for solution. When George Joseph took over the lead after, the arrest of Menon, Gandhi wrote to him thus : 'As to Vykom, I think that you shall let the Hindus do the work. It is they who have to purify themselves. You can help by your sympathy and by your pen, but not by organizing the movement and certainly not by offering *Satyagraha*. If you refer to the Congress resolution of Nagpur. It calls upon the Hindu members to remove the curse of Untouchability. It was surprised to learn that Mr. Andrews said that the disease had infected even the Syrian Christians.'

The use of the road was the final goal of the *Satyagrahis*. Gandhi was quite optimistic about the fact that the present movement throughout India was to throw open to the suppressed classes all the public roads, public schools, public wells and public temples which were accessible to non-Brahmins. *Satyagraha* in an Indian State by the Congress for the attainment of its object was forbidden. But *Satyagraha* in an Indian State in concoction with local abuses could be legitimately taken up at any time provided the other necessary conditions were fulfilled. As in an Indian State, there could be no question of non-cooperation, the device of petitions and deputations was not only always open, but it was obligatory. In a letter to George Joseph, Gandhi explained thus : 'You must be patient. You are in an Indian State. Therefore, you may wait in deputation on the Dewan and the Maharaja. Get up a monster petition by the orthodox Hindus who may be well-disposed towards the movement. See also those who are opposing. You can support the gentle direct action in a variety of ways. You have already drawn public attention to the matter by preliminary *Satyagraha*. Above all see to it that it neither dies nor by impatience becomes violent.'

At one point of time, His Holiness Shri Narayan Guru, the spiritual leader of the Tiyas, was reported to have disapproved the methods of *Satyagraha* practised at Vykom. He suggested that volunteers should advance along barricaded roads and scale the barricades. They should enter temples and sit with others to dine. Gandhi did not agree with this kind of suggestion and contradicted it in an article entitled 'Vykom *Satyagraha'* in the issue of *Young India* dated 19 June 1924. He opined that the action proposed by Shri Narayan Guru was not *Satyagraha* which he professed and preached. He argued that scaling barricades was tantamount to open violence. 'If you may scale barricades, why not break open temple doors and even pierce through temple walls? How were volunteers to pierce through a row of policemen except by using physical force? I do not for one moment suggest that by the methods proposed the Tiyas if they are strong and are willing to die in sufficient numbers cannot gain their point. All I submit is that they will have gained it by something the reverse of *Satyagraha;* and then too they would not have converted the orthodox to their view but would have imposed it on them by force .... I would, therefore, urge the organizers at Vykom to make redoubled efforts and at the same time keep stricter watch on the conduct of those who take part in the movement. Whether it takes long or short to reach the goal, the way is the way of peaceful conversion of the orthodox by self-suffering and self purification and no other.'

At the last stage of the *Satyagraha,* the Travancore authorities practically abandoned the *Satyagraha* to the tender mercies of goondas. This was emphernistically called the organised opposition of the orthodox section. Besides the violence of the *goondas* was said to be of a particularly barbarous type. They blinded the eyes of volunteers by throwing lime into them. At this point of time, Gandhi advised the volunteers not to lose their nerves sand instead resort to methods in accordance with his creed and philosophy of non-violence. "The challenge of the *goondas* must be taken up. But the *Satyagrahis* must not lose their heads. The *khaddar* dress of the volunteers is said to have been torn from them, and burnt. This is all provoking. They must remain cool under every provocation and courageous under the hottest fire. Loss even of a few hundred lives will not be too great a price to pay for the freedom of the 'unapproachable'. Only the martyrs must die clean. *Satyagrahis* like Caesar's wife must be above suspicion."

Gandhi gave a word of advice and warning to the Hindu reformers who were intent on removal of untouchability. The immediate goal of the *Satyargahis* was the opening of the roads surrounding the temple, not their entry into the latter. Their contention was that the roads should be opened to the so-called untouchables as they were to all other Hindus and even-non-Hindus. That point was completely gained. But whilst *Satyagraha* was directed to the opening of roads, the ultimate aim of reformers was undoubtedly removal of every disability that 'the untouchables' were labouring under which the other Hindus were not. It, therefore, included access to temples, wells, schools etc. to which other non-Brahmins were freely admitted. *Satyagraha* is never adopted abruptly and never till all other and milder methods had been tried. The reformers of the South have to cultivate public opinion in the matter of temple-entry etc. This is, moreover, a disability not peculiar to the South but unfortunately and to our shame, it must be admitted, common, to more or less extent, to Hinduism throughout India, "I therefore, welcome the decision of St. Kelappen Nayar who was in charge of the camp at Ykom to concentrate his effort on working among the unhappiest and the most suppressed among 'the untouchables' *i.e.* Puliyas whose very Shadow defiles. . .. Reform has to be undertaken at both ends to make *savarnas* do their duty by the 'untouchables' whom they have so cruelly suppressed and to help the latter to become more presentable and to shed habits for which they can in no way be held accountable but which nevertheless have to be given up if they are to occupy their proper place in the social scale."

Gandhi elaborated his point of view in respect of a temple entry programme at Deoli, 'I take the masses only so far as they are prepared to go. I do not want to injure their susceptibilities. I open temples with the utmost caution. I refused to open a temple at Deoli because the trustees were said to be sharply divided over the issue, though the vast majority of temple-goers were in favour of opening the temple to the Harijans immediately.

Some of the leaders of the untouchables, especially B.R. Ambedkar, opined that Gandhi and his associates were paying too much attention to the problem of temple entry and less attention to the improvement of their economic status and upliftment of their educational standards. To this Gandhi replied that temple entry was the decisive test to the fact whether the mind of the orthodox Hindus had changed or not, and its achievement would strike the imagination of all most effectively. His line of thinking was thus concerned as much with the *savarna* Hindus as with the untouchables. Indeed what he ardently desired was a change of heart. He argued that political and economic betterment would be far more quickly brought about if religious equality were attained.

In May 1924, Gandhi admitted in the *Navajivan* about the pitiable plight of untouchables. ". . . . not a single school for untouchables could be started, for our work among them is yet to be considered as 'popular'. Moreover, in many villages all the Hindus are opposed to such an activity or, if not actually opposed to it, are indifferent in the matter .... So far as the untouchables are concerned, we have really clipped their wings. We have crushed better sentiments out of them, so that much of our work among them has to be done by way of atonement. All this is a debt we own them. Moreover, this obligation may not become 'popular'. Those to whom it appeals may spend their money on it and work without hoping for reward . . .."

Gandhi did not believe that interdining or even intermarriage necessarily deprived a man of his status that his birth had given him. The four divisions, defined a man's calling, they did not restrict or regulate social intercourse.

He argued that the divisions defined duties and did not confer any privilege. It was, he held, against the 'genius' of Hinduism to arrogate to oneself a higher status or assign to another a lower. 'All are born to serve God's Creation .... There is nothing, again, to prevent the *Shudra* from acquiring all the knowledge he wishes .... *Varnashvama* is self-restraint and conservation and economy of energy .... I do not want *Moksha.* I do not want to be reborn. But I have to be reborn, I should be born as an untouchable, so that I may share their sorrows, sufferings, and the affronts levelled at them in order that I may endeavour to free myself and them from that miserable condition .... if I should die with any of my desires unfulfilled, with my service of the untouchables unfinished, with my Hinduism unfilled, I may be born again amongst the untouchables to bring my Hinduism to fulfilment.'

'As a lay human student of Hinduism and claming to be one desirous of practising Hinduism in the spirit and to the letter, let me tell you that I have found no warrant or support for this terrible doctrine. Let us not deceive ourselves into the belief that everything that is written in Sanskrit and printed in *Shastra* and has any binding effect upon us .... Untouchability poisons Hinduism as a drop of arsenic poisons milk. Knowing the quality of milk, and the use of milk and knowing the quality of arsenic, we should be impatient with the man sitting near a pitcher of milk and trying to remove arsenic grain by grain, and we should throw the whole pitcher overboard. Even so do I, as a Hindu, feel that the curse of untouchabiliy is rendering the milk of Hinduism altogether poisoned and impure .... Patience with evil is really trifling with evil and with ourselves

You must remember that all the great religions of the world are at the present time in the melting pot. Let us not ostrich-like hide our faces and ignore the danger that lies at the back of us. I have not a shadow of doubt that in the great tuamoil now taking place either untouchability has to die or Hinduism has to disappear. But I do know that Hinduism is not dying, is not going to die, because I see untouchability is a corpse struggling with its last breath to hold on for a little while.

'Untouchability is a snake with a thousand mouths, though each of which it shows its poisonous fangs .... It need no sanction from Manu or the other ancient law-givers .... Reformers are trying to cope with the evil. I feel, however, that much more drastic methods are needed than are employed to rid Hinduism of the blot. We are needlessly afraid to mould the susceptibilities of orthodoxy . .. This untouchability naturally recoils on the heads of those who are responsible for It.'

Indeed the Mahatma very much wanted to uplift Hinduism, and, therefore, he regarded the untouchables as an integral part of the Hindu community. He was pained when he happened to see a single *Bhangi* driven out of the fold of Hinduism. But he did not believe that all class distinctions could be obliterated. He had deep faith in the Doctrine of Equality as taught by Lord Krishna in the *Gita*. The *Gita* teaches us that members of all the four castes should be treated on an equal basis. It insists that the Bhangi should be entitled to the same measure of consideration, and esteem as the former with all his superior learning. 'It is, therefore, our duty to see that the untouchables do not feel that they are despised or looked down upon. Let them not be offered leavings from our plates for their subsistence.'

Gandhi narrates how he was touched by the deplorable plight of a scavenger when he was hardly twelve years old. In his later career, he challenged the artificial religious norms imposed by the Hindu society on millions of untouchables. He stated, "A scavenger named Uka, an 'untouchable' used to attend our house for cleaning latrines. Often I would ask my mother why it was wrong to touch him, why I was forbidden to touch him. If I accidentally touched Uka, I was asked to. perform ablutions and though I naturally obeyed, it was not without smilingly protesting that untouchability was not sanctioned by religion .... I often had tussles with them on this matter. I told my mother that she was entirely wrong in considering physical contact with Uka as sinful. While at school, I would often happen to touch the 'untouchables'."[28]

He drew a sharp distinction between untouchability and *Varna* or caste. The caste system, in his opinion, had a scientific basis. Reason does not revolt against it. 'Caste creates a social and moral restraint. The doctrine of caste cannot be extended. I would restrict it to four divisions. Any multiplication would be an evil. I would reform the castes and rid them of undoubted abuses, but I can hand no reason for their abolition. For me there is no question of superiority or inferiority. A Brahmin who regards himself as superior being born to look down upon the other castes is not a Brahmin. If he is first he is so by right of service. "

Gandhi wrote in 1931, 'Untouchability cannot long endure. Some years ago we obstinately clung to it, today we are indifferent. It will be a thing of the past only when the indifference is translated into a conscious, deliberate awakening to a sense of the duty of selfpurification. Even the indifference or of sufferance would have been impossible fifteen years ago,/?0 was of the firm conviction that if untouchabitity was an integral part of Hinduism, the latter was a spent bullet'. But untouchability, he stated, was a hideous untruth. What he was aiming at was not every Hindu touching an 'untouchable', but every touchable Hindu driving out untouchability from his heart, going through a complete change of heart. In fact interdining or intermarrying was not the main point. "I may not dine with you, but I ought not to harbour the feeling that if I dined with you I should be polluted. If I was a woman to be married, I should not say : "I cannot marry a man because he is an untouchable' . . .. Instead of being the dead faith that it threatens to be, I want it to be a living faith, so that it may exist side by side with other religions of the world."

Thus, to remove untouchability was a penance that caste Hindus owed to Hinduism and to themselves. The purification required was not of untouchables, but of the so called superior castes. Indeed, there was no vice that was special to the untouchables, not even dirt and insanitation. "It is our arrogance which blinds us, 'superior' Hindus, to our own blemishes and which magnifies those of our down-trodden brethren, whom we have suppressed and whom we keep under suppression . . .. God's grace and revelation are the monopoly of no race or nation. They descend equally upon all who wait upon God. That religion and that nation will be blotted out of the face of the earth which pins its faith to injustice, untruth or violence. God is Light, no darkness. God is love, not hate. God is Truth, not untruth. God alone is Great. We his creatures are but dust. Let us be humble and recognize the place of the lowliest of His creatures. Krishna honoured Sudama in his rags, as he honoured no one else .... The Hindus have to purify themselves before they can hope to revive the Vedic philosophy and make it a living reality."

During the second phase of the Civil Disobedience Movement, Gandhi had been kept in jail under the usual rules.. But during his fast, these had been relaxed and he had Kasturba to attend upon him and many visitors. After his contact with the authorities through correspondence, he was permitted from 7 November to conduct the Harijan movement from within the jail, to receive visitors freely and to write. In May 1933 sixteen months after his arrest, he decided again to fast for twenty-one days. This was his only fast of any length since his experimental fasts in South Africa. His explanation is as follows :

"A tempest has been raging within me for some days. I have been struggling against it. On the eve of the 'Harijan Day' (April 30) the voice became insistent and said, 'Why don't you do it?' I resisted it. But the resistance was vain .... The fast is against nobody in particular .... But it is particularly against myself. If is a heart-prayer for the purification of self and associates, for greater vigilance and watchfulness. But nobody who appreciates the step about to be taken is to join me .... Let the fast however be a preparation for many such fasts to be taken by purer and more deserving persons than myself ....

> ". . . . I have no desire to die. I want to live for the cause. But I need for me and my fellow-workers greater purity, greater application and dedication. I want more workers of unassaiblable purity. Shocking cases of impurity have come under my notice. I would like my fast to be an urgent appeal to such people to leave the cause alone.

"I know that many of my *sanatanist* friends and other think that the movement is a deep political game. How I wish this fast would convince them that it is purely religious."[33]

In a public meeting in Nagpur on 8 November, 1933, the Mahatma explained thus : "I am deeply grateful to you for the manifestation of this great affection. Thanks be to God that you have assembled in such numbers to listen to my message. The Chairman is right when he says that this Harijan work is essentially religious from my standpoint. That it has many other results is equally true. There never has been a single truly religious activity but has had its influence on many departments of life. That perhaps is one of the tests by which we recognize a great religious movement. I would like to say in all humility, but with perfect confidence, that I have taken up this movement in no spirit of antagonism to any other religion or community. It would be impossible for any person to point to a single act of mine during the past 50 years which could be proved to have been antagonistic to any person or community. I have never believed anyone to be my enemy. My faith demands that I should consider no one as such. I may not wish ill to anything that lives. It is my certain conviction that, if the Hindu heart is completely purged of the taint of untouchability, the event will have its inevitable influence not only upon all the communities in India but on the whole world. This belief is daily becoming stronger. I cannot remove from my heart untouchability regarding several millions of human beings and harbour it towards some other millions. The very act of the Hindu heart getting rid of distinctions of high and low must cure us of mutual jealousies and distrust of and among other communities. It is for that reason that I have staked my life on his issue. In fighting this battle against untouchability. I am fighting for unity not only between Hindu touchables and Hindu untouchables but among Hindus, Muslims, Christians and all other different religious communities. Do not for one moment believe that I am interested in the numerical strength of Hindus. I have never throughout my life laid stress upon quantity. I have ever insisted upon quality at the scarifices of quantity. If I collected a million false coins they would be a worthless burden to me. One true coin would be worth its value. A religion cannot be sustained by the number of its lip-followers denying in their lives its tenets. This great Hindu religion itself will perish, in spite of its so-called millions of followers, if its voteries persist in harbouring the evil of untouchability. Not because untouchables can be counted by the millions. It would perish even if they were a handful. Milk is poisoned and has to be thrown away whether you put a little or much arsenic in it. If we believe that we are all children of one and same God and that God is Truth and Justice, how can there be untouchability amongst us, His children? God of Truth and Justice can never create distinctions of high and low among his own children. I, therefore, invite all without distinction of race and religion to assist this movement by praying for its complete success, so that we may all live in peace and friendship.

"And if I want concord amongst all the communities professing different faiths. I cannot desire discord between the so-called *sanatanists* and reformers. I can harbour no ill-will against *sanatanists,* I ask them to extend the same toleration to reformers that they would have the latter extend towards themselves. If they tolerate the faith and practice of others, why will they not tolerate the faith and practice of the reformers? They may not help so long as they regard untouchability as an integral part of Hinduism. I and fellow reformers firmly believe that untouchability is an evil; and if it is so and if the reformers will continue to exercise patience and gentleness, the heart of the *sanatanists must melt* There can be no room for compulsion or violence in this great movement. I endeavor to place before the vast mass of Hindus the results of a belief derived from such prayerful study of the Hindu scriptures as has been possible for me, and from association with those who are learned in them and, what is more, from my practice based upon that belief. Surely, that cannot promote internal dissensions. I observe that many who oppose this movement have not taken the trouble to understand its implications. The object of this tour is to place the position of the reformers clearly before the public. And I am hoping that, as the scope of the activities of the Servants of Untouchables Society becomes known, the position to it will melt away. We want to change the hearts of those who today oppose the movement. We want to remove their distrust. We do not desire to compel them to act against their belief. We want to win them over to the reform by gentlest persuasion, by appealing to their reason and to their hearts. Love can never express itself by imposing sufferings on others. It can only express itself by self-suffering, by self-purification. I am convinced that, if the reformers will show in their own lives an increasing purity, self-denial, and capacity for suffering, they will be sure to melt the hearts of those who are today saturated with untouchability, believing it to be a desirable part of Hinduism.

"It is said that untouchables are so because of the evil in them. But are the 'touchables' better? Are they sinless? Indeed, defenders of untouchability claim that some people are always untouchables and that no amount of pure conduct can cure them of the taint with which they are born. They must remain social lepers for ever. The fact is that whatever weaknesses we may notice about untouchables are a reflection of our own weaknesses and sins. They are a direct result of the ill-treatment that we have heaped upon their devoted heads. Their real rise, therefore, depends upon the removing of untouchability root and branch and upon showing a growing purity in our own lives. Thus the movement is dependent, not so much upon pecuniary help, as upon correct conduct. Pecuniary help is to be an earnest of our determination to rid ourselves of the evil and to achieve self-purification.

"The question is repeatedly asked whether the reform includes inter-dining. Though I have answered this question repeatedly, I must continue to repeat the answer as long as the question continues to be asked. Everybody knows what my personal views are. Since my youth upward I have consistently dined with all so long as the rules of cleanliness have been observed. But that has nothing to do with the present movement. Interdining and the rest is a question for each individual to determine for himself. The movement organized by the Servants of Untouchables Society stands for simple removal of untouchability in every shape and form, in so far as it is special to the so-called untouchables. They would have the same public rights and facilities as are enjoyed by every other Hindu, that is to say, they should have access to all public institutions, such as wells, schools, roads, temples, etc.

"One word as to the objections raised against Anti-untouchability Bills. *Sanatanists* have contended that they constitute State interference in matters of religion. I suppose by interference is meant that which is undue. For it is possible to quote instances where State interference has been sought and has been inevitable in matters of religion. What is sought is freedom from external compulsion. I am no more in favour of such compulsion in matters affecting religion, than *sanatanists.* These Bills involve no such compulsion, no undue interference. The interference sought is beneficial and unavoidable. If the State compelled the opening of temples to Harijans, it would without doubt be undue interference, but it cannot be undue when the State is called upon to legalize the voluntary opening by a stated majority of temple-goers or the trustees. Not to do so would be compulsion. The Temple-entry Bill merely seeks to legalize the action of a majority. The other bill has been long overdue. It does not abolish untouchability altogether. It seeks to rob it of secular consequence. To clothe it with such consequences is to constitute an intolerable interference with the free exercise of religion. Nobody will deny that to make a religious obligation an obligation in law would be a gross and undue interference by the State. The observance of untouchabiltiy requires the voluntary recognition of it by both touchables and untouchables. For the State to compel observance by untouchables would be a gross interference in matters of religion. The Bill, therefore, seeks to remove the secular recognition of uotouchability, without in any way interfering with the religious observance of it or the religious consequences of the breach of it. If the objectors mean, therefore, what they say and on a careful study should find that the Bills involve no Compulsion, they should waive their objection.

"The poor man perhaps had nothing else to pay and he

seems to have paid his all. It is an unsoiled *cowrie,* as Malaviyaji would call it. We attribute our earnings to fate, but what we give in the name of God, and for the service of his creatures bring us merit. Looking at it as a symbol of sacrifice, it is more precious than gold."[34]

The same sentiments were expressed by him in public meetings at, Amraoti and Calicut. 'I have visited many places throughout the length and breadth of this country and such big meetings are to me the manifestations of the grace of God. I believe that with God's favour only can we conduct such huge assemblies. With His grace also I have taken up the Harijan work. It is a religious work and should therefore be done with truth, peace and sacrifice. It could not be done otherwise. If we want to expiate for the injustice done to the Harijans and if we want to atone for the wrongs we, the *savarna* Hindus, are still doing them, we must treat them as we treat other *savarna* Hindus. I would like to tell you all that, unless we behave with them on equal terms, there is no chance of our improvement also. I visited the Harijan quarters with the help of Dr. Patwardhan, and have also seen other work here, and have now heard the address read out to me by the local Municipal Committee. If the Municipality of this place could not do anything in this matter, it is not to be blamed. I have seen many other municipal committees and the conditions are just the same all over. But I must say that now even the Western scientists after their research have come to the conclusion that if we leave out any particular section of our society out of our fold, we are sure to go down economically. After these 25 years of observations, my belief is being strengthened that wealth should always go hand in hand with religion. There should be harmony between religion and wealth. I have come to realize from my Harijan work that one who tries for wealth in accordance with religion gets both. I believe it to be the duty of every *savarna* Hindus that should try to take up the Harijan into his fold. If we do our duty towards the Harijans, all of us, Hindus, Moslems, Parsis, Christians, will live peacefully. To my mind there is no better way to unity of these people than Harijan work. Now I must tell you what every one of you can do in this respect. The Harijan movement is a great yajna and each of you can put his little bit in it. Those who have money can give it for this cause. Those who have the leisure and intelligence to spare can teach the Harijan boys and give them lessons in personal hygiene and cleanliness. The Congressmen are doing this work at present. But I want that non-Congressmen also should undertake this work. It is the religious duty of every one of you to do this work.

T do not value politics as much as I value this work. Politics is nothing to me. It is my belief that if we do this work with religious fervour everything will be obtained. I am not travelling with any other intention in this work. And when I see people assemble in such large numbers to hear me, I hope they will stand by rne in this work. In July last the Harijan Sevak Sangh was started and some of you must have taken the vow to wipe out this curse of untouchability. It is the birthright of the Harijans to make use of public institutions and to enter into the temples. But as long as there is a single soul boycotted as being a Harijan, I shall not regard untouchability as being wiped out totally. It is up to you, therefore, to change your hearts and consider the Harijans as your brethren.

'The Harijan Sevak Sangh is composed of people of different schools of thought but they can do this work together. The workers in this fields should not aspire after any kind of honour or title. They should not have the slightest tinge of personal interest or selfish motive. This work should also be free from any sort of political colour. There is no doubt that it will have some political meaning but I do not value political things as much as this. The Harijan work is for the purification of the Hindu religion. I have great hopes in this matter. I have always been an optimist and my optimism in this case is increasing every day. But even if I fail it remains my duty to continue this work. Very few sincere workers have so far come forward. I therefore, pray to God that He should give you all the necessary strength and guidance to do your duty in this respect. I must remind you of the ledge given last year in you name. You will remember that a meeting of representatives of Hindus was held in Bombay in September last year, Pandit Malaviyaji being in the chair. Among other things they resolved that untouchability, being a blot on the Hindu religion had to be removed and that Harijans were entitled to the same public utilities, and in the same manner, as caste Hindus. There was in that resolution a special reference to Hindu temples, and legislation was contemplated if it was found to be necessary for attaining the end. It is, therefore, the bounden duty of every caste Hindu *to* fulfil the pledge by throwing open to the Harijans temples, wells and other institutions precisely on the same terms as they are open to caste Hindus.

'We are the cause of the degradation to which the Harijans are reduced. We must spend money if the wrong is to be redressed. He who will give to the cause will gain. We may not be satisfied, therefore, with giving out of superfluous cash, we have to give even if we have to stint ourselves, some of us will have to give our all for Harijan service.

'It gladdens me to find both Congressmen and non-Congressmen working together in this movement. Since questions are being asked as to how far Congressmen can join this movement, I would like to reiterate what I have said before. The Congress adopted removal of untouchability as an integral part of its programme in 1920. It is, therefore, the duty of every Hindu Congressman to fight untouchability and help Harijans in every way open to him. But, if the movement were confined *to* Congressmen alone, it could not make the headway we all desire. Every *savarna* Hindu has to do his bit in the movement. But whilst every Congress member is expected to fight the evil, he or she is not expected officially to join the Harijan Sevak Sangh. If they are active civil registers, they ought not to hold office in these organizations. And no Congressman who believes in and wants to offer civil resistance need in any way feel constrained to suspend or give it up altogether. The case is wholly different with those who feel the call to give up civil resistance for the sake of Harijan service or who lost faith in the former.

'In this movement of self-purification as in *satyagraha* there is no room for camouflage. Harijans have complained that some self-seekers have crept into the movement. In a purely religious movement there is no room for such people. Only those can or should take office who have the spirit of service in them.

'Some of the ladies of this place have offered me ornaments and the little children have given me a little silver casket which 1 wish to put for auction. I shall accept money from you all, be it even a *cowriehut* it should be given with a pure heart. I assure you that it will make you happy and will be helpful to the Harijans.'[35]

I have just got several purses on behalf of the citizens of Calicut which amount to Rs. 4,388-5-9. On the principle that you may not look a gift horse in the mouth I must in all courtesy thank you for the gifts that you have given on behalf of the Harijan cause. But as a self-chosen or self-appointed Harijan servant, I must lodge my respectful protest against the leanness of the purses from the capital of Malabar. You will be surprised to learn that Bangalore, not the capital of Mysore, but the second city in Mysore, not as big as Malabar, produced much more than you have given this evening. And I am fully aware of the capacity of Calicut to give for the Harijan cause. But nothing is lost yet. You have got here many tempting things, and at the end of a few remarks that I want to make, it is open to you and perfectly possible for you to make up for the deficiency and what is today undoubtedly a lean purse can be turned by you into a fat purse.

"As I have said from many a platform after entering Malabar, if there was a map of untouchability made for the whole of India, Malabar would be marked as the blackest spot in all the land; and as matters stand today, I suppose you will admit that you will have to plead guilty to the charge. Then if you are convinced of the sin of Malabar, as confessedly you are convinced by the very fact of your giving me this purse, you will admit that Malabar has to make the greatest reparation in order to rid itself of the greatest sin. It does not matter, and if ought not to matter, the least little bit that some of you who are monied men do not originally come from Malabar. Those who make their livelihood or their fortunes in Malabar should realize that every pie they get is trained with this sin. Therefore, in the matter of reparation and repentance, they stand exactly on the same footing as the original Malayalis.

"This morning they took me to a most beautiful bit of Malabar; they took me up the hills with the most romantic scenery. There I was taken to a village called Kalpetta, and I recalled a hymn-I think it was composed by Bishop Heber. But whether it was composed by him or some other bishop, this is the line that I single out from that hymn for your edification. It is said that, as he was approaching this Western coast of India, involuntarily this line came to his lips, or to his pen : 'Every prospect pleases, man alone is Vila.' I have no doubt that he had not this black spot of untouchability in his mind when he wrote this line. The orthodox interpretation of this line is wholly different from the one that I put upon it. But poets can never be confined even in cases of their own construction. Poets write for eternity. Their words are charged with a meaning of which they have no conception when they utter or write them. Scented breezes come from plantations that Nature has designed for man in Malabar. But through untouchability he has violated Nature and thus become vile. We have endeavored to disfigure God's mightiest creation, namely, man. The soul of man presents a beauty never to be surpassed by any ravishing beauty of vegetation. But the so called *savarna* Hindu or the so called high class Hindus arrogated to themselves the right of suppressing a portion of Hindu humanity. They endeavoured, however, vainly, as we shall presently see in a few years, perhaps. But man has left no stone unturned to suppress, in the mane of Divinity itself, the soul of man by putting thousands outside the pale of society.

'I will tell you what I saw today in Kalpetta in the midst of the ravishing beauty of vegetation. I saw wild specimens of humanity, with a stinking odour. Please do not say hastily that is why they are untouchables. I want you to think with me a little more deeply than possibly you are prepared to do and realize with me that for this indescribably painful scene you and I are responsible. These very men, in an hour's time, if you desire, can be transformed into beings cleanly and outwardly as respectable as you and I may be. A little hot water, or soap, a little white *khaddar* and you will immediately find that they are just as presentable as you and I are. Internally, God alone can be the judge between them and us. It is quite possible, in fact, in my opinion it is quite certain, that we are much more sinful or much viler than they can be. Our slates are sullied with writings not particularly creditable to us. Their slates have still to be written upon. Are you now surprised that, when I saw these countrymen of ours, I involuntarily said in my mind to the poet, "you were right in saying, 'Every prospect pleases, and alone is vile'." Now, put your hands upon your hearts and tell me whether, if you gave up all your wealth and all sisters discarded every article of jewellery of which they are possessed, would it be a sufficient reparation for the injuries that you have been partners in inflicting on these countrymen of ours? I wish to suggest you that you will be fit servants of Harijans when you have begun the act of reparation by discarding all your possessions for their sake. But I know that is an ideal state of things, and I know also that, if I could possibly carry you along those ideals, then India would again be really a land of thirty crores of gods.

'But I am labouring under no such delusion. I consider myself a practical idealist. I take from human nature what it yields and go my way. My business is to present to you the realities of the situation, to stimulate your intelligence and your imagination, to touch your hearts and then leave you to do the very best that you can possibly do for a cause so noble and so sacred as that of the Harijans.

'I would like you, lastly, to realize that if we, the so-called *savarna* Hindus, failed in this elementary duty by the Harijans during this brief period of probation, Hinduism will be a thing of the past. History teaches us that many a civilization, many a culture perished beyond redemption because of the inherent weakness of their presentatives of those bygone civilizations.

Do not, therefore, run away with the belief that Hinduism will be an exception and escape the impending doom, if we, Hindus, prove unworthy representatives of the priceless treasures that the *rishis* have left for us.'[36]

When Seth Ghanshyamdas Birla, President of the Harijan Sevak Sangh wrote to Gandhi for starting a few residential schools for Harijan boys, he whole-heartedly supported his idea and wished him all success in his efforts. In fact Gandhi knew well that these schools would greatly enhance their academic standard and would enable them to become better citizens for India. G.D. Birla wrote thus :

'We are thinking of establishing a few residential schools mainly for educating Harijan boys, though not exclusively. So far, whenever we have talked of Harijan hostels or schools, we have thereby meant cheap schools or cheap hostels conducted by ill-educated and ill-paid teachers and wardens with boys half-starved. So long as we educate Harijans or children of poor parents in these cheap institutions, the boys will never succeed in shedding the inferiority complex from which they often suffer. And what will they learn from these unqualified and ill-paid teachers? These boys never get the opportunity to mix with the other boys. The harm due to this lack of contact between the poor and the well-to-do or between Harijans and *Savarnas* is mutual. I therefore propose that we should have a few residential schools established in pleasing environment. They should be of a standard that would compare favourably in every respect with a well-conducted public school. We should start a few such schools first of all as a trial.

They should be of the matriculation standard and affiliated to a university. They should, of course, be mostly residential. Personal attention to students should be a speciality. Education should be imparted through the medium of the mother tongue. English should be taught as a second language. During the period of this education, the boys should be taught useful handicrafts chosen for their educative value.

In order to make this education thorough and self-sufficient, we should take two years more than the time needed for the matriculation examination. These two years should be utilized in giving extra training to the boys besides what they learn for the matriculation course.

We propose to have three crafts, one of which will be taken up by every boy at his option. These will be :

> Either (1) Carding, Spinning, Weaving, Dyeing and Bleaching; or (2) Carpentry and Smithy; or (3) Paper-making, Book-binding and Ordinary Composing.

It is intended to employ a superior staff, adequately paid, to ensure good qualifications. The underlying idea is that the boys may not feel the want of a college education. There will be no bar to such. The boys, it is hoped, will not find it difficult to earn an honest livelihood after finishing the course. It will be the duty of the Board to accommodate such boys as may like to be.

Besides the university course and craft, special attention will be given to increasing the general knowledge and hygiene. Music, games, exercises, riding, swimming, etc. should be taught. Religious or moral training should not be neglected. Equal respect for all religions should be inculcated, along with a good grounding in the principles of Hinduism and the peculiar beauties of our own culture.

Half the number of the students should be Harijans who would have free education and free boarding and lodging. The other half of the students, *i.e. savamas,* should be charged fees.

This is a very rough and brief outline of my idea of a good high school.

But there is difference amongst us about this outline. Some say : why should we have the matriculation course?

Others say: we should not undertake costly education as this will be a bad example to set. It is urged that we may employ most qualified men, but only if they come on a bare maintenance and out of a spirit of sacrifice. In other words, in their opinion, in this school there would be no room for teachers other than those prepared to lead a simple life of sacrifice. Some go to the extent of saying that we should rather have no school than start one which is not manned by as highly self-sacrificing staff.

I consider all this unpractical. I need not give my arguments. They are obvious.

Will you express your views on this question?

I whole-heartedly support Seth Ghanshyamdas's scheme. The arguments advanced in opposition seem to be based more on caution than on principle. I too should side with the opposition, if the scheme was to be financed out of the meagre funds of the Harijan Board. But I assume that the model schools would be financed by special donations enough to guarantee their full working. Having lived in South Africa for twenty years where every Indian is treated almost as a Pariah, I know how sensitive the mind becomes under unnatural treatment. I took some time to regain my balance though I never lost the sensitiveness. I felt that I was a strange creature in the company of the general body of Europeans. The plight of Harijans in India is much worse because of their much greater ignorance and still greater poverty. Therefore, if we are to break down the double complex, we have to bring up a fair number of Harijan lads in surroundings in no way inferior to those that are available to the well-to-do classboys. The scheme under examination does not contemplate the production of clerks who would be too big for their boots and who would be naturally discontented because no one would have them as clerks. Boys trained under the scheme would be in no way inferior in knowledge to the other matriculates. But these will be better placed because their bodies will be specially looked after and their hands will have their cunning fully developed. Such boys will have their future assured. They will have self-confidence. They will not be torn from their kith and kin on the contrary, they will be expected to serve fellow Harijans and give them the benefit of the teaching they have received.

It may be objected that I am inconsistent in that I have written and spoken against the present system of education.

The objection would be superficial. In the first place, the worst features of the system will be eliminated in that the training will be in the mother-tongue and the boys will be taught handicrafts which should enable them to earn an independent and decent living. Secondly, an objection that may be applicable to boys who can be better educated cannot be held good in the case of boys who have no choice and who smart under the knowledge that they cannot have the education that thousands of other boys have simply because they are not Harijans. I would not insult Harijan lads by arguing with them that what the thousands of non-Harijan lads are doing is wrong, and that therefore they had better be satisfied with the shanties which Seth Ghanshyamdas has referred to in his letter.

I plump for his scheme. I wish him all success. The sooner it is launched, the better for Harijans and better for India. These schools will be potent instruments for exercising the demand of untouchability.

Thus he recommended higher education for Harijans.

"I hope all those who are interested in the removal of untouchability are familiar with Mr. David's scheme for the higher education of selected Harijans by caste Hindus. In Mr. David's words, 'it aims at enabling a large number of untouchables to enjoy the benefits of the best higher education (including technical instruction) possible in this country/ Under it, 'well-to-do caste Hindus are expected throughout India each to bear the expenses for such education of at least one Harijan student for a period of five years. Scholarships should be given to selected candidates and the expenses imply the provision of educational fees, books and living expenses on a modest scale.' Mr. David thinks that Rs. 500 per year per Harijan would be required for college education and half as much for high school education. He advised donors to subscribe, wherever it is possible, the whole amount covering five years in one lump sum.

'In order to build up the self-respect of Harijan scholars,' says Mr. David, 'it should be laid down that each scholar would be expected to reimburse the amount originally advanced for his education as soon as he is in a position to do so. Thus a student is provided by means of a loan and not a gift.' And if a large number of students discharge these debts of honour Mr. David anticipates that a permanent fund will be created.

Mr. David advises the formation of Committee or Committees in provinces which will frame rules for the selection of candidates, and the disbursements of subscriptions will be subject to the recommendation of such Committee or Committees. He is emphatic that the scheme, if carried out, should 'produce important and sustained results', and make possible within a comparatively short period the creation of a large number of lawyers, teachers, doctors and engineers from among Harijans. The existence of a considerable number of such persons would be of material help in raising the social status of the depressed classes, and, he adds, 'it is framed on strictly non-controversial lines, thus widening to the maximum its potential field of response. It should win the support of even the staunchest Sanatanists .... It is an opportunity at hand for caste Hindus to give concrete expressions of their feeling towards 'untouchables'.'

Let me hope, with Mr. David, that the scheme will commend itself to the 'staunchest Sanatanists' and that in any case it would receive liberal support."

'A Harijan if it was right to encourage Harijan boys to

become B.A.s', or M.A.s, when unemployment was rife among graduates, and whether it would not be better if they took to technical education. Gandhiji replied that they could hardly expect Harijans to go in for industrial education before it had successfully appealed to the *Savarnas.* And it was possible that, even if mere academic training was now no good for Savarna, it had its own value for Harijans. For instance, he had long thought Dr. Ambedkar to be a Brahmana. He was equal in intelligence and ability to the tallest among us. Such distinction had its undoubted use for Harijans. Gandhiji himself fully believed in industrial education and wished the numerous Harijan students would turn their attention to it. Harijan Sevak Sangh could not force Harijans to such education. They had to encourage the academical side by side with the industrial. It was for the Harijans to preach the gospel of industrial training.'

According to Gandhi Vykom Satyagraha was intended to be of an educative force. A *satyagrahistrived* to reach the reason through the heart.

To make bold to state that from the very outset Satyagraha at Vykom was intended to be an educative force and never an instrument of coercion of the orthodox. It was for that reason that the fast against the orthodox was abandoned. It was to avoid coercion of the Government by embarrassment that the barricades have been scrupulously respected. It was for that reason that no attempt was made to dodge the police. It has been recognized that what appears to the reformers as a gross and sinful superstition is to the orthodox a part of their faith. The satyagrahi's appeal has therefore been to the reason of the orthodox. But experience has shown that mere appeal to the reason produces no effect upon those who have settled convictions. The eyes of their understanding are opened not by argument but by the suffering of the Satyagrahi. The Satyagrahi strives to reach the reason through the heart. The method of reaching the heart is to awaken public opinion. Public opinion for which one cares is a mightier force than that of gunpowder. The Vykom Satyagraha has vindicated itself in that it has drawn the attention of the whole of India to the cause, and it has been instrumental in the Travancore Assembly considering in a remarkable debate a resolution favouring the reform sought for and lastly in eliciting a considered reply from the Dewan of Travancore. I am sure victory is a certainty if only the Satyagrahis will retain their patience and their spirit of suffering.

'Vykom of which till lately no one outside Travancore, at most the Madras Presidency, knew anything has suddenly leapt to fame because it has become the seat of Satyagraha. The press contains daily bulletins of the progress of the movement. It has been undertaken on behalf of the 'untouchables' of Travancore. The movement has given us another word to describe the condition of the suppressed classes. It is unapproachability. These poor countrymen of ours may not only not touch any other caste Hindus but they may not even approach them within a stated distance. The leaders of the movement with a view to remedying the evil have taken up only a fragment of the evil, hoping no doubt that if they deal with it successfully they will have dealt it a death-blow at least in that part of India in which direct action is now going on. In the prosecution of the campaign some of the staunchest workers of Malabar have been imprisoned. There can now be no receding. The struggle may last long if orthodox Hindu opinion is actively hostile to the movement. The Satyagrahis are certain to break down the wall of prejudice, no matter how strong and solid it may be if they continue firm, but humble, truthful and non-violent. They have faith enough in these qualities to know that they will melt the stoniest hearts.

'The Vykom Satyagraha has perhaps a meaning deeper than is generally realized. The young men who have organized it are stern in discipline and gentle in their dealings with the orthodox section. But this is the least part of their trials. Some of them suffering too the persecution of social boycott. We of the Western Presidency have no idea of what this persecution can mean. These young men who are taking part in the movement are not only being denied social amenities but are threatened even with the deprivation of their share in the family property. If they would go to law, probably they would get their due. But a Satyagrahi cannot go to law for a personal wrong. He sets out with the idea of suffering persecution. In a reform that the Vykom struggle seeks to achieve, the Satyagrahi seeks to convert his opponent by sheer force of character and suffering. The purer he is and the more he suffers, the quicker the progress. He must therefore resign himself to being excommunicated, debarred from the family privileges and deprived of his share in the family property. He must not only bear such hardships cheerfully but he must actively love his persecutors. The latter honestly believe that the reformer is doing something sinful and therefore resort to the only means they know to be effective to wean him from his supposed error.

The Satyagrahi, on the other hand, does not seek to carry out his reform by a system of punishments but by penance, self-purification and suffering. Any resentment of the persecution, therefore, would be an interruption of the course of discipline he has imposed upon himself. It may be a prolonged course, it may even seem to be never ending 'Vykom Satyagraha has attracted such wide public attention, and though restricted to a small area, presents so many problems for solution that I offer no apology to the reader for constantly engaging his attention for it.

'I have received several important and well-thought-out letters protesting against my countenancing it in any way whatsoever. One such letter even urges me to use whatever influence I may have, for stopping it altogether. I am sorry that I am unable to publish all these letters. But I hope to cover all the points raised in these letters or otherwise brought to my notice.'

The first may be cleared at once. Exception has been taken to Shri George Joseph—a Christian—having been allowed to replace Shri Menon as leader and organizer. In my humble opinion the exception is perfectly valid. As soon as I heard that Shri Joseph was 'invited to take the lead' and he contemplated taking it, I wrote to him as follows on 6th April:

"As to Vykom, I think that you should let the Hindus do the work. It is they who have to purify themselves. You can help by your sympathy and by your pen, but not by organizing the movement and certainly not by offering Satyagraha. If you refer to the Congress resolution of Nagpur, it calls upon the Hindu members to remove the curse of untouchability. I was surprised to learn from Mr. Andrews that the disease had infected even the Syrian Christians."

Unfortunately before the letter could reach him, Shri Menon was arrested and Shri George Joseph had taken his place. But he had nothing to expiate, as every Hindu has in the matter of untouchability as countenanced by the Hindus. His sacrifice cannot be appropriated by the Hindus in general as expiation made, say by Malaviyaji would be. Untouchability is the sin of the Hindus. They must suffer for it, they must purify themselves, they must pay the debt they owe to their suppressed brothers and sisters. Theirs is the shame and theirs must be the glory when they have purged themselves of the black sin. The silent, loving, suffering of one single pure Hindu as such will be enough to melt the heart of millions of Hindus; but the sufferings of thousands of non-Hindus on behalf of the 'untouchables' will leave the Hindus unmoved. Their blind eyes will not be opened by outside interference, however well-intentioned and generous it may be; for it will not bring home to them the sense of guilt. On the contrary they would probably hug the sin all the more for such interference. All reforms to be sincere and lasting must come from within.

But why may the Vykom Satyagrahis not receive

monetary aid from outside, especially if it be from Hindus? So far as non-Hindus assistance is concerned, I am as clear about such pecuniary help as I am about such personal help. I may not build my Hindu temple with non-Hindu money. If I desire a place of worship I must pay for it. This removal of untouchability is much more than building a temple of brick and mortar. Hindus must bleed for it, must pay for it. They must be prepared to forsake wife, children and all for the sake of removing the curse. As for accepting assistance from Hindus from outside, such acceptance would betray unreadiness on the part of the local Hindus for the reform. If the Satyagrahis have the sympathy of the local Hindus, they must get locally all the money they may need. If they have not, the very few who may offe. *satyagraha* must be content to starve. If they are not, it is clear that they will evoke no sympathy among the local Hindus, whom they want to convert, Styagraha is a process of conversion. The reformers, I am sure, do not seek to force their views upon the community; they strive to touch its heart. Outside pecuniary help must interfere with the love process if I may so describe the method of *Satyagraha.* Thus viewed, the proposed Sikh free kitchen, I can only regard, as a menance to the frightened Hindus of Vykom.

There is no doubt in my mind about it that the orthodox Hindus, who still think that worship of God is inconsistent with touching a portion of their own co-religionists and that a religious life is summed up in ablutions and avoidance of physical pollutions merely, are alarmed at the development of the movement at Vykom. They believe that their religion is in danger. It behoves the organizers, therefore, to set even the most orthodox and the most bigoted at ease and to assure them that they do not seek to bring about the reform the compulsion. The Vykom Satyagrahis must stoop to conquer. They must submit to insult and worse at the hands of the bigoted and yet love them, if they will change their hearts.

But a telegram says in effect, 'the authorities are

barricading the roads; may we not break or scale the fences? May we not fast? For we find that fasting is effective.'

My answer is, if we are *Satyagrahis,* we dare not scale or break fences. Breaking or scaling fences will certainly bring about imprisonment but the breaking will not be civil disobedience. It will be essentially incivil and criminal. Nor may we fast. I observe that my letter to Shri Joseph with reference to fasting has been misunderstood. For the sake of ready reference I reproduce below the relevant part:

> 'Omit fasting but stand or squat in relays with quiet submission till arrested.'

"The above is the wire sent to you in reply to yours. Fasting in Satyagraha has well-defined limits. You cannot fast against a tyrant, for it will be a species of violence done to him. You invite penalty from him for disobedience of his orders but you cannot inflict on yourselves penalties when he refuses to punish, and renders it impossible for you to disobey his orders so as to compel infliction of penalty. Fasting can only be resorted to against a lover, not to extort rights but to reform him, as when a son fasts for a father who drinks. My fast at Bombay and then at Bardoli was of that Character. I fasted to reform those who loved me. But I will not fast to reform, say, General Dyer, who not only does not love me but who regards himself as my enemy. Am I quite clear?"

It need not be pointed out that the above remarks are of a general character. The words 'tyrant' and 'lover' have also a general application. The one who does an injustice is styled 'tyrant'. The one who is in sympathy with you is the 'lover'. In my opinion, in the Vykom movement opponents of the reform are the 'tyrant'. The state may or may not be that. In this connection I have considered the state as merely the police striving to keep the peace. In no case is the State or the opponents in the position of 'lover'. The supporters of Vykom *satyagrahis*enjoy that status. There are two conditions attached to a *satyagrahi*fast. It should be against the lover-and for his reform, not for extorting rights from him. The only possible case in the Vykom movement when a fast will be justified, would be when the local supporters go back upon their promise to suffer. I can fast against my father to cure him of a vice, but I may not in order to get from him an inheritance. The beggars of India who sometimes fast against those who do not satisfy them are no more *satyagrahis* than children who fast against a parent for a fine dress. The former are impudent, the latter are childish. My Bardoli fast was against fellow-workers who ignited the Chauri Chaura spark and for the sake of reforming them. If the Vykom *satyagrahis* fast because the authorities will not arrest them, it will be, I must say in all humility, the beggar's fast described above. If it proves effective it shows the goodness of the authorities, not that of the cause or of the actors. A *satyagrahi's* first concern is not the effect of his action. It must always be its propriety. He must have faith enough in his case and his means, and know that success will be achieved in the end.

But, say some of my correspondents, the conditions for lawful *satyagraha* do not exist in Vykom. They ask :

1. Is unapproachability exclusively observed at Vykom or is it general throughout Kerala?
2. If it is general, then what is the special reason for selecting Vykom in preference to places within the British territory in Kerala?
3. Did the satyagrahis petition the Maharaja, the local Assembly etc.?
4. Did they consult the orthodox sections?
5. Is not the use of the road the thin end of the wedge, is it not a step towards the abolition of caste altogether?
6. Is not the road a private road?

The first two questions are irrelevant.

Unapproachability and untouchability have to be tackled wherever they exist. Wherever the workers consider a place or time suitable, it is their duty to start work whether by *Satyagraha* or other legitimate means.

My information goes to show that the method of petition etc., was tried not once but often. They did consult the orthodox people and thought that they had the latter's support.

I am assured that the use of the road is the final goal of the *satyagraha.* It is however not to be denied that the present movement throughout India is to throw open to the suppressed classes all the public and public schools, public wells and public temples which are accessible to non-Brahmanas.

It is in fact a movement to purify caste by ridding it of its most pernicious result

I have letters which protest that the road in question is a public road. In fact my informations tell me it was some years ago even accessible to the unapproachables as to other non-Brahmanas.

In my opinion, therefore, there is a just cause for the Vykom Satyagraha, and so far as it is kept within limits and conducted with the strictest regard to non-violence and truth, it deserves full public sympathy.

Thus the steps for the upliftment of Harijans taken by Gandhi were unique in our history. Along withnumerous other issues—political, social, economic, cultural and others—he ardently identified himself with numerous causes which had deep linkage with the daily life of a down-trodden member of our society. He always wished to give the Harijan a place of honour and respect in our society which was denied to him since centuries. In this task what he preached, he professed. He spoke much in their favour by undertaking strenuous tours of all the regions of India. He castigated caste-Hindus and criticised their behaviour towards the untouchables. By doing so, he demanded their financial and social co-operation for the upliftment of this neglected community. At Mahatma' persuasion, numerous affluent persons came forward and funded his schemes of reform. The money thus raised was spent on their educational, moral, social, economic and religious development, undoubtedly much progress was visible in this regard with the passage of time. The Hindu orthodoxy in many areas had to bow down before Mahatma's humanitarian gestures.

Gandhi used to spend some time with the Harijans by living himself with them. This kind of personal identification of the Mahatma made the Harijans realise their sense of importance in our society. He taught them the sense of cleanliness and advised them to raise their economic and social standards by hard work and honest means. He raised their colonies and advised the workers to devise schemes of their upliftment.

After incessant work for more than three decades, it was realized that much headway was made in this regard. They were given numerous concessions in the educational institutions, reservations in government departments, ministerial positions, reserved seats in the provincial legislatures and Lok Sabha. By doing so, the social status of a sizeable population in this community has been raised.

10

Mahatma Gandhi Challenge to British Imperialism

Introduction

Massive humanitarian crisis was occurring in British dominated South Asia (India, Bangladesh, Pakistan, Sri Lanka & other countries) from 1765 to 1947. Resistance to foreign rule began mid- 19th century, even though the first War of Independence failed in 1857, the dreams and sacrifices of its leaders inspired the generations to come. In the late 19th century and early 20th century, political aspirations were shaped by solid work for the country's social reform of the Congress Party founder Surnendranath Bannerjee and his team leaders. First Indian National Congress meets in Bombay. Great writer Bankim Chandra Chattopadhay wrote "Vande Mataram,' the wonderful national Song -that soon became the famous among several generations that bravely fought the British Crown. It defied India, its fertile soil, beautiful landscape and relegated its governance and defense to no emperor or general but its masses.[ii] Logic is: if there is foreign rule, we have to fight for Home Rule (Swaraj). Arabian and Turks Muslim soldiers and rulers conquered India and Islamic Mogul Empire was established in South Asia before the British took over it. Is Muslims' rule foreign in India? Was there Home Rule in Moghul Empire? In Sonar Ga Bengali Nawab Isha khan was revolt against the Emperor Akbar's Commander- in -Chief Man Singh and fought against of

Mogul crown. There are two main faces (Hindu & Muslim) of India. Alongside "Allah ho Akbar" with Vande Mataram was the slogan of the Khilafat movement in 1920. Might is Right. Today's Taliban, Al- Quida and Pakistan's Red mosque problems are the results of blind Islamic radicalism. Even Mohammad Ali Jinnah banned the Bengali language in 1948 to save Pakistan brand Islam. Such a great man (Mr. Jinnah, National Father of Pakistan), forgot the universality of Islam. Mr. Jinnah did not get any lesson from the non-violence movement. He had sinister conspiracy to rob Bangladesh. Gandhi came to Noakhali to stop Hindu - Muslim riot. Mr. Jinnah came to Dhaka to confiscate Bangladesh people's mother tongue in the name of Islam. Bangladesh people express shame on him. The people of Bangladesh have been suffering by the Jamat and Islamic Fundamentalists ages after ages.

Mohandas Karamchand Gandhi (1869 - 1948) fought to defend the East Indians at home and South Africa. He was combined brilliance, humanism and courage with indomitable will brought a revolutionary change in the East Indian Community in South Africa and India. He became an icon of world peace and India. He brought a dignity of Man to the East Indian Community. Gandhi encouraged us that the triumph over prejudice and ignorance is a triumph for us all. Humanity is like the ocean. Nobody could divide it in a name of politics and religion. Greed and hatred are roots of many problems, it is necessary to bring greed and hatred under control. This is message of Gandhi for his Swaraj or Home Rule. It is remarkable that the author Michael Adas writes, "In the long term interests of the peoples brought under European rule." It quotes in his famous book entitled "Machines as the Measure of Men: Science, Technology and Ideologies of Western Dominance." Gandhi protested against of Britain's injustice.

Gandhi said, "Great as the Buddha's contribution to humanity was in resorting God to His eternal place, in my opinion, greater still was his contribution to humanity in his exacting regard for all life, be it ever so low. The Buddha said, if you want to do any sacrifice, sacrifice yourself, your lust, all your material ambition, all worldly ambition. That will be an ennobling sacrifice."

Setting the Scene

Indian community at home and abroad truly amazed to see Gandhi's commitments by dedicating his time, money and life. He was the supreme leader of the Congress Party of India years 1918 - 22, who could lead India as he iii(Gandhi) wished. In simple words everyone is free in his home and country. We want our rule in our country. Gandhi discovered his country's self rule (sawraj or home rule) and his leadership helped introduce to India and the world a completely new set of opinions to fight foreign rule, namely civil disobedience based on truth and non-violence and mass participation in peaceful, political action against colonialism. In "Gandhi" (through Richard Attenbourough's 1982) film as we watched, "They (police) beat us, but should not beat them." It is impossible for human nature. But Gandhi found the kingdom of God in human minds. So we respect Gandhi for his self rule (swaraj) relating to India's freedom.

Under Mahatma Gandhi, a unique mass mobilization was started to take shape. The foundation of Gandhi's advocacy for freedom and self-rule was based on the truth and Ahimsa or non-violent protest revolution against the British Government. India's independence movement is also characterized by largely nonviolently methods of resistance to the British rule. The Indians adopted the West minister parliamentary model as their ideal. It reminds me the 1916 Rising and the Irish War of Independence. When I study Gandhi's self rule in India, then I discover similarity relating to Northern Ireland and IRA terrorism, political prisoners and hunger strikes.

Gandhi is a Challenge to Violent World

Many freedom fighters became terrorists in India,

Ireland and other countries who dedicated their lives for the sake of their mother lands or home land's home Rule (Swaraj). The purpose of this essay is to give a short outlines of "Mahatma Gandhi's (1869 - 1948) freedom struggle was started with Home Rule (Swaraj) movement in South Africa and Non-cooperation movement (Satyagraha) including Crime and Society in British India. Mohandas Karamchand Gandhi (Sanskrit word Mahatma means in English language great mind) ever to have walked on the planet who is one of the most famous Indians who followed Buddha, Jesus and Tolstoy.[iv] East India Company and British corrupt bureaucrats made irregularities and corruption in the administration.

Mohandas Karamchand Gandhi (Mahatma Gandhi) designed a campaign which came to known as the "Rowlatt Satyagraha" the first experiment with non-violent resistance on a national scale. I have to define Gandhi's Sawraj or Indian Home Rule in the British India. As we study on Michael Collins (1890 - 1922) leader of Irish Revolution and watched his (M. Collins) movie in our class, feelings of freedom in Ireland and India alike. British Government tortured us (Indians and Irish people). Our events and modes of expression of freedom are parts and parcels.

Crime and Society in British India

Native East Indians are over represented as victims, offenders, and prison inmates, due to (1) unemployment and homeless create higher rtes of criminal activity and (2) discrimination in the system of colonial criminal justice. There are hypocrisy of

British Justice, Law and order. There was the Mutiny of the Indian soldiers of the army of the East India Company and revolt of Oudh and of some Indian princes.

Gandhi in South Africa (1893 -1914) & 'self rule'

In May 1893 Gandhi arrived in Cape Town, South Africa. Later in Durban, South Africa, Gandhi wore a turban and entered into the Court and the British judge ordered him (Gandhi) to remove the turban. Gandhi refused to do so and left the chamber in protest. Due to racism a British ticket master insulted Gandhi and he was ejected from the train at Pietermaritzburg Railway station despite holding a first class ticket. Gandhi was insulted by the South African Government and he became the victim of racism as he discovered the 'deep disease of color prejudice'[vi] in British dominated South Africa.

Deeply influenced by the South Africa's racism toward East Indians, Gandhi founded Natal Indian Congress to agitate for Indian Rights in 1894. In retaliation British Government imprisoned Gandhi and he was harshly beaten several times and he was twice imprisoned. During the Boer War in 1899 Gandhi raised an ambulance corps and sincerely he served the South African British Government. There were thousands of Indians joined him in civil disobedience campaign.

In India Swaraj (home Rule or Independent, May 1921) in one year

There were Gandhi's "the Rowlatt Satyagraha (Resistance of tyranny through civil disobedience)" and Swaraj (Home Rule) are adding fuel to the fire in the Crown of British India. The leadership of Mohandas Karamchand Gandhi (Mahatma Gandhi) helped introduce to India and the world a completely new set of weapons to fight foreign rule, namely civil disobedience based on Truth and Non-violence and mass participation in peaceful political action against colonialism.

The historic movement in 1920 Gandhi launched a non-cooperation movement against British Government and urging Indians to spin their own cotton and boycott British goods, courts and government. He was arrested and confined in jail from 1920 -1924. In the history of man so many conflicts and persecutions have been provoked and so many wars precipitated in the name of politics or religions. Gandhi researched and found all human beings equally worthy of dignity and respects. Another important in protest of a salt tax movement was launched by Gandhi and thousands of Indians on the 200 miles (320 k.m.) march to the Indian Ocean to make their own salt. British Government arrested him again. Lord Irwin's declaration on 'Dominion status' does not satisfy Indian Congress. [vii]

Gandhi conquered hearts of East Indian people by his highly compassion, sincerity and honesty. Relating to the Sawraj (Indian home Rule) Gandhi explained, "My countrymen impute the evils of modern civilization to the English people and, therefore, believe that the English people are bad, and not the civilization they represent. My countrymen, therefore, believe that they should adopt modern civilization and modern methods of violence to drive out the English. 'Hind Swaraj' has been written in order show that they are following a suicidal policy, and that, if they would but revert to their own glorious civilization, either the English would adopt the later and become Indianized or find their occupation in India gone."

> "I (Gandhi) have written some chapters on the subject of Indian Home Rule which I venture to place before the readers of Indian Opinion. ...

He added. "I should prefer to be killed by the arrow of a tribal person (Bhil) than to seek unmanly protection. Macaulay betrayed gross ignorance when he labeled Indians as being practically cowards." (Hind Swaraj, p. Gandhi writes to J. Nehru, (first prime minister of India), "The real question, according to you, is how to bring about man's highest intellectual, economic, political and moral development. I agree entirely. (2) In this there should be equal right and opportunity for all. (3) In other words, there should be equality between the town dwellers and the villagers in the standard of food and drink, clothing and other living conditions. In order to achieve this equality today people should be able to produce for themselves the necessaries of life, i. e. clothing, foodstuffs, dwellings, lighting and water.

Man is not born to live in isolation but is essentially a social animal independent and interdependent. No one can or should ride on another's back. If we try to work out the\ necessary conditions for such a life, we are forced to the conclusion that the unit of society should be a village, or call it a small and manageable group of people who would, in the ideal, self sufficient (in the matter of their vital requirements) as a unit and bound together its bonds of mutual cooperation and inter-dependence.").

Abuse was Wrong in British India (1757 - 1947)

East Indian people had been abused by the rulers of East India Company, British Army & its Government for 200 hundred years. The abuse could be physical, sexual, emotional, psychological or financial. Indian people experienced more than one type of abuse. Examples of physical abuse were (1) hitting (2) pinching (3) slapping (4) (5) pushing punching, (6) kicking (7) burning (8)shooting (9) stabbing and (10) cutting.

According to the British law Gandhi could not enter into Punjab state due to the general strike (haratal). There were about 10,000 people gathered on the13 April 1919 in the Jalianwala Bagh square, Amritsar, Punjab. Without any warning suddenly Brigadier General Reginald Dyer ordered his troops to open fire on the unarmed crowd. There was no moral value in British Army. There were 379 civilians were killed and 1000 wounded. British Government wanted India for money and its wealth, not its people.[xi] Gandhi's social movements are enduring collective attempts to change all of the social order by means of non-violence.

It is also remarkable that military's demands get articulated and implemented, while public demands get ignored and suppressed. It is abundantly clear that British Government made a mockery of civilization and its principles by hypocritical actions through out India and the World. It was no exaggeration to say that the concept of

British democracy has been one of the most tossed about misused, confused, misunderstood and abused terms ever since it came into use and applied specially to governance.

1906 - 1907 Recording companies recorded the first national song (Vande Mataram) in the voice of Rabindranath Tagore and other artists released a version commercially in 1907. Police destroy the factory, as well as the disc, however, survived in Belgium and Paris, where the record was released.

Gandhi in South Africa and India : Comparative Study

To my mind, in South Africa Gandhi "Learned to see all Indians as one, regardless of class and caste, religion and regional origins." *nn* (p. 49, Gandhi, David Arnold). But in India when Gandhi demanded immediate Independence as India price for helping Britain during World War II. British Government imprisoned Gandhi from 1942 - 1947. Gandhi could not save in one India as Muslims created Pakistan by Muhammad Ali Jinnah. Again Gandhi was started fasting for non-violence until Delhi rioters pleaded peace to him. On the January 30, 1948 while Gandhi way to prayer Nathuram Godse assassinated Mahatma Gandhi by three bullets. Life of Gandhi mirrors the fate of violence, "As war begins in the minds of men, it is in the minds of men that the defenses of peace of must be constructed." Gandhi said, "Hinduism absorbs the best in other religions and there is a scope for expansion in it."

Conclusion

However, everyday we discover Gandhi's dream of happiness for mankind in his thoughts. Gandhi said, "A time is coming when those who are in the mad rush today of multiplying their wants, vanity thinking that they add to the real substance, real knowledge of the world, will retrace their steps and say what have we done? Civilizations have come and gone and in spite of all our vaunted progress, I am tempted to ask again and again: To what purpose?"

Recently U.N. declares Gandhi's birthday "International Day of Non Violence." M.K Gandhi said, "An eye for an eye makes the whole world blind." Mahatma Gandhi's philosophy of brother hood and peace was immortalized when the UN General Assembly declared October 2, Mahatma Gandhi's birth anniversary as the International Day of Non-violence." My interpretations of Gandhi's Home Rule (or self rule Swaraj) and his freedom struggle followed several books, experiences and exhibitions etc. I respect the glorious remarks of Albert Einstein in 1944, "Generations to come, it may be, will scarce believe that such a one as this ever in flesh and blood walked upon this earth."

Historians have judged India's National Movement as a unique struggle by a people, inspired by a shared vision. Mahatma Gandhi's teaching inspired us according to the International law, Universal Declaration of Human Rights, Convention against torture and crimes against humanity to which Britain is a signatory. Home Rule (Swaraj), Indian and Ireland people's rights had been severely violated by the British Government. We have to recognize all human beings are endowed with dignities of equality and uniqueness which makes each of us precious beyond measure. We are governed by our compassion each other, our humanity and common family in our "Home Rule (Swaraj)."

REFERENCES

Desi Talk, Indian community News Weekly, Toronto, p. 15, dated May 11, 2007.

David Arnold, Gandhi p. 105

David Arnold, Gandhi, p.61.

Autobiography by M. K. Gandhi, p. 114

Hermann Kulke and Dietmar Rothermund, *A History of India, p. 358.*

H. Kulke and D. Tothermund, *A History of India, p. 357*

Instructor V. Ravindiran, History of India, Part II, Summer Term 2000, U of T. page.66 - 71

V. Ravindiran, *History of India, Tutorial 7, : Gandhi's Vision of India, 12 - 57,*

V. Ravindran, History of India, suplementary writings, University of Toronto, p. 155

Hermann Kulke and Dietmar Rothermund, *A history of India,* p246 & 267.

Desi Talk, Indian Community Weekly, Toronto, Toronto, p. 15, dated May 11, 2007.

David Arnold, *Gandhi p. 41*

Anthony Copley, *Against the Tide, p. 65, Oxford, 1987.*

11

Mahatma Gandhi : The Philosopher

Gandhi's thought and his ideas about specific political strategies in specific contexts flowed from ideas that were very remote from politics; instead they flowed from and were integrated to the most abstract epistemological and methodological commitments. The quality of his thought has sometimes been lost because of the other images Gandhi evolves? a shrewd politician and a deeply spiritual figure. Gandhi's view of moral sense, his denial of the assumed connection between moral sense and moral judgment, is of considerable philosophical interest and in his writings, take on a fascinating theoretical consolidation. In Gandhi's highly 'integrating' suggestion, as this paper suggests, there is no true non-violence until criticism is removed from the scope of moral; the ideal of non-violence is thus part of a moral position in which moral principles, which lead us to criticise others, are eschewed.

We were once asked by a literary magazine to write a review essay on Nehru. Some weeks later, I was asked by the editor if I would throw in Gandhi as well. As it happened I never wrote the piece, but I remember thinking that it was like being asked while climbing the Western Ghats whether I would take a detour and climb Mount Everest as well. I am not now trying to scale any great peak or to give a defining interpretation to Gandhi. Its generally foolhardy to write about Gandhi, not only because you are never certain you've got him right, but because you are almost sure to have him wrong. There is a lack of plain argument in his writing and there is an insouciance about fundamental objections, which he himself raises, to his own intuitive ideas. The truth of his claims seem to him so instinctive and certain that mere arguments seem frivolous even to readers who disagree with them. Being trained in a discipline of philosophy of a quite different temperament, I will try to not get distracted by the irritation I sometimes feel about this.

In reading Gandhi recently I have been struck by the integrity of his ideas. I don't mean simply that he was a man of integrity in the sense that he tried to make his actions live up to his ideals, though perhaps in fact he tried more than most to do so. I mean something more abstract: that his thought itself was highly integrated, his ideas about very specific political strategies in specific contexts flowed (and in his mind necessarily flowed) from ideas that were very remote from politics. They flowed from the most abstract epistemological and methodological commitments. This quality of his thought sometimes gets lost because, on the one hand, the popular interest in him has been keen to find a man of great spirituality and uniqueness and, on the other, the social scientist's and historian's interest in him has sought out a nationalist leader with a strikingly effective method of non-violent political action. It has been common for some decades now to swing from a sentimental perception of him as a 'Mahatma' to a cooler assessment of Gandhi as 'the shrewd politician'. I will steer past this oscillation because it hides the very qualities of his thought I want to uncover. The essay is not so much (in fact hardly at all) inspired by the plausibility of the philosophy that emerges as by the stunning intellectual ambition and originality that this 'integrity'displays.

Violence has many sides. It can be spontaneous or planned, it can be individual or institutional, it can be physical or psychological, it can be delinquent or adult, it can be revolutionary or authoritarian. A great deal has been written on violence: on its psychology, on its possible philosophical justifications under certain circumstances, and of course on its long career in military history. Non-violence has no sides at all. Being negatively defined, it is indivisible. It began to be a subject of study much more recently and there is much less written on it, not merely because it is defined in negative terms but because until it became a self-conscious instrument in politics in this century, it was really constituted as or in something else. It was studied under different names, first usually as part of religious or contemplative ways of life remote from the public affairs of men and state, and later with the coming of romantic thought in Europe, under the rubric of critiques of industrial civilisation.

For Gandhi, both these contexts were absolutely essential to his conception of non-violence. Non-violence was central in his nationalist mobilisation against British rule in India. But the concept is also situated in an essentially religious temperament as well as in a thoroughgoing critique of ideas and ideologies of the Enlightenment and of an intellectual paradigm of perhaps a century earlier than the Enlightenment. This is a paradigm in which science became set on a path, which seemed destined to lead to cumulative results, building to a progressively complete understanding of the world in which we lived, a world which we could as a result control. It is a familiar point that there is no understanding Gandhi, the anti-colonial nationalist, without situating him in these larger trajectories of his thought.

The strategy of non-violent resistance was first introduced by him so as to bring into the nationalist efforts against the British, an element beyond making only constitutional demands. On the face of it, for those reared on western political ideas, this seemed very odd. Constitutional demands, as they are understood in liberal political theory, are the essence of non-violent politics; as is well known the great early propounders of liberal democratic thought conceived and still conceive of constitutions and their constraints on human public action as a constraint against tendencies toward violence in the form of coercion of individuals by states and other collectivities, not to mention by other individuals. So why did Gandhi, the prophet of non-violence, think that the Indian people, in their demands for greater self-determination, needed more than constitutional demands? And why did he think that this is best called 'non-violent' action' The obvious answer is the instrumental and strategic one: he knew that making demands for constitutional change had not been particularly effective or swift in the first two decades of this century, and that since the conventionally conceived alternative was violent revolutionary action ' which found advocates on the fringes of nationalist sentiment in India ' he instead introduced his own strategy of civil disobedience, at once a non-violent and yet a non- or extra-constitutional strategy. But, of course, he had more in mind than this obvious motive.

First, Gandhi wanted all of India to be involved in the movement, in particular the vast mass of its peasant population. He did not want the nationalist achievement to be the effort of a group of elite, legally and constitutionally trained, upper-middle class Indian men ('Macaulay's bastards'), who argued in assemblies and round-table conferences. He almost single-handedly transformed a movement conceived and promoted along those lines by the Congress Party into a mass movement of enormous scale, and he did so within a few years of arriving from South Africa on Indian soil. Non-violent action was the central idea of this vast mobilisation. Second, he knew that violent revolutionary action could not possibly carry the mass of people with it. Revolutionary action was mostly conceived hugger-mugger in underground cells and took the form of isolated subversive terrorist action against key focal points of government power and interest, it was not conceived as a mass movement. He was not unaware that there existed in the west ideologies of revolutionary violence which were geared to mass movements, but he was not unaware either, that these were conceived in terms of middle class leadership vanguards that were the fonts of authority. Peasant consciousness mattered very little to them. In Gandhi there was not a trace of this vanguard mentality of a Lenin. He did indeed think that his 'satyagrahis' ' the non-violent activists whom he described, with that term, as 'seekers of truth' ' would provide leadership which the masses would follow, but it was absolutely crucial to him that these were not to be the vanguard of a revolutionary party along Leninist lines. They were to be thought of along entirely different lines, they were to be moral exemplars, not ideologues who claimed to know history and its forward movement better than the peasants to whom they were giving the lead. Third, Gandhi chose his version of non-violent civil disobedience instead of the constitutional demands of the Congress leadership because he thought that the Indian people should not merely ask the British to leave their soil. It was important that they should do so by means that were not dependent and derivative of ideas and institutions that the British had imposed on them. Otherwise, even if the British left, the Indian populations would remain a subject people. This went very deep in Gandhi and his book Hind Swaraj, is full of a detailed anxiety about the cognitive enslavement even of the nationalist and anti-colonial Indian mind, which might, even after independence, never recover from that enslavement.

These points are well known, and they raise the roughly political considerations which underlie his commitment to non-violence. As I said, they give only a first glimpse of the integrity of his ideas. There are deeper and more ambitious underlying grounds than these in his writing.

The idea that non-violence was of a piece with the search for truth was central to what I have called his 'integrity' and to these more ambitious and abstract considerations than the ones I have just discussed. Gandhi was explicit about this, even in the terminology he adopted, linking ahimsa (non-violence) with satyagraha (literally, 'truth-force', or more liberally, a tenacity in the pursuit of truth). There is a standard and entrenched reading of Gandhi which understands the link as follows (and I am quoting from what is perhaps the most widely read textbook of modern Indian history, Sumit Sarkar's, Modern India): 'Non-violence or ahimsa and satyagraha to Gandhi personally constituted a deeply-felt and worked-out philosophy owing something to Emerson, Thoreau and Tolstoy but also revealing considerable originality. The search for truth was the goal of human life, and as no one could ever be sure of having attained the truth, use of violence to enforce one's own view of it was sinful.' (p 179; the emphasis is mine) I have no doubt that Gandhi says things that could lead to such a reading, and for years, I assumed that it was more or less uncontroversially, what he had in mind. After scrutiny of his writings however, especially his many dispatches to Young India, it seems to me now a spectacular misreading. It fails to cohere with his most fundamental thinking.

Notice that according to this reading, or misreading, his view is no different from one of the most celebrated liberal arguments for tolerance ' the meta-inductive argument of Mill's On Liberty. Mill contends that since much that we have thought to be true in the past has turned out to be wrong, this in itself suggests that what we presently think true might also be wrong. We should therefore tolerate not repress dissent from our present convictions just in case they are not true. According to Mill, and according to Gandhi on this widespread misreading of him, truth is never something we are sure we have attained. We must therefore be made modest in the way we hold our present opinions, and we must not impose our own conceptions of the truth on others. To do so would be a form of violence, especially if it was enforced by the apparatus of the state.

The modesty would appeal to Gandhi, but he would find something very alien in Mill's argument for it. There is no echo in Gandhi of the idea that the source of this modesty is that however much we seek truth, we cannot attain it, which is what Sarkar contends is the ground of his non-violence. In fact, it makes little sense to say that truth (or anything else) is something we should seek, even if we can never attain it. How can we intend to attain what we know we cannot attain? It would be bootless to protest that Gandhi and Mill are not saying that we can never attain the truth, only that we cannot know if we have attained it ? so there is still point in the search for truth. That does little to improve matters. What sort of a goal or search is that? On this epistemological view, our inquiry and search for truth would be analogous to sending a message in a bottle out to sea, a search that is blinded about its own possible success, making all success a sort of bonus or fluke.

In any case, there is something rather odd in Mill's argument for tolerance. There is an unsettling tension between the argument?s first two premises. The first premise is that our past beliefs have often turned out to be wrong. The second, is that this is grounds for thinking that our present opinions might be wrong. And the conclusion is that we should therefore be tolerant of dissent from current opinion. But the fact is that when past opinions are said to be wrong, that is a judgment made from the present point of view, and we cannot make that judgment unless we have the conviction in the present opinions which Mill is asking us not to have. It is all right to be asked to be diffident about our present opinions, but then we should, at least to that extent, be diffident about our judgment made on their basis, viz, that our past opinions are wrong. And if so, the first premise is shakier than he presents it as being.

The pervasive diffidence and lack of conviction in our opinions which is the character of the epistemology that Mill's argument presupposes, is entirely alien to Gandhi;

and though he is all in favour of the modesty with which we should be holding our opinions, that modesty does not have its source in such an epistemology and such a conception of unattainable truth. What, then, is its source?

It is quite elsewhere than where Sarkar and everybody else who has written on Gandhi has located it; its source is to be found in his conception of the very nature of moral response and moral judgment. The 'satyagrahi' or non-violent activist has to show a certain kind of self-restraint, in which it was not enough simply not to commit violence. It is equally important not to bear hostility to others or even to criticise them; it is only required that one not follow these others, if conscience doesn't permit it. To show hostility and contempt, to speak or even to think negatively and critically, would be to give in to the spiritual flaws that underlie violence, to have the wrong conception of moral judgment. For it is not the point of moral judgment to criticise. (In the section called 'Ashram Vows' of his book Hindu Dharma, he says ?Ahimsa is not the crude thing it has been made to appear. Not to hurt any living thing is no doubt part of ahimsa. But it is its least expression. It is hurt by hatred of any kind, by wishing ill of anybody, by making negative criticisms of others.') This entails the modesty with which one must hold one's moral opinions, and which Mill sought in a quite different source: in a notion of truth which we are never sure we have attained and therefore (from Gandhi?s point of view) in a quite untenable epistemology. The alternative source of the modesty in Gandhi has less to do with issues about truth, and more to do with the way we must hold our moral values.

Despite the modesty, one could, of course, resist those with whom one disagrees, and Gandhi made an art out of refusal and resistance and disobedience. But resistance is not the same as criticism. It can be done with a 'pure heart'. Criticism reflects an impurity of heart, and is easily corrupted to breed hostility and, eventually, violence. With an impure heart you could still indulge in non-violent political activism, but that activism would be strategic, merely a means to a political end. In the long run it would, just as surely as violence, land you in a midden. Even the following sensible sounding argument for his own conclusion, often given by many of his political colleagues who found his moral attitudes obscure, did not satisfy Gandhi: 'Let us adopt non-violent and passive resistance instead of criticising the British colonial government. Because to assert a criticism of one's oppressor would usually have the effect of getting his back up, or of making him defensive, it would end up making things harder for oneself.' Gandhi himself did occasionally say things of that sort, but he thought that colleagues who wanted to rest with such arguments as the foundation of non-violence were viewing it too much as an instrument and they were not going deep enough into the spiritual nature of the moral sense required of the satyagrahi. One did not go deep enough until one severed the assumed theoretical connection between moral judgment and moral criticism, the connection which, in our analytical terms, we would describe by saying that if one judges that ?x is good?, then we are obliged to find morally wrong those who in relevant circumstances, .judge otherwise or fail to act on x. For Gandhi this does not follow. The right moral sense, the morally pure-hearted satyagrahi, sees no such connection between moral judgment and moral criticism. Of course, we cannot and must not cease to be moral subjects; we cannot stop judging morally about what is and is not worthy, cannot fail to have moral values. But none of that requires us to be critical of others who disagree with our values or who fail to act in accord with them. That is the relevant modesty which Mill sought to justify by a different argument.

This view of the moral sense might well seem frustratingly namby-pamby now as it certairly did to those around him at the time. Can?t it be argued then that Gandhi is shrewdly placing a screen of piety around the highly creative political instrument he is creating, both to confuse his colonial masters and to tap the religious emotions of the Indian masses? This is the oscillating interpretation I have been inveighing against, which, finding his religiosity too remote from politics, then fails to take his philosophical ideas as being intended seriously and views him only as a crafty and effective nationalist politician. It sells short both his moral philosophy and his politics. The fact is that his view of moral sense is of considerable philosophical interest, and is intended entirely earnestly by its author. It is given a fascinating theoretical consolidation in his writing which may be lost on his readers because it is buried in a porridge of saintly rhetoric, of 'purity of heart'.

What is the assumed theoretical connection between moral judgment and moral criticism, which Gandhi seems to be denying? It has a long history in the western tradition of moral philosophy. Our moral judgments or values are the basis of our moral choices and actions. Unlike judgments of taste which are the basis, say, for choosing a flavour of ice cream, moral judgments have a certain feature which is often called 'universalisability'. To chose an action on moral grounds under certain circumstances is to generate a principle which we think applies as an 'ought' or an imperative to all others faced with relevantly similar circumstances.

Universalisability is not to be confused with universality. Universality suggests that a moral value, whether or not someone in particular holds it, applies to all persons. Universalisability suggests merely that if someone in particular holds a moral value, then he must think that it applies to all others (in relevantly similar situations). Yet despite the fact that it is much weaker than universality in this sense, it still generates the critical power which Gandhi finds disquieting. If moral judgments are universalisable, one cannot make a judgment that something is morally worthy and then shrug off the fact that others similarly situated might not think so. They (unlike those who might differ with one on the flavour of ice cream) must be deemed wrong not to think so.

Gandhi repudiates this entire tradition. His integrating thought is that violence owes to something as seemingly remote from it as this assumed theoretical connection between values and criticism. Take the wrong view of moral value and judgment, and you will inevitably encourage violence in society. There is no other way to understand his insistence that the satyagrahi has not eschewed violence until he has removed criticism from his lips and heart and mind.

But there is an interpretative challenge hidden here. If the idea of a moral value or judgment has no implication that one find those who disagree with one's moral judgments, to be wrong, then that suggests that one's moral choices and moral values are rather like one's choice of a flavour of ice cream, rather like one's judgments of taste. In other words, the worry is that these Gandhian ideas suggest that one need not find one's moral choices and the values they reflect relevant to others at all, that one's moral thinking is closed off from others. But Gandhi was avowedly a humanist, and repeatedly said things reminiscent of humanist slogans along the order of 'Nothing human is alien to me'. Far from encouraging self-enclosed moral subjects, he thought it the essence of a moral attitude that it take in all within its concern and its relevance. How, then, to reconcile the rejection of universalisability and of a value's potential for being wielded in criticism of others with this yearning for the significance of one?s choices to others? That is among the hardest questions in understanding the philosophy behind his politics, and there are some very original and striking remarks in his writing which hint at a reconciliation.

So far, I have presented the challenge of providing such a reconciliation as a philosophically motivated task. But it is more than that. It is part of the 'integrity' that I am pursuing in my interpretation of Gandhi that it also had a practical urgency in the political and cultural circumstances in which he found himself. We know very well that it was close to this man's heart to improve India in two ways which, on the face of it, were pointing in somewhat opposite directions. On the one hand there was the violence of religious intolerance, found most vividly in the relations between Hindus and Muslims. This especially wounded him. Religious intolerance is the attitude that the other must not remain other, he must become like one in belief and in way of life. It is an inclusionary, homogenising attitude, usually pursued with physical and psychological violence toward the other. On the other hand, for all his traditionalism about caste, there was something offensive to Gandhi within Hinduism itself. The social psychology of the Hindu caste system consists of an exclusionary attitude. For each caste, there was a lower caste which constituted the other and which was to be excluded from one's way of life, again by the most brutal physical and psychological violence. When I think sometimes about caste in India ' without a doubt the most resilient form of exclusionary social inegalitarianism in the history of the world ' its hard to avoid the conclusion that even the most alarming aspects of religious intolerance is preferable to it. To say 'You must be my brother', however wrong, is better than saying, 'You will never be my brother.' In religious intolerance there is at least a small core which is highly attractive. The intolerant person cares enough about the truth as he sees it, to want to share it with others. Of course, that he should want to use force and violence in order to make the other share in it, spoils what is attractive about this core. It was Gandhi?s humanistic mission to retain the core for it showed that one? conception of the truth was not self-enclosed, that it spoke with a relevance to all others, even others who differed from one. How to prevent this relevance to others from degenerating into criticism of others who differed from one and eventually violence towards them, is just the reconciliation we are seeking.

In the philosophical tradition Gandhi is opposing, others are potential objects of criticism in the sense that one's particular choices, one's acts of moral conscience, generate moral principles or imperatives which others can potentially disobey. For him, conscience and its deliverances, though relevant to others, are not the well-spring of principles. Morals is only about conscience, not at all about principles.

There is an amusing story about two Oxford philosophers which makes this distinction vivid. In a seminar, the formidable J L Austin having become exasperated with Richard Hare's huffing on about how moral choices reveal principles, decided to set him up with a question. 'Hare?, he asked, 'if a student came to you after an examination and offered you five pounds in return for the mark alpha, what would you say' Predictably, Hare replied, 'I would tell him that I do not take bribes, on principle!'

Austin's acid response was, 'Really' I think I would myself say, 'No thanks'. 'Austin was being merely deflationary in denying that an act of conscience had to have a principle underlying it. Gandhi erects the denial into a radical alternative to a (western) tradition of moral thinking. An honoured slogan of that tradition says, 'When one chooses for oneself, one chooses for everyone'. The first half of the slogan describes a particular person's act of conscience. The second half of the slogan transforms the act of conscience to a universalised principle, an imperative which others must follow or be criticised. Gandhi embraces the slogan too, but he understands the second half of it differently. He too wants one's acts of conscience to have a universal relevance, so he too thinks one chooses for everyone, but he does not see that as meaning that one generates a principle or imperative for everyone. What other interpretation can be given to the words 'One chooses for everyone' in the slogan, except the principled one'

In Gandhi's writing there is an implicit but bold

proposal: 'When one chooses for oneself, one sets an example to everyone.' That is the role of the satyagrahi. To lead exemplary lives, to set examples to everyone by their actions. And the concept of the exemplar is intended to provide a wholesale alternative to the concept of principle in moral philosophy. It retains what is right in Mill (the importance of being modest in one's moral opinions) while rejecting what is unsatisfactory (any compromise in our conviction in them). There is no Millian diffidence conveyed by the idea that one is only setting an example by one's choices, as opposed to laying down principles. One is fully confident in the choices one wants to set up as exemplars, and in the moral values they exemplify. On the other hand, because no principle is generated, the conviction and confidence in one's opinions does not arrogate, it puts us in no position to be critical of others because there is no generality in their truth, of which others may fall afoul. Others may not follow. Our example may not set. But that is not the same as disobeying an imperative, violating a principle. As a result, the entire moral psychology of our response to others who depart from us is necessarily much weaker. At most we may be disappointed in others that they will not follow our example, and at least part of the disappointment is in ourselves that our example has not taken hold. And the crucial point is that disappointment is measurably weaker than criticism, it is not the paler shade of contempt, hostility, and eventual violence.

This is a subtle distinction, perhaps too subtle to do all the work we want from morals. But that there is a real distinction here is undeniable as is its theoretical power to claim an alternative way of thinking about morals. It is a commonplace in our understanding of the western moral tradition to think of Kant's moral philosophy as the full and philosophical flowering of a core of Christian thought. But Gandhi fractures that historical understanding. By stressing the deep incompatibility between categorical imperatives and universalisable maxims on the one hand, and Christian humility on the other, he makes two moral doctrines and methods out of what the tradition represents as a single historically consolidated one. And discarding one of them as lending itself ultimately to violence, he fashions a remarkable political philosophy and national movement out of the other.

I want to stress how original Gandhi is here as a philosopher and theoretician. The point is not that the idea of the 'exemplary' is missing in the intellectual history of morals before Gandhi. What is missing, and what he first brings to our attention, is how much theoretical possibility there is in that idea. It can be wielded to make the psychology surrounding our morals a more tolerant one. If exemplars replace principles, then it cannot any longer be the business of morals to put us in the position of moralising against others in forms of behaviour (criticism) that have in them the potential to generate other psychological attitudes (resentment, hostility) which underlie inter-personal violence. Opposition to moralising is not what is original in Gandhi either. There are many in the tradition Gandhi is opposing who recoiled from it; but if my interpretation is right, his distinction between principle and exemplar and the use he puts it to, provides a theoretical basis for that recoil, which otherwise would simply be the expression of a distaste. That distaste is a distaste for something that is itself entailed by a moral theory deeply entrenched in a tradition, and Gandhi is confronting that theory with a wholesale alternative.

This conception of moral judgment puzzles me, even while I find it of great interest. It has puzzled me for a long time. Before I became a teenager (when I began to find it insufferably uncool) I would sometimes go on long walks with my father in the early mornings. One day, walking on a path alongside a beach we came across a wallet with some rupees sticking visibly out of it. With a certain amount of drama, my father said: 'Akeel, why should we not take that' Flustered at first, I then said something like, 'Gee (actually I am sure I didn''t say 'gee'), I think we should take it'. My father looked most irritated, and asked, 'Why'?

And I am pretty sure I remember saying words more or less amounting to the classic response: 'Because if we don't take it then I suppose someone else will.' My father, looking as if he were going to mount to great heights of denunciation, suddenly changed his expression, and he said magnificently, but without logic (or so it seemed to me then): 'If we don't take it, nobody else will.' As a boy of 12, I thought this was a non-sequitur designed to end the conversation. In fact I had no idea what he meant, and was too nervous to ask him to explain himself. Only much later, in fact only while thinking about how to fit together the various elements in Gandhi's thought, did I see in his remark, the claims for a moral ideal of exemplary action. But notice how puzzling the idea is. Here is a wallet, abandoned, and we should not take it. This would set an example to others, though no one is around to witness it. The romance in this morality is radiant. Somehow goodness, good acts, enter the world and affect everyone else. To ask how exactly they do that is to be vulgar, to spoil the romance. Goodness is a sort of mysterious contagion.

The idea is as attractive as it is romantic. The question is, how attractive? I will leave the question hanging since all I want to do in this short essay is to present Gandhi's highly 'integrating' suggestion that there is no true non-violence until criticism is removed from the scope of morals. This is to see the ideal of non-violence as being part of a moral position in which moral principles, by the lights of which we criticise, are eschewed. Exemplary action takes the place of principles. If someone fails to follow your example, you may be disappointed but you would no longer have the conceptual basis to see them as transgressive and wrong and subject to criticism. So the integration Gandhi wishes to achieve (the integration of non-violence with total non-criticism) is as plausible as is the moral position stressing exemplars. The plausibility of the moral position depends a great deal on the degree to which the moral action and judgment is made visible. How else would an example be set except through public visibility' Gandhi was of course fully aware of this as a political thinker and leader, which is why it is even possible to integrate the detail of his political ideas with the moral philosophy I have been sketching. He was fully aware that the smaller the community of individuals, the more likelihood there is of setting examples. In the context of family life, for example, one might see how parents by their actions may think or hope that they are setting examples to their children.

Gandhi's ideal of peasant communities organised in small panchayat or village units could perhaps at least approximate the family, where examples could be visibly set. That is, in part, why Gandhi strenuously argued that flows of populations to metropoles where there was far less scope for public perception of individual action, was destructive of the moral life. Indeed, once such metropolitan tendencies had been unleashed, it is easy to understand his habit of going on publicised fasts. It was a way of making visible some moral stance that could reach a larger public in the form of example rather than principles.

We have been arguing that the standard view, which presents Gandhi as essentially applying Mills argument for tolerance to an argument for non-violence, is very wide of the mark. They exhibit diverging attitudes towards the concept of truth, and the epistemology it entails. Gandhi, like Mill, wants our own opinions to be held with modesty, but, unlike him, with an accompanying epistemology that does not discourage conviction or confidence. To that end, Gandhi rejects the notion of truth that Mill seems to presuppose in his argument for tolerance. He replaces the entire argument, as I have been indicating, with another that seems to have less to do with the notion of truth per se than with the nature of moral judgment.

But now a question arises. How can this argument have less to do with truth and one's search for it, when the term 'satyagraha' with which 'ahimsa' is constantly linked in his thinking, has truth as its target?

It is in answer to this question that his final and most audacious step of theoretical integration takes place. For him, truth is a moral notion, and it is exclusively a moral notion. So there is no possibility of having misrepresented his argument in the way that I am worrying. The worry I have just expressed is that once Gandhi repudiates Mill?s basis for tolerance and non-violence (that we may never be confident that we have arrived at the truth in our search for it) and once he replaces it with his own basis (the separability of moral value and judgment from moral principle and moral criticism), truth then drops out of the Gandhian picture in a way that seems un-Gandhian. It in fact does not drop out since truth in the first place is not, for Gandhi, a notion independent of what his argument rests on, the nature of our own experience of moral value.

What this means is that truth for Gandhi is not a cognitive notion at all. It is an experiential notion. It is not propositions purporting to describe the world of which truth is predicated, it is only our own moral experience which is capable of being true. This was of the utmost importance for him. It is what in the end underlies his opposition to the Enlightenment, despite the undeniably Enlightenment elements in his thought including his humanism and the concern that our moral judgments be relevant to all people. Those who have seen him as an anti-Enlightenment thinker usually point to the fact that he is opposed to the political and technological developments which, he insists, issue inevitably from the very conception of Reason as it is understood in scientific terms. So understood, some time in the 17th century, with the rise of the scientific method in Europe, all the predispositions to modern government and technology came into place. All that was needed for those predispositions to be triggered in our sustained efforts to organise and control our physical and social environment, was for the Enlightenment to articulate the idea of Reason as it affects social life and the polity. But this familiar understanding of his view of the Enlightenment does not take in what I have called his final and audacious integrating? philosophical move. This conception which set in sometime in the 17th century itself owes much to a more abstract element in our thinking, which is that truth is a cognitive notion, not a moral one. Only if truth is so conceived can science become the paradigmatic pursuit of our culture, without it the scientific outlook lacks its deepest theoretical source. And it is a mark of his intellectual ambition that by making it an exclusively and exhaustively moral and experiential notion instead, Gandhi was attempting to repudiate the paradigm at the deepest possible conceptual level.

What I mean by truth as a cognitive notion is that it is a property of sentences or propositions that describe the world. Thus when we have reason to think that the sentences to which we give assent exhibit this property, then we have knowledge of the world, a knowledge that can then be progressively accumulated and put to use through continuing inquiry building on past knowledge. His recoil from such a notion of truth, which intellectualises our relations to the world, is that it views the world as the object of study, study that makes it alien to our moral experience of it, to our most everyday practical relations to it. He symbolically conveyed this by his own daily act of spinning cotton. This idea of truth, unlike our quotidian practical relations to nature, makes nature out to be the sort of distant thing to be studied by scientific methods. Reality will then not be the reality of moral experience. It will become something alien to that experience, wholly external and objectified. It is no surprise then that we will look upon reality as something to be mastered and conquered, an attitude that leads directly to the technological frame of mind that governs modern societies, and which in turn takes us away from our communal localities where moral experience and our practical relations to the world flourish. It takes us towards increasingly abstract places and structures such as nations and eventually global economies. In such places and such forms of life, there is no scope for exemplary action to take hold, and no basis possible for a moral vision in which value is not linked to 'imperative' and 'principle', and then, inevitably, to the attitudes of criticism and the entire moral psychology which ultimately underlies violence in our social relations. To find a basis for tolerance and non-violence under circumstances such as these, we are compelled to turn to arguments of the sort Mill tried to provide in which modesty and tolerance are supposed to derive from a notion of truth (cognitively understood) which is always elusive, never something which we can be confident of having achieved because it is not given in our moral experience, but is predicated of propositions that purport to describe a reality which is distant from our own practical and moral experience of it.

All these various elements of his opposition to Mill and his own alternative conception of tolerance and non-violence were laid open by Gandhi and systematically integrated by these arguments implicit in his many scattered writings. The only other philosopher who came close to such a sustained integration of political, moral, and epistemological themes was Heidegger, whatever the fundamental differences between them, not least of which is that Gandhi presents his ideas in clear, civil and bracing prose.

There remains the question whether such an integrated position is at all plausible. It should be a matter of some intellectual urgency to ask whether our interests in politics, moral philosophy, and notions of truth and epistemology, are not more fragmented or more miscellaneous than his integrations propose. Is it not a wiser and more illuminating methodological stance sometimes to recognise that there is often a lack of connection in our ideas and our interests and that to register that lack is sometimes more important and revealing than to seek a strained connection? We will resist answering these questions, except to say that Gandhi's idea ' the idea that it is a matter of great moment, both for epistemology and for society and politics and morals, that truth is not a cognitive notion ' is impeached by the worst aspects of our intellectual culture.

If Gandhi is right and if truth is an exclusively moral notion, then when we seek truth, we are pursuing only a moral value. (Actually Gandhi's writings leave it a little unclear whether he is making the steepest claim that truth is not a cognitive notion at all, or the more cautious one that even if there is such a notion, it yields no special value of its own for us, a specifically cognitive value. The texts don't decide this matter, but it is obviously more sympathetic to read him as making the latter claim, and in the rest of this discussion, I will assume that that is so.) This leaves a great deal out of our normative interest in truth, which, as we have seen, Gandhi is perfectly willing to do. He is quite happy to discard as illusory our tendency to think that apart from the moral virtues involving truth (such as that of telling the truth, and living by and exemplifying our moral values) there is also in some sense a value or virtue in getting things right about the world and discovering the general principles that explain its varied phenomena. This latter is not a moral virtue, it is a cognitive virtue, and for Gandhi, cognitive virtues are a chimera. For him truth?s relationship to virtue cannot consist at all in the supposed virtue of acquiring truths of this kind; it is instead entirely to be understood in how truth surfaces in our practical and moral relations. That is why truth itself will have no value for us other than the value of such things as truth-telling, which does involve our practical and moral relations. To tell the truth is among other things (such as, say, generosity or kindness or considerateness) a way of being moral, and it was an aspect of morals that Gandhi himself was keen to stress. But the point is that truth being only a moral notion, there is no other value to truth than the value of such things as telling the truth, no more abstract value that it has.

There is a palpable mistake in collapsing the cognitive value of truth into the moral value of truth-telling, a mistake evident in the fact that somebody who fails to tell the truth can, in doing so, still value truth. That is to say, the liar often values truth and often values it greatly, and precisely because he does so, he wants to conceal it or invent it. The liar indeed has a moral failing in that he disvalues truth-telling, but he still values truth, and what he values in doing so therefore cannot be a moral value. It cannot be what Gandhi (and more recently Richard Rorty) insist is the only value that attaches to truth. To put it very schematically and crudely, truth has to be a more abstract value than a moral value because both the (moral) truth-teller and the (immoral) liar share it.

So what is this more abstract value of truth, which even the liar shares? If there is this abstract value to truth, and if even the liar values it, someone must surely in principle be able to fail to value it, else how can it be a value? How can there be a value if no one can fail to value it?

This is indeed a good question and only by answering it can we come close to grasping the value of truth that is not a moral value. The answer is: yes, someone does indeed fail to value truth in this more abstract sense. But it is not the liar. It is the equally common sort of person in our midst: the bullshitter. This is the person who merely sounds off on public occasions or who gets published in some academic journals simply because he is prepared to speak or write in the requisite jargon, without any goal of getting things right nor even (like the liar) concealing the right things which he thinks he knows.

The so-called Sokal hoax on which so much has been written, allows this lesson to be sharply drawn. I don't want to get into a long discussion about this incident both because it is remote from Gandhi's interests but also because I think that it has become a mildly distasteful site for people making careers out of its propagandist and polemical potential. Everything that I have read on the subject of this hoax, including Sokal?s own contribution, takes up the issue of how Sokal exposed the rampant and uncritical relativism of postmodern literary disciplines. I don't doubt that literary people in the academy have recently shown a relativist tendency, and yet I wonder if that is really what is at stake. The point is analogous to the one I just made about the liar. The relativist also does value truth in the abstract sense I have in mind, even if he has a somewhat different gloss on it from his opponents. In fact it is because he does value truth in this sense that he wishes to urgently put this different gloss on it. I believe it quite likely that the journal in which Sokal propagated his hoax would have been happy (at least before the controversy began) to publish a similarly dissimulating hoax reply to his paper in which all kinds of utterly ridiculous arguments were given, this time for an anti-relativist and objective notion of truth, so long as these arguments were presented in the glamorous jargon and with the familiar dialectical moves that command currency in the discipline. If so, the lesson to be learnt from the hoax is not that relativism is rampant in those disciplines but that very often bullshit is quite acceptable, if presented in the requisite way. To set oneself against that is to endorse the value of truth in our culture, truth over and above truth-telling, for a bullshitter is not a liar. Living and working in the context in which I do ' contemporary American academic culture ' I feel almost as strongly about the value of truth in this sense as I do about moral values surrounding truth, such as telling the truth or indeed many of the other moral values one can think of. That it might have mattered less to Gandhi is of course a matter of context, a matter of the quite different and much more impressive political concerns and interests of the Indian nationalist movement. But the philosophical lesson is a perfectly general one, and the very fact that he himself had gathered the strands of his political concerns and interests and tied them into 'integral' relations with these more abstract issues about truth and epistemology, make it impossible for us to dismiss the lesson as being irrelevant to him. So I must conclude by saying that I don?t think that Gandhi should have denied this cognitive value of truth. He should in fact have allowed that it defines the very possibility of his own philosophical undertakings and that it underlies his own yearning to find for his philosophical ideas the highest levels of what I have called 'integrity'. These undertakings and yearnings are all signs of a commitment to the very notion of truth which he wishes to repudiate. Whether allowing it will in the end have unravelled that integrity must remain a question for another occasion.

But I will end by saying that what that question will turn on is really the underlying question of this essay: How much integrity can these themes tolerate' It is Gandhi's essentially religious temperament that motivates the extraordinary ambitions of his integrations of these themes. What I mean here is that for all his romanticism about the power of exemplary actions to generate a moral community, Gandhi, like many religious people, is deeply pessimistic in one sense. He is convinced of the inherent corruptibility of our moral psyches. This surfaces at two crucial places, which are the well-springs of his integrity. It is what lies behind his fear that criticism will descend inevitably into violence, and it is also what underlies his fear that the intellectualisation of the notion of truth to include a cognitive value, will descend inevitably into an elevation of science into the paradigmatic intellectual pursuit of our culture, and thus descend further in turn to our alienation from nature with the wish to conquer and control it without forgiveness and with the most destructive technologies. The modern secular habits of thinking on these themes simply do not share this pessimism. Neither descent is inevitable, we will say. We can block the rise of bad technologies by good politics. There is no reason to see it as inevitable once we think of truth in cognitive terms, not even inevitable if we value scientific inquiry. So also we can block violence with good constitutional politics and the rule of law, and there is no reason to think it inevitable just because we think of values as entailing the exercise of our critical capacities towards one another. This modernist faith in politics to control and via this control to instil cognitive and moral habits in us which distract us from what might otherwise be seen as our corruptible nature is the real achievement, if that is what it is, of the Enlightenment. It is only this faith that convinces us that the integrations which Gandhi's pessimism force on him are not compulsory.

It needs a large and elaborate stock-taking of modernity to figure out whether the faith is justified, one in which philosophy and moral psychology will play as large a part as history and political economy. I have only raised the issue at stake at the highest level of generality. It is in the details, however, that it will be decided, and those really must await another occasion.

12

Gandhian Interpretative Repertoires

Gandhi's *truth* was and in my opinion still is - of an evolving nature. Thus Gandhian interpretative repertoires are immersed in an infinite semiosis of meaning. Yet, to make things intelligible, there is a need for full stops, albeit provisionally. That is, the slowly evolving nature of communicative resources should be acknowledged. In this chapter, I intend to shed light on the unfinished closures in Gandhian interpretative repertoires of *swaraj, satyagraha* and *sarvodaya.* Thus, I would like to show how Gandhian interpretative repertoires are relatively solid points of departure.

Discontinuities of East and West

Swaraj, satyagraha and *sarvodaya* are points of relative discontinuity, to use the term Ulf Hannerz has coined. Gandhi, and people who draw on Gandhian interpretative repertoires as resources, act as mediators between these and other points. However blurred discontinuities might be, we would like to show how Gandhian interpretative repertoires often involve *East/West* dichotomies.

In *Hind Swaraj,* Gandhi normalizes discontinuities of *East* and *West.* According to Rajmohan Gandhi, his grandfather pursued a separation of the *civilizations,* in an attempt to prove *Eastern* superiority. Gandhi believed in the eventual meeting of *East* and *West.* However, in his view, people's rejection *of modern civilization* is crucial to attain successful rapprochement. In the supposed conflict between *civilizations,* India has to be itself. Indeed, Gandhi went far beyond the commonsensical meaning of *civilization* - a singular noun - as progress. The Gujarati word *sudharo* supposedly is the equivalent for *civilization,* meaning good conduct. In this radically novel definition, Gandhi replaced material desire and technology fetishizing by an emphasis on duty and morality.

He presented good conduct as an ancient essential of Indian *civilization.* To prevent the coming of an Englishtan, pre-colonial, Hindustani Wisdom-Land has to be evoked. Authentic Indians practice an authentic Indian nationalism, which would lead to the reenactment of the spirituality and organic structure of immovable India:

> 'In the midst of all this India remains immovable and that is her glory. It is a charge against India that her people are so uncivilized, ignorant and stolid, that it is not possible to induce them to adopt any changes. It is a charge really against our merit. What we have tested and found true on the anvil of experience, we dare not change. Many thrust their advice upon India, and she remains steady. This is her beauty: It is the sheet-anchor of our hope'.

There are people who have been tempted to lift the anchor and they are alleged to have become civilized out of savagery. However, many Indians are untouched by *civilization.* In Gandhi's view, these people 'conscientiously believe that Indian civilization is the best and that the European is a nine days' wonder'. He even went as far as to state that the tendency of the former is to uphold morality, while the latter propagates the opposite.

By now, I think it has become clear that Gandhian interpretative repertoires can be characterized by an emphasis on supposed discontinuities of Indian/Eastern and European/Western *civilizations.* These dual oppositions do not do full justice to what was the heart of the matter for Gandhi: He had fundamental problems with uncritical assimilation of *civilizational* values he hold to be dominant in the *West*. After I have presented three possible readings of discontinuities of *East* and *West* in Gandhi's constructed history and resulting utopia, I will therefore reconsider them.

Swaraj Versus Statism

Hind Swaraj can be seen as 'the East's assertion of identity in a world and an age dominated by the West'[1]. While I consider this statement of Rajmohan Gandhi a very bold one, I do think Gandhi was involved in nationalist identity politics. He sought to mobilize *Hind* - India - against British tyranny, and for *swaraj2* or home rule. He thereby brought forth the imagined political community of Hindustan.

Benedict Anderson conceptualizes the imagined nation as limited, sovereign and as a community. As I have set out to show above, discontinuities of *East* and *West* abound in Gandhian interpretative repertoires. These pertain to a sharp limitation of what a Wisdom-land utopia founded on ancient cultural essentials is. Moreover, the utopian organic structure I mentioned, implies the allegedly communitarian character of Indian society. Gandhi maintains that, though colonial powers divided the one Indian nation, characterized by one inspirational thought and an identical mode of life, 'India is still, somehow or other, sound at the foundation'. To conclude the application of Anderson's frequently quoted theory, I would like to mention the sovereignty of the imagined nation. In his view, the sovereign state is the hallmark of a nation's freedom.

As the nation in *Hind Swaraj* is not the state, the Andersonian concept of the sovereign state does not to apply to *swaraj*. Gandhi envisioned *ramrajya* or divine rule. This utopia pertains to *self-contained* villages, and such that Gandhi typified it as ordered anarchy. In this kingdom of Ram on earth, oceanic circles will ripple from individual centers to villages, and circles of villages. Obviously, state centralism has no place in this vision. The sole purpose of the state's existence will ultimately be the representation of the communal will. For the time being, the state has to be minimized.

According to Gandhi, India's organic structure is not built on any *potentat*. He describes the pre-colonial situation as one in which peasants lived independently. His concept of *gram swaraj* is closely connected to this vision.

It is often translated as village republic and comes down to self-reliance in - among other things – governance[4]. Enjoying true Home Rule, people avoided courts. These evil institutions were solely found in urban areas.

With the advent of the British Raj came parasitical professions such as law and medicine. In *Hind Swaraj,* Gandhi dedicated several chapters to these supposedly malignant forces[5], already lurking in the cities. In Gandhi's opinion, lawyers advance quarrels instead of solving them, and doctors propagate the sin of indulgence. Gandhi writes that at the end of what he calls the Black Age, the axe of true religion will be raised over the trunk of which these undertakings are branches.

True religion still prevails in Indian villages, where people ridicule new-fangled notions such as inherently urban[6] machinery. In the nineteenth chapter of *Hind Swaraj,* he sets out to show that machinery has impoverished India. For Gandhi, the Bombay textile mills epitomize this chief symbol of modern *civilization*. He movingly shows his concern for the workers. As Rajmohan Gandhi maintains, his sentences on *Verelendung* inherent in the machinery mania still make sense. It is supposed to be a sign of progress, that people formerly working in the open air, now have no choice but to work in factories or mines.

Gandhi called on all Indians to cease to use machine-made goods. He hoped mill owners would establish handlooms, which he considered ancient and sacred. As part of the *Constructive Programme,* Gandhi introduced the principle of *swadeshi* or home-based production. Exalting the local, the native, and the national over the *Western* and the foreign, Gandhi set out to nurture appropriate technologies like *khadi* or hand-loomed cloth. Working towards full decentralization of production, village industries will be installed.

Gandhi concluded: 'We shall save our eyes and money and support Swadeshi and so shall we attain Home Rule'.

Satyagraha versus Struggle

While the *Constructive Programme* was crucial to attain *swaraj,* Gandhi emphasized that '[r]eal Home Rule is possible only where passive resistance is the guiding force of the people'. He took great pains to underline discontinuity of expedient nonviolence - which he associated with self-interest - and *satyagraha* or soul-force. The latter would signify moral commitment towards *satya - truth* - which Gandhi equated with God.

Gandhi stressed the authentically Indian character of the *satyagrahic* method of resistance. The nation as a whole has generally been involved with inherently irenic non-cooperation with rulers. Again, the ordered anarchic character of *swaraj* is visible in his renunciation of the new-fangled notion of complying with *leges* without taking *mores* into account. However, Indians do not break laws and lawgivers, if these do not appeal to them. While it remains to be seen whether this does not amount to breaking, Gandhi said Indians suffer and do not submit to laws. He advocated campaigning for equality beyond personal advantage, sacrificing the Self and not the Other. Practitioners of *ahimsa* avoid inflicting *himsa* or injury[7].

Hind Swaraj seems to suggest that the guiding force present in foreign - that is *Western* - rule comes down to violence instead of *ahimsa.* Rajmohan Gandhi even goes as far as to summarize its thesis as a dichotomy of violence and *Western civilization* on the one hand and *satyagraha* and Indian *civilization* on the other. Being the only weapon that is suited to the genius of India and its people, 'spiritual and spirited resistance against inequality and domination is the Indian way, not the violent resistance of the West'.

Gandhi pitted *satyagrahic* pity against Machiavellian opportunism. For him, *(Western)* pacifism in fact pertained to expedient nonviolence. He wrote in his *Anasaktiyoga,* that 'the extreme of means is salvation' and 'salvation of the Gita is perfect peace'. Indeed, the Editor of *Hind Swaraj* — Gandhi himself - rebukes the Reader - his discussant - for believing that the means and the end are not connected. In so doing, Gandhi renounces the adage *'Si vis pacem, para bellum'. Satyagraha,* then, can be seen as both the end and the means and it has to be practiced immediately.

Sarvodaya versus Socialism

For Gandhi, class struggle seems to have been the epitome of brute force. While *Hind Swaraj* does not deal with this specific form of violent resistance, his later criticism seems to go back to earlier concerns. He emerges to be opposed to Bolshevist mobocracy. In reply to an article by M.N. Roy - who would become leader of the Radical Democratic Party - he wrote: 'I believe in *conversion* of mankind, not its destruction'. David Hardiman mentions the Gandhian contrast between class struggle and *satyagraha,* the latter being moral conversion *par excellence.*

Just months before his passing, Gandhi expressed his fundamental discomfort with socialism. This, however, is not to be seen as an outward rejection of its *ends.* As Krishorlal Mashruwala - a loyal interpreter of Gandhi - has it, 'he was a communist minus their violence'. According to him, 'truth and ahimsa must come alive in [it]'. He reckoned this only to be possible, 'when there is a living faith in God'. In *Hind Swaraj,* he had stated 'religions teach [...] that we should set a limit to our worldly ambition and that our religious ambition should be illimitable'. On the contrary, *civilization* overlooks both morality and religion. As a result of this lack of *dharma* or duty, neither capitalists nor communists believe in living a simple, hard and laborious life.

Gandhi said he did not propagate *samyavada* - the theory or ideology of communism - but *samyadharma* - the practice or duty of equality. This creative negotiation is closely related to his *sarvodaya* tenet. Particularly stressing spiritual satisfaction, he took this to mean the welfare of all. While the fundamentally different conception of communism of the *West* is the belief in the essential selfishness of human nature, Indian socialism should be founded in non-violence and harmonious co-operation of labor and capital, landlord and tenant.

The distinct *Eastern* tradition with its *varnashrama*[12] division of labor - contributes to Gandhi's doctrine of trusteeship. India's organic structure provides for a spiritual regeneration of the rich, who will provide for the poor. As part of a reciprocal system of gift giving - *dan* - rather than impersonal market relations, capital will be communalized in a spiritual, non-violent way. The intention was not to destroy the capitalist, but to destroy capitalism.

Reconsidering Gandhian Discontinuities

We realize the above Gandhian discontinuities do not do full justice to Gandhi's critique of *civilizational* assimilation. As Rajmohan Gandhi remarks, 'if we go by what Gandhi did and how he lived, then it is obvious that his aim was to modify modern civilization, not to uproot it'. The problem here is that if we go by what he *said, East/ West* dichotomies are almost ever-present.

After heaving read *Hind Swaraj,* strongly simplified, I was inclined to see it as an anti-Western and anti-modern manifesto. David Hardiman, however, warns for such a reading, as it amounts to a questionable a dichotomy between *Western civilizational* values and Gandhi's alternative morality. For him, Gandhi related to *modernity* in a dialogic, rather than an antagonistic way. Apart from his critique *of civilization,* he deployed some Enlightenment values, such as the doctrines of human rights, egalitarianism and democracy against Indian society. Ashis Nandy argues in a similar vein, when he finds a critique of *tradition* coupled with a critique of *modernity*. Indian traditionalists actually accused Gandhi of being a destroyer of social harmony, while modernizers called him a backward looking crank. Gandhi said to defend immovable India. He actually went far beyond conserving *Eastern tradition,* but not so much *towards modernity.*

We have been concerned with the question as to which unfinished closures in Gandhian interpretative repertoires of *swaraj, satyagraha* and *sarvodaya* can be discerned. However fluid these schemes might be, there is slowness in the flux. Thus, I have tried to get a grasp of the closures Gandhi himself identified in his political vocabulary. He distinguished his concepts by dual opposition of Indian/Eastern to European/Western civilization. Apart from his critique of the latter *civilization,* he radically reformulated the singular term, meaning progress, as good conduct.

One of Gandhi's discontinuities of *East* and *West* amounts to rethinking the role of the state. Following *Hind Swaraj,* the concept of home rule *(swaraj)* does not pertain to top-down power. Instead, *ramrajya* implies the rule of God, rippling from individual centers to a mere representative communal organ. New-fangled notions, present in *modern civilization,* such as the need for machinery, are to be disenchanted by the *Constructive Programme. Swadeshi* or home based production is to be the key in decentralization of power, ranging from economics to politics.

For Gandhi, *swaraj* cannot be dissociated from the

essentially Indian means of attaining it; that is, *satyagraha* or soul-force in non-violence. Practicing *ahimsa* or avoidance of injury, Indians choose to suffer as a result of their disobeying laws which do not appeal to them. In *Hind Swaraj,* Gandhi maintained that this attitude is opposed to

Western inclinations. In his view, pacifists pursue opportunistic non-violence. Like the belligerent means of fellow *Westerners,* their quest amounts to struggle instead of *satyagraha.*

Claiming to be a communist minus their violence, Gandhi rejected socialism in favor of *sarvodaya* or the welfare of all. While the former espouses destruction, the latter involves conversion. In his plea for the duty of communism, Gandhi believed in harmonious cooperation of landlords and tenants. He held the doctrine of trusteeship to be part and parcel of such a system. This amounts to non-violent communalization, initiated by affluent trustees.

Reading *behind* Gandhi's lines offers a more nuanced construction of Gandhian interpretative repertoires than reading the lines themselves. He seems to have meant that the actual practitioners of the *Constructive Programme* continually mediate between different viewpoints. In the following chapter, I will look at ways thinkers have theorized in positive and normative terms, respectively, the institutions Gandhi assigned a crucial role in this dialogical reconstruction of India: Voluntary associations.

Social Theory

As part of his reluctance to create any isms, Gandhi did not claim to have innovated any social theory. He, however, did discuss social change. Crucially, volunteers would be vital in social reconstruction. Indeed, Indians commonly refer to their nonprofit sector organizations as *seshcha sevi* or *voluntary* associations. In the following discussion, I will mainly use the latter conventional Indian English term. First, I will consider positive, etic perspectives on voluntary associations. Then, normative views - including emic

Gandhian ones - will add to an understanding of Indian voluntary associations. While I outwardly acknowledge Thomas Kuhn's position that Is and Ought are often more related than scholars have noticed, I propose this distinction for the sake of analytical convenience.

Civil Society

Voluntary associations can generally be thought of as being part of civil society. Thus, We will start the discussion by shedding light on perspectives concerning this societal realm. Roughly speaking, there are two approaches to it. As J. Singh Uberoi purports, analysis of civil society is either focused on culture or on power.

Approached from the aspect of culture, civil society is imagined as 'a natural and universal development of intermediary institutions between the priest and the prince or between the household and the state'. Uberoi hereby follows in the wake of James Frazer, who describes these segments as being part of a triple unity of the love of God, king, and country'. He, however, critically reflects on Frazer's findings. For him, to analyze the establishment of civil society, the allegedly essential separation of sacral and profane kingship should be taken into account.

The opposite approach Uberoi discerns is focused upon power, authority or hierarchy and sovereignty; the latter including the legitimacy of the use of force. Thomas Hobbes most famously formulates this side of the question of civil society. He and his followers argue that the human species only emerges out of its supposedly pre-social state of nature, when the Self and the Other surrender liberty to the sovereign apparatus of the Leviathan state. Human beings sign the social contract to move from the brutish state of nature to the graceful state of civil society and good government. Hobbes describes the premises of the agreement as the supposition that the many are one, and that a part, constituting its sovereign, represents the whole.

It is useful to supplement Uberoi's review of Hobbes with an outline of Jean-Jacques Rousseau's *contrat social.* In his view, human society is not built on the pillars of insecurity and mutual distrust - as Hobbes claims - but on humans' desire to attain a higher moral nature. As citizens and participants in the *volonté générale,* people enjoy the freedom to apply laws on themselves and to remain as independent as in the natural state. Hence, the essential *Western* ideal of individual autonomy harmoniously coexists with the legitimacy of the state.

From the early 1800s onwards, European scholars continue to view civil society as representing the general will and the common good, and start to associate it with political economic innovations such as industrial democracy. This in turn triggers Georg Hegel to transcend legal reductionism and to include morality, ethical life and world-history in the realm of civil society, which is the territory of mediation. Crucially, *modern* capitalist societies possess this ability to develop a moral sphere, which Karl Marx views to be dominated by the commodity principle.

Endorsing the Hegelian paradigm to a significant degree, Neera Chandoke conceptualizes civil society as a level of mediation between the private and the public. It is therefore the site of expressed politics, either affirming or contesting the projects of the state. Participants aggregate for various purposes, both to nurture their self-interest and the reproduction of society. Thus, Chandoke does not make the distinction commonly accepted in European and American research between movements aiming at personal change and those pursuing political revolution. Indeed, for Martin Fuchs and Antje Linkenbach, this separation is less suited to Indian contexts.

Social Movements

Now that I have introduced some of the leitmotivs in the general debate on civil society, it is useful to specify the concept under consideration. Following Fuchs and

Linkenbach, We would like to focus on social movements, which I assume to amount to human initiatives, mediating between highly personal and overtly impersonal aggregation. While many researchers use this term in a naively descriptive manner to refer to an allegedly unified collective, We think civil society is an even bolder denomination.

Be this as it may, aspects which are generally associated with social movements are anti-establishment social contents, evocation of ideas of autonomy, equity, human dignity and fundamental rights, and links to social change through *modernization* as part of the participants' quest. The eventual definition formulated by the authors amounts to 'collective self-organizations for the attainment of social recognition and the assertion of rights or existential interest hitherto denied to a group or category of people'.

Fuchs & Linkenbach offer a comprehensive review of social movement theory, in which two basic lines of thought can be discerned. Whereas one strand focuses on the behavior of movement participants, the other takes the socio-political system as point of departure. The former implies social movements to be exceptions to the rule of adherence to institutionalized behavior, while the latter seems to follow in the wake of the Hobbesian war of all against all, in which conflict and antagonism are regular features of social life.

As the first strand of research is concerned, early protagonists of the theory of collective behavior attribute the rise of social movements to extensive disorder inherent

in *modernization* and (colonial) political repression. Thus, scholars see them as reactions to social disintegration. They are singular phenomena, pertaining to the uncoordinated accumulation of individual actions. It is only from the 1920s onwards, that sociologists of the Chicago School enrich this model by acknowledging social innovation.

The renewal of the theory of collective behavior pertains to the recognition of the individually coordinated nature of collective action and the identification of a particular foundation of social movements. Consequently, the behaviorist emphasis moves from a frustration-aggression paradigm to the rationalist assumptions of a strategic action model. A bottom-up resource mobilization theory hereby replaces a top-down perspective in which the elite's views are also taken to be held by other participants. However, the individualistic instrumentalism inherent in the model downplays the role of ideology.

The second strand of research, then, rehabilitates social movements as historical actors. Subsequently, apart from characterizing society as structurally conflictual, scholars adhering to this approach view movements as macro subjects. In the 1960s and '70s, this particularly holds true for *Third World* peasants, who carry the same historical projects as previous revolutionary subjects in the *West*. For many authors, the concomitant correlation of objective, structural constraints with historically encountered social conflicts looks convincing. Nevertheless, as post-classical capitalist contexts are concerned, there is a need to recognize movements in their own right.

New social movement or identity-oriented approaches reinvest the macro-sociological approach with meaning. From the late-capitalist 1980s onwards, the struggle does not solely amount to class, but to numerous conflicts. The significant scholarly attention to new social movements includes a re-invention of particular moral economics and their confrontations with rising market economy and capitalism. Thus, religious and other *non-modern* cultural forms of opposition or subalternity are no longer ignored.

Finally, several contemporary scholars realize that neither the novel new social movement theory nor the focus on resource mobilization is an adequate model of the dynamics involved. Instead, Ananta Kumar Giri and Thomas Rochon plead for a dialectics of the perspectives.

Giri clarifies the point in his newest volume. Dialects are both visible in the application of participants' identities to the mobilization of resources, and in the increasingly non-physical nature of resources.

Voluntary Associations in India

To get a grasp of the complex ways voluntary workers constitute their movements, it is necessary to focus on the specific context. Therefore, I would like to provide an overview of the history of voluntary associations in India. However, as Siddharta Sen underlines, India's complexity implies that attempts to provides an overview of the nonprofit sector in India is problematic, for no master narrative can be discerned. It is not my intention, then, to give insight in the whole of India's voluntary associations. Instead, I will focus on some important trends.

Sen locates the initial voluntary efforts in social development in the early 1810s. The Christian missionaries involved in these endeavors focused on *modernization* and empowerment, which pertained to credit, health care and training, and adult literacy and *panchayats,* respectively. In the latter half of the 1820s, modern Indian elites tried to surpass the English clergy with a genuine *mission civilisatrice.* In the 1870, *caste sabha* associations emerged to promote caste affiliates' social and political mobility. Interestingly, Gandhi actually offered an alternative to issue-based voluntary efforts like these. He can be said to have contributed to the twentieth century introduction of political contents within voluntary work in India.

Indeed, Sen calls the early post-independence period the era of religion-based and *Gandhian* nonprofit organizations (NPOs). Nonetheless, he indicates that the rise of Gandian NPOs is attributable to the early Indian state's promotion of NPO participation in development work. Crucially, Prime Minister Jawaharlal Nehru was of the opinion that the state should provide technical and financial support to the voluntary sector. Yet, Seth and Sethi view this enduring dependence of Gandhian associations on the state as detracting from the sector's vibrancy.

In the 1960s and '70s, many welfare-oriented associations emerged. Unemployment among the educated youth and malcontent as the institutional status quo was concerned provided these organizations with a breeding ground. Among the diverse groups of participants were young Sarvodaya workers focused on voluntary land reforms, and Naxalite revolutionaries. In the decades that followed, numerous action groups like these disintegrated. In parallel with this development, the government regained its grip on the sector and promoted apolitical associations. Moreover, organizations professionalized.

In order to arrive at a situational theory of voluntary associations in late twentieth and early twenty-first century India, I would like to turn to the theory of voluntary associations in a cross-cultural perspective, as reviewed by Thomas Oommen. In the first part of his article, Oommen presents this as a scheme consisting of two dimensions developed in two specific contexts. One dimension is associated with the context of rising statist autocracy. Following Alexis de Tocqueville, this theoretical aspect holds voluntary associations to be essential instruments of pluralism as they facilitate people's influence on the government.

The dimension Oomen is primarily concerned with, however, lies within the context of dehumanization caused by industrial urbanization. This model assumes *traditional* primary groups to have disappeared, and alienated, atomized and free-floating individuals to participate in voluntary associations to mend the situation. Oommen, however, is at great pains to deconstruct what he calls the myth of urban-industrial tyranny. According to him, scholars criticizing mass society romantically adore rural society. Furthermore, 'urban-industrial society is not as cruel, as impersonal and as loose-knit as it is usually made out to be, and primary groups and penetrating interpersonal relations form an important aspect of urban life'.

In the second part of his article, Oommen aims at the formulation of a typology of voluntary associations, based on functional variations. Following Gordon and Babchuck, he differentiates between the instrumental type - aimed at the maintenance or the creation of conditions of social change - and the expressive type -focused on the fulfillment of individual needs for fellowship. Finally, the instrumental-expressive type combines the functions of these orientations.

Oommen ascribes different degrees of associational probability to different types of societies. For him, voluntary associations in *traditional* societies will instrumentally function to bring about social change and structural differentiation. Those operating in *urban-industrial* societies, on the other hand, will expressively mend the weakening of *traditional* primary group ties. Additionally, 'in *transitional societies* which have partially moved out of their *traditional* value system and yet have *not fully modernized,* the voluntary associations are likely to combine both instrumental and expressive functions thereby operating as *"links" between tradition and modernity,* as integrating mechanisms between the past and the present'. From this, it is clear that Oommen implicitly clings to a *modernization* discourse.

The author pursues his evolutionary development paradigm in his discussion of two main types of urban voluntary associations in contemporary India. In his opinion, there are those which have originated in *traditional* particularistic structures, such as religious and caste associations, and organizations which are newly inducted into the system, such as youth clubs, cooperatives and trade unions. He assumes the former type to *modernize traditional* structures and the latter to get *traditionalized* while performing *modern* functions. The originally *modern* associations are mostly instrumental in nature. They boost the process of economic development and emancipate the individual from collective tyranny. The originally *traditional* organizations, on the other hand, are expressive in nature. They function as alternative primary groups for their participants. Be this as it may, Oommen still acknowledges the situationality of voluntary associations in urban India, as they combine instrumentality and expressivity.

Normative Perspectives on Voluntary Associations

We have been concerned with positive sociological theories. For Bijyanand Kar, these do generally pertain to an emphasis on society as an agent of social change. However, Gandhi maintained that 'the freedom of the individual cannot be surrendered for any cause of mechanization'. His pursuit to harmonize social and personal interests is to be seen in this light. I think Gandhi's conviction that social reform must ultimately aim at a change of heart amounts to a normative juncture in social theory. In this subchapter, I will therefore take into account practical idealism or practical spirituality.

As Alain Tourain clarifies, 'practical spirituality transgresses easy and familiar boundaries between material and spiritual, social welfare and devotional compassion, and politics and ethics'. It is a key concept for Ananta Kumar Giri, an innovative social scientist from India, who aims to trigger dialogues with voluntary workers. His primary point is the alleged lack of concern about self-development on their part. In his impression, participants generally consider their practice an other-regarding, altruistic act. For him, however, 'other-regarding action has a source in the aspiration and the happiness of the *self* and if this source is not identified and properly nurtured then the actors of voluntary action are bound to feel depressed and dissatisfied'.

In Giri's vision, genuine identification of the recognized Self with the Other will dissolve paternalism, inherently present in supposedly other-regarding voluntary work. In *concreto,* the author urges voluntary workers to identify with the people with whom they work. While this is to imply the genesis of deep rapport between voluntary workers and commons, it will be reflected in cadres' outward lifestyles. A first advice Giri directs at voluntary workers, is to live together with the people they claim to represent.

Similarly, Gandhi called on a rural volunteer to make her life resemble that of a villager. Wearing a 'low paid peon['s]' *khadi* dress, she joins the people in their *charka* spinning and observes simplicity, sincerity and regularity.

In so doing, she works and lives in a spirit of renunciation and selflessness. Gandhi's adage that '[she] who serves the poor serves God' thus applies, and her spiritual quest therefore is an act of self-purification. The *yogi-like* volunteer, then, would attend only to herself and her work.

Indeed, Swadhyaya seems to resemble the Gandhian attitude of detachment Dadage and Jena describe. Participants in this socio-spiritual mass movement conduct community farming, which they consider labor of devotion. These *bhaktas* work because of an unconditional ethical obligation, both to the Self and to the Other. The *impact* on the Other, though, is not a point of reference for them. As Giri rightly remarks, 'in the process the problem of the other is in danger of being marginalized'. Thus, the author warns that the quest for self-development he prescribes should not mean a sole focus on the Self.

Self-development does not pertain to a mere act of *bhakti* or devotion on the part of the Self, but to an interactional process, closely connected with dialogical democracy. Thus, Giri incites voluntary workers to associate in an egalitarian way with the people they usually consider objects of charity. Felix Wilfred maintains that this ability implies self-emptying or *kenosis* in the use of power. Following Anthony Giddens, Giri holds this is to be a move from party-political domination to service oriented life-politics. This amounts to a shift from a clinical search for programs of social change, which is part and parcel of the bureaucracy present both in governmental *and* in nongovernmental associations.

Likewise, Vijay Kumar - himself a Gandhian - reflects on the confrontation of community action groups with power politics. In his view, these associations have moved from imposed *development* towards the alternative model of indigenization. Consequently, community action workers are supposed to be non-authoritarian and sharing moral and idealistic values. Yet, however voluntary in name, these individuals are increasingly professionalized. Kumar maintains that even Gandhians have assumed that the state is a legitimate instrument of power. Thus, 'most organizations in India accommodate themselves to the dominant ideology and political structure'.

By contrast, Gandhi said he had 'no doubt that the ideal [...] for public institutions is to live, like nature, from day to day'. Judging from this statement, he denounced far-reaching institutionalization. He favored a non-violent, small and local organization of workers who are acquainted with each other, and only permitted a more sizable association that is genuinely voluntary in nature, and solely giving advice. The decentralized organization he had in mind is one in which the essentially individual voluntary effort is 'channelized through organization which has the benefit of group thinking for the welfare of the community', as Sudhira Jena has it. Gandhi hereby differed from Henry David Thoreau and Leo Tolstoy - two famous European pacifists with whom he corresponded - who were rather *individualistically* oriented in their protest. Speaking in a similar vein as Gandhi, Jiddu Krishnamurti said in a memorable speech about the legitimacy of institutionalization:

'Those who really desire to understand, who are looking to find that which is eternal, without beginning and without an end, will walk together with a great intensity, will be a danger to everything that is unessential, to unrealities, to shadows. And they will concentrate, they will become the flame, because they understand. Such a body we must create, and that is my purpose'.

In this chapter, We have conceptually interrogated Indian voluntary associations, to whom Gandhi ascribed a critical role in his *Constructive Programme*. Thus, I have set out to answer the question as to how thinkers have theorized Indian voluntary associations in positive and normative terms, respectively.

As part of my initial engagement with positive perspectives on voluntary associations, I have presented an outline of some relevant classical social theory. Understandings of civil society have roughly taken either of two distinct foci as points of departure. The focus on culture amounts to a developmental perspective, in which civil society develops as an intermediary realm between profane and sacral power. The more notable concern with power, on the other hand, proceeds from the relevancy of the struggle *between* the state and the people on the battlefield of civil society.

However, both Hobbes' belief in he desperate foundation of the domain and Rousseau's contention that it is built on a genuinely voluntary will, dubiously take its support of state power for granted. While civil actors either affirm or contest state projects, they do not question its very existence. They thus crucially share the premise of centralism with their counteragent in the process of political expression in civil society. Hence, it seems most scholars endorsing this view overlook the possibility of aggregation of anarchistly inclined actors, radically pursuing decentralism.

As opposed to major strands of thought on civil society, theories of social movements more fully take into account anti-establishment social contents. Within the latter, sociologists endorsing behaviorist paradigms view people's collectives as reactions to social disintegration. While recognizing individuals' strategic action, scholars have theoretically extended their views in the resource mobilization approach.

Diverting from the above creeds, macro-sociologists conceptualize society as *structurally* disintegrated. Within this perspective, movements are historical actors, objectively defined according to class. New social movement or identity orientations add subjective dimensions to subalternity. In any application of theory on social movements, there is, however, a need for a dialectics of resource mobilization and identity approaches. This is to say that participants often mobilize immaterial resources, and they regularly apply their very identities to their rallies.

New social movement theory allows for concrete Indian contexts to add to the complexity of voluntary associations in the country. Among diverse themes, an interesting feature of national nonprofit sector history amounts to Gandhi's introduction of political content within voluntary work. The subsequent early post-independence period was characterized by the rise of state-backed Gandhian organizations.

As for localized theories of Indian voluntary associations, several dimensions and functions can be identified. A dimensional framework pertains to growing statist autocracy, and dehumanization as a result of industrial urbanization. Functional axis

amount to instrumental and expressive types of voluntary associations in India. It is, however, highly questionable that these are characteristic of *traditional* and *modern* societies, respectively, and that instrumental-expressive types epitomize transitionality. The distinction originates in modernization discourse, taking for granted development towards urban-industrialism.

A normative alternative for developmentalist approaches is to be found in Gandhi's concept of practical idealism, which focuses on identification of the Self with the Other. In this model of self-development, voluntary workers and people they work with are engaged in a process of dialogical democracy. Instead of clinically applying their skills in a hierarchical way, movement participants present themselves as servants, aiming at indigenization. It must be noted that party-politics and professionalization disenchant the decentral organization of individual volunteers Gandhi had in mind. In what follows, I will deal with these and other dilemmas surrounding Neo-Gandhian voluntary work for people's development.

Gandhian Interpretative Repertoires in Practice

Contemporary Gandhians view *sarvodaya* - the welfare of all - as the only feasible scenario for Indian society. Otherwise, people head straight for *sarvnash* or the destruction of all. Indeed, a motto *sarvodayis* have expressed for years is *'vikas chahiye, vinash nahin'* - 'we want development, not destruction'[15] . First, I will make an attempt to account for the presence of such universal foci within Indian voluntary associations. Then, I will give an outline of Gandhian agenda points. This is followed by a discussion of the Neo-Gandhian National Alliance of People's Movements and some of its constituents. Finally, I will provide an ethnographical record of a Post-Gandhian's voluntary work in the Mumbai Eco Friendly Centre.

Struggles Particular and Universal

The contemporary world can be thought of as a global ecumene. That is, it amounts to 'an area of persistent social interaction and cultural flow'. Voluntary workers form part of the extensive range of actors who mediate between points of relative discontinuity in this flux. They negotiate nodes present in a cosmopolitan struggle for meaning.

Accordingly, Indian activists have realized that, while non-committal engagement with others on specific issues is insufficient, they have to challenge more encompassing structures. For example, the campaign against the Sardar Sarovar dam has come to transcend the campaign for a particular river. Movement participants have begun to critically interrogate an entire system. The struggle thus powerfully exemplifies the 'war for the rivers and the mountains and the forests of the world', as Arundhati Roy has it. David Hardiman, however, points to the status quo, the immense power of which often implies marginalization. Consequently, voluntary workers generally have to focus on particular issues. Still, specific successes can inspire people into action both narrow and wide.

At the same time, Arundhati Roy expresses her doubts about the effectiveness of the pursuit of large issues. As in the case of the river Narmada, it can blunt information concerning specific facts about specific issues - a most substantial instrument. Moreover, many grassroots activists fear involvement in overarching formations will result in alienation from people's every-day struggles. Therefore, it seems fair to say that a majority of Indian voluntary workers are determined to act locally, while not all of them intend to think globally.

Indeed, the ecofeminist activist Vandana Shiva applies Gandhian interpretative repertoires to the fight against *globalization,* which she perceives to amount to colonialism. She conceptualizes *swadeshi* as indigenous economic freedom. Furthermore, for her, *ahimsa* implies small economics, not dominant and destructive to any life form. While she thus follows in the wake of Schumacher's *Small is Beautiful,* Shiva strongly refutes mainstream Indian journalists' contention that *swadeshi* is a form of xenophobia. Instead, the author maintains that *globalization* is 'a project of total global control, arising from a fear of everything that is alive, free and autonomous'.

Luuk Middelaar, however, questions the very concept of *globalization* as object of contemporary struggles. Crucially, activists such as Vandana Shiva - publishing in the international *Ecologist* magazine - are themselves very globalized. Following Naomi Klein, some people engaged in anti-globalism now refer to The Movement. Similarly, activists in the Netherlands and Flanders have coined *anders-globalisme* -alternative globalism. In so doing, people express the idea that their object of dissent is not *globalization* in general, but neo-liberal *mondialisation marchande.* Admittedly, Shiva's emphasis on *swaraj* as an interactional basis implicitly coincides with more nuanced counterconcepts.

Running parallel with this, in present India, *satyagrahic* activists make use of global information networks, which paradoxically facilitate the spread of foreign capital. Indeed, David Hardiman maintains that electronic communications have increased the efficacy *of satyagraha,* in that they facilitate people's ability to extend a non-violent struggle which appears to be solely local into national or even international territory. In this respect, Ishwar Harris even identifies the globalization of Gandhism.

In fact, my very ethnography in cyberspace illustrates the point that global media further the expansion of Gandhian evocations. Websites of *sarvodayic* organizations in themselves testify the spread of repertoires to which they pertain. Moreover, I *digitally* conducted the interview we had with Daniel - a voluntary worker in the Mumbai Eco Friendly Centre. However, the reluctance of some Gandhi-inspired activists to use the internet for communication - which Daniel and Dana van Breukelen told me about -points to their critique of the allegedly un-Indian character of such practices.

Gandhian Agenda Points

There can be said to be a number of common causes contemporary Gandhians have taken up. Harris questionably identifies these as aimed at the retrieval of the Indian *civilization.* The first and foremost is their critique of the un-Indian economic development practice, which for them has neglected agriculture and exploited the poor. Another, related common cause is the issue of the reckless pursuit of technology, which they say has replaced man with machine. A third joint concern is their opposition to the Indian government's liberalization policies and the subsequent rise of multinational companies, which they see as a threat to *swaraj*. Finally, they share serious doubts about what they see as the economic exploitation of villages, and centralization of power.

While Ishwar Harris enumerates common points rather abstract in nature, Jeanet van der Woude (1996) ethnographically identifies a number of more or less concrete Gandhian elements. When she is participant-observing the Anti Tehri Dam movement, she is wondering where Gandhi is. A superficial Gandhian element she distinguishes, then, pertains to the *khadi* clothes the activists are wearing. An additional, more crucial issue is the emphasis on harmony between people and nature as the foundational principle of Gandhian involvement in the ecology movements she observes.

Strikingly, Van der Woude expresses her doubts about the Gandhian quality of the non-violent struggle within the movements. She recognizes the practice of *satyagraha*. Activities such as demonstrations and fasts are strongly focused on ethics and morals. Yet, the researcher critically examines whether their non-violent character is a direct adoption of *satyagraha*. The movement participants in Dhauntri village eventually tell they would indeed switch to belligerent means, when their soul-force would not be effective anymore. The cadre *sarvodayis,* however, consider non-violence first priority.

While the uphold of *satyagraha* among *sarvodayic* ecology movements seems to be sustainable, there are many issues which are by no means agreed upon within the Gandhian network. Van der Woude relates this to Gandhi's multiplicity of principles. The different ways two voluntary workers deal with the issue of finance exemplifies this point. Whereas Suresh Nautiyal advances Gandhi's doctrine of trusteeship in his acceptance of non-governmental and even governmental funds, Sunderlal Bahuguna embraces the principle of self-reliance in his refusal to accept financial support of 'any institution related to the structure that [stimulates] destruction in the name of "development"'. Similarly, as opposed to Raksha Sutra movement participants, people affiliated with the Save the Himalaya movement disapprove of even the alternative, small-scale form of industrialization suggested by Gandhi.

Interestingly, Jeanet van der Woude concludes that 'it is difficult to stipulate exactly how far the similarities [of ecology movements' ideologies with Gandhism] are the result of a direct link, an adoption, or that they are based on logic because of the same orientation towards problems'. Tridip Suhrud goes as far as to state that related evocations of Gandhian interpretative repertoires often remain symbolic. For him, there is a call to take constructive work seriously, and to translate Gandhi's life and thought into politics.

Towards Jan Vikas

Ishwar Harris argues that there is a call for a new generation of Gandhians, who are able to evoke a whole range of interpretative repertoires, while still referring to Gandhi. These Neo-Gandhians 'do not follow the Gandhian dogmas but are committed to experiments in the quest for truth and building an equitable society'. Indeed, ever since *satyagrahic* activism began to braid with the new social movements, many Indian voluntary workers have rejected a doctrinaire approach.

The Indian new social movements which form the National Alliance of People's Movements (NAPM) can be said to epitomize Neo-Gandhism. While participants in NSMs like these have drawn on Gandhian interpretative repertoires, they have also been inspired by numerous other strands of thought. This implies both intra-, and interorganizational hibridity. Constituting a multiheaded swarm network, affiliated associations exhibit collective diversity and coordinated anarchy.

United under one platform in a somewhat desperate way, NAPM constituents share convergent political ideals. They hereby pursue *jan vikas* or people's development, which amounts to a negotiated alternative for the evolutionist *development* paradigm. Voluntary worker have outlined a number of principles as its foundations. These include people's control over natural resources in their vicinity and their involvement in decision-making. Although Rajni Bakshi does not use the phrase, Gandhi's emphasis on the need of all, instead of on the greed of some seems to have been inspirational in the formulation of this principle. Stressing 'non-violence and dialogue as a means to change individuals and societies', people evoke Gandhi in a more explicit way.

Arguably the core principle of *jan vikas* is observance of austerity and simplicity as opposed to consumerism. Commemorating Gandhi's martyrdom, participants in a national tour put forward *'Equality, simplicity, selfreliance for proper development'* as a rallying call. This amounts to sustainable use and conservation of resources in labor-intensive, decentralized production, based on renewable energy.

Crucially, the simple life - as Gandhi had it - applies to both commons *and* cadres within the NAPM. First, it is essential to note that the latter are not contenders for power. Medha Patkar - convener of the alliance - underlines their reluctance to join a party. The self-emptying in the use of power they can be said to pursue implies close contact with commons, instead of distant party politics. Still, during the 1989 Harsud rally of Indian voluntary associations, some people suggested the foundation of an Indian Green Party. Both Ishwar Harris and Rajni Bakshi urge workers to consider this possibility 'to place their agenda of concerns at the centre-stage of the political mainstream'.

While many people within the NAPM are reluctant to enter external power structures, some even oppose internal institutionalization. As Sanjay - a voluntary worker associated with the alliance - puts it during a conference in Chennai:

People will do from different places, whatever it is. While it is still small then we have this mazza, doing it from our own houses, spending our own money, this that. This is the spirit, joy, volunteerism. When there is institutional structure, this mazza peters out'.

Whereas Sanjay states that the NAPM 'is not an organisation if one wishes', for Ramanujam - another conference participant - there is a call to institutionalize, in order to achieve sustainability.

Finally, NAPM affiliates consider it to be important that cadres' lifestyles amount to simplicity. More or less following Gandhi in his belief that 'change is possible only by being one with the pain, suffering and misery of people', Gabriele urges participants to 'start thinking of scaling down lifestyle and consumption'. While, for her, an anti-plastic campaign was a great leap forward, she suggests an enduring emphasis on energy- and transport alternatives. Sanjay credits Neo-Gandhians for bringing the issue of simplicity onto the agenda. For him, it is both 'a social policy, and a way to enrich the individual life'. He concludes by stressing that there is a need to halt the post-modern practice of separating 'our politics and our ethics'.

It is interesting to note how voluntary workers in particular NAPM constituents put some of the above, Neo-Gandhian principles of *jan vikas* into practice. The most famous of hundreds of affiliated associations is the Narmada Bachao Andolan (NBA) or the Save the (River) Narmada Movement. While the NBA has frequently been characterized as environmental, its emic goal pertains to 'creating an alternative political culture based on Gandhian principles'. Participants view *satyagraha* as the only way to counter statist development tyranny. Medha Patkar - both convening the NAPM and the NBA - '[advances] the Gandhian argument that the struggle is for decentralisation of power, with local people having the right to decide how their resources should be utilised'. While she does not claim to be a Gandhian herself, Patkar has participated in various *satyagrahic* fasts and joined *satyagrahis* in their submerged villages.

Another voluntary association affiliated with the NAPM is the Aazadi Bachao Andolan. According to its website, the ABA is 'the all India organization striving for achieving *Real Swaraj* cherished by Mahatma Gandhiji'. It covers 300 Indian districts, in which a total of ten thousand patriotic workers are volunteering. Rajiv Dixit, 'who has renunciated all worldly affairs', is leading the association. As can be read in the ABA's Appeal to Patriotic Workers and to the True Indian, participants 'have wrath against bureaucracy, politics, capitalism and policy of globalization, liberalization and foreignization'. Interestingly, workers 'have indignation against bureaucracy but not against bureaucrats'. Similarly, industrialists and politicians 'are not without hearts'. This is the typically Gandhian approach of 'hating the sin, not the sinner', and 'trying to convert the opponent into a friend'. Mass voluntary action to disenchant the 'empire of injustice and exploitation' implies propaganda of *swadeshi* goods and boycott of 'all foreign goods and commodities produced by big factories'. ABA participants argue in favor of economic, political, educational, agricultural, and health localization[22]. Talking in a similar vein, Medha Patkar urges 'the simple-living human communities' to take action against 'the globalization/liberalization policies - imposed by our own politicians, a handful of elites fulfilling the desires of the global powers'.

As a third example of a NAPM-affiliated voluntary associations, I would like to mention the Bombay Sarvodaya Mandal. This *mandal* or society is 'a *Gandhian charitable trust* having noted Gandhians amongst its midst and undertakes various constructive programmes, seminars, workshops, meetings and youth camps [..] in pursuance of the teachings of Gandhiji, Vinobaji and Jayaprakash Narayan', the latter two being disciples of the former. Apart from the propagation of Gandhian literature, voluntary workers' activities include 'organizing peace marches and mass-walks with the focus on crucial global issues like a nuclear free world, nonviolence, communal harmony, and international peace'. Furthermore, workers motivate students on Gandhian philosophies, during youth camps in tribal villages. Finally, 'to provide the village with a means to arrest the exodus of their youngsters to the city for employment', volunteers promote village industries, by encouraging production and sale of *khadi* clothes. In so doing, *'samata sadgi svavalamsam, lake rehaga jan andolan'* - 'equality, simplicity, self-sufficiency, will be achieved by people's movements'.

A Post-Gandhian in the Eco Friendly Centre

The Eco Friendly Centre was an Association for India's Development initiative within the Bombay Sarvodaya Mandal. It was similar to *khadi bhandars,* stores which voluntary workers opened to market village industries' produce and nationalist literature in Gandhi's time. Participants in the Eco Friendly Centre, however, not only focused on *swadeshi* and *khadi,* but also on *eco-friendly, organic* agriculture. Daniel - one of the people that used to be involved in the shop - shared both his personal story as an activist, and the story of the Eco Friendly Centre with me in two online interviews.

Post-Gandhian Foundations

In the first interview, Daniel proposes to start by introducing himself. Belonging to a progressive Jewish-Indian middle class family, he helped his sister to sell socialist newspapers when he was approximately twelve years old. In the 1950s, he and his peers in the Land Gift movement of Vinoba Bhave belonged to the generation of Post-Gandhians. They 'were actually inspired by Vinobaji and Gandhiji was at the back of all philosophy which Vinobaji very ably put up before the people of our country'. When Daniel was at college, he had met 'young people who had already given full time to the movement'. He had talked with them and began to read literature on the Land Gift Movement at their suggestion. The movement meant for him 'that the landlessness of the village people shall be removed that they will get some land to work on and that they and their family will be able to live in a slightly better condition'.

Daniel had eventually read all important books on the Land Gift movement and had started attending and organizing meetings of workers, selling literature and doing office work for it. Back then, the now 70-year-old voluntary worker was 19 years of age, and he soon left his university. The talks by movement participants made him realize Gandhi and Roy were very much alike. While the latter was more of an 'ethical and moral revolutionary' and the former and Vinoba were spiritual, all three did not have any faith in party politics.

In Daniel's opinion, party politics are not suited to 'the Indian ethos'. The party system is opposed to 'the tradition [of] *panch* (five) *bole* (speak) *parmeshwar* "god speaks through them"' (my emphasis). In the powerful unit of the village, people took care of the poor. In his view, 'the villages remained untouched', and small industries flourished. British Raj representatives, however, 'purposely broke the whole economy based on village industry'. Daniel says this can be read in *The Early Phase,* written by Pyarelal, Gandhi's personal secretary.

When I asked him whether *Hind Swaraj* is similar in contents, he answered that this is very much the case and that 'in fact for us it is the Bible of India's freedom and freedom struggle and the road map of economic, political, social and spiritual emancipation'. Although, for him, 'the style is a bit oldish', 'Gandhi said that he did not find any need for changing the basic thoughts mentioned in that book, even after many years'. Daniel mourns Nehru's ' [acceptance of] all the western models of progress, reforms, rule of law, rule of planning for five years etc.'. In his view, 'slowly we left Gandhi in the ditch, and that is what we now see around us, all, consumerism and competition, market has become the most powerful thing, and everything is for sell here and all over, in the new globalisation policies'. He however, nuances his position, in that he 'not only [opposes] western [practices] but [any] that creates classes, rich and poor, competition, violence [...] even if that is made in India [...], for 'India is going by the western standards, and [is] now part of the global process by which the poor get poorer and the [rich] get richer'[27].

The Eco Friendly Centre

In the second interview, Daniel talks about the Eco Friendly Centre in detail. Friends of Daniel and his fellow *sarvodayis* in Mumbai, who were active in the Narmada Bachao Andolan and had founded the Association for India's Development, proposed to finance an ecological shop. Daniel took interest, because the subject was close to his heart. His colleagues in the Sarvodaya movement contributed the space needed and Medha Patkar inaugurated the store. In it, voluntary workers 'were working for social change through nonviolence'.

They aimed at the survival of 'village people and village life' by providing a market without middlemen/women to earn profit. *Khadi* or *charka* was crucial in their vision of 'village life'. Daniel cites Gandhi in his depiction *of khadi* as 'the sun [...] around [which] all the village industries revolve, evolve'. He further states, that 'it can provide the poorest of the poor some living wage, something to cling on, something which will give them cloth and little money if they are able to spin and weave more'. Daniel and his fellow voluntary workers were doing the marketing of the items purchased by friends of the Association for India's Development. The hand-made objects and organically produced food came from the Indian states of Maharashtra, Andhra Pradesh, Tamil Nadu, Kerala, Gujarat and Madhya Pradesh.

Elaborating on their focus on ecology, Daniel stresses the fact that 'chemical fertilizers spoil the earth' and '[t]hey may create, in the long run, some bad effects on health'. For him, this critique 'was in [Gandhi's] thinking, but at that time, there was not much of a talk of machine made fertilizers'. Gandhi, however, did talk of 'cow, bullocks and manure'. After Gandhi, Vinoba Bhave initiated the Sarvodaya movement, which 'tries to protect villages from the encroachments of big industries, big ideas of dams, big factories, big and big and big'. Daniel hereby refers to Schumacher's *Small is Beautiful,* which matches 'with what Gandhi, Vinoba and Jayaprakash Narayan were talking about. All of them envisioned 'a sort of neighbourliness [as] the spirit of life style, and not depending on big ideas of development'.

As for the Eco Friendly Centre, the voluntary workers unfortunately were not able to sustain it. While at first, there was a young woman who looked after it for well over nine months, no one was able to volunteer full-time later on. Furthermore, storage space and financial support were limited. Thus, the committed workers of the Eco Friendly Centre eventually had to stop their experiment.

In the preceding, I have discussed the question as to how Neo-Gandhian voluntary workers pursue people's development. These *sarvodayis* have themselves conceptualized their struggle as one against the destruction of all, and in favor of the welfare of all.

In the present global ecumene, voluntary workers are engaged in a cosmopolitan struggle for meaning. Correspondingly, realizing their critical immersion in encompassing systems, Indian activists have begun to expand their particular struggles into universal ones. Commentators have, however, expressed their doubts as to the effectiveness of large issues. This is to say that universal action can imply the demise of crucial *specific* information, and rapport between cadres and commons.

Certain Indian voluntary workers' reluctance to think globally has its roots in their critique of globalization. Some refer to the term as a whole as colonialism. Yet, many are themselves highly globalized. Their severe appraisal, then, amounts to a rejection of particular processes of *mondialisation;* that is, those neo-liberal in nature. Other operations have actually proven to serve as vessels to facilitate struggles like *satyagraha.*

Accordingly, while questionably alleged to be aimed at the retrieval of the Indian civilization, contemporary Gandhians have rejected government's liberalization policies. They countervail this threat to *swaraj* by upholding the practice of *satyagraha.* As for the application of various other Gandhian interpretative repertoires, voluntary workers do not consense. For example, many pit Gandhi's doctrine of trusteeship against his principle of self-reliance. Moreover, some commentators deconstruct evocations of Gandhian interpretative repertoires as rather symbolic - that is, superficial - in nature.

Running somewhat parallel with the observance of ostensible superficiality, it seems that nowadays, most Indian voluntary workers do not draw on Gandhian interpretative repertoires in a dogmatic way. Many analysts have therefore ascribed these movement participants a Neo-Gandhian denomination. The approach to which it pertains can be traced back to the interbraiding of Gandhi-inspired activism with the hybrid modes of the new social movements.

A multiheaded swarm network, the National Alliance of People's Movements (NAPM) is constituted by pivotally Neo-Gandhian voluntary associations. Its affiliates have jointly formulated a number of principles of *jan vikas* or people's development. Among these postulates are people's control over natural resources and their inclusion in decision-making. Apart from NAPM constituents' drawing on Gandhian interpretative repertoires in the identification of the former view, the observation is the more justified as their emphasis on non-violence is concerned.

Crucially, voluntary workers associated with NAPM affiliates draw on Gandhian interpretative repertoires surrounding the observance of simplicity. This includes the ideals of sustainability, labor-intensiveness and decentralization. As for the essential application of the value to the ways of voluntary workers, cadres do not contend for power. Moreover, some participants even oppose internal institutionalization. Finally, their shared emphasis on scaling down cadres' lifestyle amounts to the Gandhi-inspired belief in identification with commons.

The Narmada Bachao Andolan, the Aazadi Bachao Andolan and the Bombay Sarvodaya Mandal are among the Neo-Gandhian voluntary associations which constitute the National Alliance of People's Movements. Using *satyagraha* as their primary modus operandi, participants in the Narmada Bachao Andolan aim at decentralization of power. Those involved in the Aazadi Bachao Andolan pursue *Real Swaraj,* while presenting *swadeshi* as the only alternative for neo-liberalism. Finally, workers in the Bombay Sarvodaya Mandal are concerned with Gandhi-inspired *Constructive Programmes.*

Daniel and other former volunteers in the Eco Friendly Centre share the focus on *Constructive Programmes* with their Bombay Sarvodaya Mandal hosts. Referring to himself as a Post-Gandhian, Daniel is very much inspired by Vinoba Bhave's vision of the Land Gift. He, additionally, outwardly agrees with Bhave in his contention that party politics are not suited to 'the Indian ethos'. For him, Gandhi was 'at the back of all philosophy', and the latter's *Hind Swaraj* is 'the Bible of India's freedom and freedom struggle'. In his ecological interpretation of these and other writings, a critique of chemical agriculture was in Gandhi's thinking. Following both Schumacher and Bhave in his *sarvodayi* endorsement of the 'small is beautiful' adage,

Daniel has set out 'to protect villages from the encroachments of big industries, big ideas of dams, big factories, big and big and big'.

Conclusions

In this paper, I have set out to answer the main question as to how Indian voluntary workers draw on Gandhian interpretative repertoires to formulate alternative concepts of development. By using the concept of interpretative repertoires, I have emphasized contextuality as evocations of discourses triggered by Gandhi are concerned. Indian voluntary workers are not only constituted by discourse, they also constitute their interpretative repertoires themselves, in specific situations.

Elaborating on Gandhian interpretative repertoires as constituting voluntary workers, a crucial characteristic of these resources is their relatively discontinuous nature. Gandhi presented his points of reference as epitomizing Indian/Eastern *civilization.* He pitted these terms against their supposed *Western* opposites. Thus, *swaraj* is antithetical to statism, *satyagraha* is antonymous to struggle and *sarvodaya* is incompatible with socialism.

While Gandhi never used the word *development,* because of its implications of evolution towards *Western modernity,* there is reason to assume that Gandhian interpretative repertoires pertain to modernization theory. In his political vocabulary, Gandhi endorsed the Enlightenment doctrines of human rights, egalitarianism and democracy. He applied these universal laws to his quest for social justice in the extremely hierarchic Indian society. Traditionalists therefore called him a destroyer of social harmony.

Similar to Gandhi's universalism, classical social theory takes for granted the constitution of civil society by modernist interpretative repertoires. Within classical positive perspectives on this societal realm, scholars view actors to either affirm or contest state projects. These theorists do not, however, consider it possible for participants to question the very universal legitimacy of the state.

While theories of social movements do take into account people's strategic action, they proceed from a similar determinism. First, behaviorists adhering to the resource mobilization approach acknowledge individuals' anti-establishment agency. Second, macro-sociologists view social actors' collectives as constituted by the allegedly objective class factor. The schools of thought these scholars relate to, assume determinative disintegration, volatile and structural in nature, respectively.

Similarly, unambiguous analysis of circumstances in which voluntary workers constitute specific themes, neglects the manifold nature of the Indian context. For example, in their ascription of instrumental-expressive functions to associations in the supposedly transitional Indian society, scholars overlook any paths other than development towards urban-industrialism.

Instead, there is a call for the recognition of interpretative repertoires' continuous nature, as they are constituted by voluntary workers. The new social movement theory, then, does acknowledge subjective dimensions of subalternity. Thus, Gandhi's concept of practical idealism is an emic view, worth considering in a conceptualization of Indian voluntary associations. As part of this model, workers continually pursue *truth* in the process of self-development.

Yet, in their evocations of Gandhian interpretative repertoires, some Indian voluntary workers seem to present these resources as discontinuities. Following Gandhi in his ostensible dichotomy of *swaraj* and statism, they see any central endeavor as a danger to maintain indigenization. Consequently, these *sarvodayis* disdain *globalization* as a whole, and are unwilling to partake in universal struggles.

However, many others have expanded their activism to embrace the global ecumene. While they reject *neo-liberal* globalization, these voluntary workers utilize the enormous potential of cosmopolitan communications to strengthen their counter-hegemonic pursuit. Thus, these activists have widened the action radius of their variously negotiated Gandhian evocations.

Indeed, aimed at people's development, many Indian voluntary workers have renounced dogmatic approaches to Gandhian interpretative repertoires. Hence, the Neo-Gandhian denomination to which their hybrid resources pertain, encompasses the new social movement perspective. It is exemplified by the National Alliance of People's Movements.

Voluntary workers affiliated with NAPM constituents have formulated several principles of *jan vikas*. Gandhi-inspired simplicity is one of the core values they observe. This crucially amounts to scaling down their lifestyles, in order to identify with commons. Additionally, as part of their genuine reluctance to appropriate power, some volunteers even oppose internal institutionalization.

Clearly, Daniel concurs with several of the principles of *jan vikas*. It follows from his contribution, that some Indians voluntary workers nowadays invest *swadeshi* with ecologist meaning. Running parallel with this observation, strands of Neo-Gandhian repertoires can be characterized as resources Indian voluntary workers draw on in their localized global struggle, in which they combine social justice and ecology.

Daniel - like the theorist Ananta Kumar Giri and AID voluntary workers - stresses the need for volunteers to reflect on their lifestyles. The concern with simplicity on their own part clearly transcends the otherizing depiction of people with whom they work as the simple-living human communities or the beneficiaries, as in the bulk of *development* theory and practice. It is crucial for voluntary workers to take action and to empower people to do so, in order to further the struggle against globalization/ liberalization policies. Yet, in order to further people's development, volunteers are to take it to encompass self-development. Thus, to quote Daniel, there is a need for 'a sort of neighbourliness [as] the spirit of life style, and not depending on big ideas of development'.

REFERENCES

Anderson, B. (2003) [1991] *Imagined Communities: Reflections on the Origin and Spread of Nationalism.* London: Verso. Bakshi, R. (1996) '"Development, Not Destruction": Alternative Politics in the Making', *Economic and Political Weekly,* 5 (31): 255-6.

Breukelen, D. van (2005) 'Dorpsbewoners Mehediganj Strijden tegen Multinational', *India Nu,* 155/156: 26-8.

Dadage, M.S. (1998) 'Gandhi's Concept of Voluntary Organization', in: J. Pandey (ed.) (1998) *Gandhi and Voluntary Organizations.* New Delhi: M.D. Publications, p. 1-9.

Fox, R.G. (1998) *Gandhian Utopia: Experiments with Culture.* Boston: Beacon Press. Fuchs, M. & A. Linkenbach (2003) 'Social Movements', in: V. Das (ed.) *The Oxford India Companion to Sociology and Social Anthropology.* New Delhi: Oxford University Press, p. 1524-63.

Gandhi, M.K. (1909) 'Hind Swaraj', in: M.K. Gandhi (ed.) *Gandhi* (10). Delhi: Publications Division, Ministry of Information and Broadcasting, Government of India, p. 245-312.

Gandhi, M.K. (1925) 'Meaning of Bolshevism', in: M.K. Gandhi (ed.) *The Collected Works of Mahatma Gandhi* (30). Delhi: Publications Division, Ministry of Information and Broadcasting, Government of India, p. 35.

Gandhi, M.K. (1927) An *Autobiography, or, The Story of* My *Experiments with Truth.* Ahmedabad: Navajivan Publishing House.

Gandhi, M.K. (1931) 'Letter to Nirmala Desai', in: M.K. Gandhi (ed.) *The Collected Works of Mahatma Gandhi* (51). Delhi: Publications Division, Ministry of Information and Broadcasting, Government of India, p. 55.

Gandhi, M.K. (1945) 'Letter to Jatindas Amin', in: M.K. Gandhi (ed.) *The Collected Works of Mahatma Gandhi* (89). Delhi: Publications Division, Ministry of Information and Broadcasting, Government of India, p. 2-3.

Gandhi, M.K. (1947) 'Socialism', in: M.K. Gandhi (ed.) *The Collected Works of Mahatma Gandhi* (96). Delhi: Publications Division, Ministry of Information and Broadcasting, Government of India, p. 37-8.

Gandhi, M.K. & B. Kumarappa (eds) (1969) *Sarvodaya: The Welfare of All.* Ahmedabad: Navajivan Publishing House.

Gandhi, R. (1995) '"Hind Swaraj"', in: *The Good Boatman: A Portrait of Gandhi.* New Delhi: Viking, p. 139-65.

Giri, A.K. (2002) *Building in the Margins of Shacks: The Vision and Projects of Habitat for Humanity.* New Delhi: Orient Longman.

Giri, A.K. (2005) *Reflections and Mobilizations: Dialogues with Movements and Voluntary Organizations.* New Delhi: Sage Publications.

Hannerz, U. (1993) 'Mediations in the Global Ecumene', in: G. Pálsson (ed.) *Beyond Boundaries: Understanding, Translation and Anthropological Discourse.*

Hardiman, D. (2003) *Gandhi in His Time and Ours.* Delhi: Permanent Black.

Harris, I.C. (1998) *Gandhians in Contemporary India: The Vision and the Visionaries.* Lewiston: Edwin Mellen Press.

Jena, S.C. (1998) 'Social Work and Rural Reconstruction in Gandhian Philosophy', in: J. Pandey (ed.) (1998) *Gandhi and Voluntary Organizations.* New Delhi: M.D. Publications, p. 61-7.

Kar, B. (1998) 'The Gandhian Approach on Individuality and Social Change. Pandey (ed.) (1998) *Gandhi and Voluntary Organizations.* New Delhi: M.D. Publications, p. 107-11.

Krishnamurti, J. 1996 [1929] 'Truth Is a Pathless Land', in: M. Cadogan c.s. (eds) (1996) *Total Freedom — The Essential Krishnamurti.* New York: HarperCollins, p. 1-7.

Kumar, V. (1998) 'Community Action Groups - The Gandhian Concept and the Indian Reality', in: J. Pandey (ed.) (1998)

Gandhi and Voluntary Organizations. New Delhi: M.D. Publications, p. 69-78.

Middelaar, L. (2002) 'On Logos and Grassroots: The Anti-Globalisation Movement Between Morals, Economics and Politics'.

Multinational Monitor (1997) 'Against Globalization - And For Power to the People: An Interview with Medha Patkar', *Multinational Monitor,* 11 (18).

Oommen, T.K. (1995) 'The Theory of Voluntary Associations in a Cross-Cultural Perspective', in: T.K. Oommen (ed.) *Alien Concepts and South Asian Reality: Responses and Reformulations.* New Delhi: Sage Publications, p. 76-89.

Pantham, T. (1995) 'Gandhi: *Swaraj, Sarvodaya* and *Satyagraha',* in: T. Pantham (ed.) *Political Theories and Social Reconstruction: A Critical Survey of the Literature on India.* New Delhi: Sage Publications, p. 102-25.

Philips, L. & M.W. Jørgensen (2002) *Discourse Analysis as Theory and Method.* London: Sage Publications. Quarles van Ufford, Ph. & M. Schoffeleers (1988) 'Towards a Rapprochement of Anthropology and Development Studies', in: Ph. Quarles van Ufford & M. Schoffeleers (eds) *Religion & Development: Towards an Integrated Approach.* Amsterdam: Free University Press, p. 1-30.

Ronfeldt, D. & Arquilla, J. (2001) *Networks and Netwars: The Future of Terror, Crime, and Militancy.* Santa Monica: Rand.

Roy, A. (1999) *The Greater Common Good.* Bombay: India Book Distributors.

Rudolph, L.I. & S.H. Rudolph (1969) [1967] *The Modernity of Tradition: Political Development in India.* Chicago: University of Chicago Press. Sen, S. (1993) 'Defining the Nonprofit Sector: India' (L.M. Salamon & H.K. Anheier (eds) *Working Papers of the Johns Hopkins Comparative Nonprofit Sector Project,* 12). Baltimore: The Johns Hopkins Institute for Policy Studies.

Shiva, V. (1999) 'Reversing Globalisation: What Gandhi Can Teach Us', *The Ecologist,* 3 (29): 224-5.

Solomon, R.C. & K.M. Higgins (1999) [1996] *Een Andere Geschiedenis van de Filosofie.* Kapellen: Uitgeverij

Pelckmans (Dutch translation of 'A Short History of Philosophy', Oxford, Oxford University Press).

Somjee, A.H. (1998) 'India: A Challenge to Western Theories of Development', in: J. Wiarda (ed.) *Non-western Theories of Development: Regional Norms Versus Global Trends*. Fort Worth: Harcourt Brace Co'lege, p. 44-63.

Suhrud, T. (2005) 'Dandi March and Gandhi's Politics', *Economic and Political Weekly,* 15 (40): 1491-2. Uberoi, J.P.S. (2003) 'Civil Society', in: V. Das (ed.) *The Oxford India Companion to Sociology and Social Anthropology*. New Delhi: Oxford University Press, p. 114-33.

Woude, J.R. van der (1996) *Think Globally, Act Locally: A Study of the Gandhian Elements in the Contemporary Ecology Movements in Uttarakhand.* Amsterdam: Free University.

13

Gandhi as a Peace Maker

On a cold night over a hundred years ago in Maritzburg, South Africa, Mohandas K. Gandhi was thrown off a train when he refused to move from his first-class seat. Gandhi's presence in that seat offended a white passenger because it was not appropriate for a "coloured person" to travel first class. This discrimination was a defining moment in Gandhi's life as it led him to develop the resolve needed to remove the injustice of color prejudice that was pervasive in South Africa at that time.

Over the next five decades Gandhi became a peacebuilder. He developed and tested methods that produced political change and reduced social injustices. Gandhi's teachings and actions had a profound effect on those around him, his country, and, in many respects, the world. In this chapter, I will outline the philosophy of Gandhi and the actions he used and advocated to estab-lish social justice. Following this, I will outline the psychological dynamics that contributed to making his peacebuilding efforts effective.

The Goal and Principles Guiding Gandhi's Actions

Gandhi's overarching goal throughout his life was *sarvodaya* which translates to "the welfare of all" or "uplift of all". To achieve this goal, three main principles guided his writings and actions. The Indian terms describing these principles are *satya* (truth), *ahimsa* (nonviolence), and *tapasya* (selfsuffering).

Satya or Truth

Satyagraha, as discussed and used by Gandhi, can be understood on at least two levels. First, it refers to the process of developing an understanding of any situation and the points of view of all individuals who are involved with it. *Satyagraha,* which can be translated to mean "Soul Force," serves in this regard as a process to vindicate the truth. In trying to understand the validity of each viewpoint, Gandhi was well aware of his limitations and those of any human being trying to establish absolute truth. Given these limitations, he believed we can never be sure if we, as one side of a conflict, are correct in our position or if our adversaries, on the other side of a conflict, have truth on their side. Therefore, while Gandhi viewed the pursuit of truth as an ongoing aspect of life which was never fully achievable in a complete sense, *satyagraha* was an important orien-tation to maintain on an individual level.

The second interpretation for the term *satyagraha* is as a positive peacebuilding strategy on a larger societal level; here, *satyagraha* is a process of civil disobedience or nonviolent resistance. It is *satyagraha* in this second sense which helped India attain independence from Great Britain and which had a profound impact on other peacebuilders such as Martin Luther King, Jr. Later in this chapter, I will describe the characteristics of a *satyagraha* movement from this perspective, and then I will provide a concrete example, the Salt *Satyagraha* campaign of 1930 to 1931. However, to fully understand the *satyagraha* method, a close look at two other principles in Gandhi's philosophy is essential.

Ahimsa or Nonviolence

An integral part of Gandhi's philosophy and life's work is the notion of *ahimsa,* which literally means "non-injury" or "nonviolence." For Gandhi, *ahimsa* was the belief in the sacredness of life and the refusal to do harm to living things, an interpretation that was based on the deep-rooted Hindu tradition of not doing harm.

Ahimsa was vital to Gandhi's peacebuilding efforts for several reasons. First, *ahimsa* means not harming others either in thought or deed. Second, Gandhi viewed *ahimsa* as also having a more dynamic and positive state which is love. Pelton describes this love as active goodwill and it also bears similarity to the Rogerian concept of unconditional positive regard. This love serves as the means to get to the ends of truth. Third, a means which uses non-violence to reveal truth has advantages to Gandhi because only relative truth can be attained for certain. Given this human limitation, the nonviolent means to realize one's goal guarantees that individuals will not hurt any adversary in a conflict who might be closer to the absolute truth than they themselves are. Excluding the use of violence is best, because humans are not capable of knowing the absolute truth and therefore are not competent to punish.

Throughout his life, Gandhi insisted that the means to get to any goal must be carefully se-lected or the attainment of the goal might be short-lived or ultimately subverted. For instance, he wanted to obtain India's independence using nonviolent means while others advocated violent rebellion. Gandhi believed the leaders who would emerge if India followed the violent path to independence would be just as tyrannical as the British leadership which they would replace. Therefore, the end result of independence would have very little impact on the common citizen of India and would not be as desirable as the leadership which would emerge if the principle of *ahimsa* was followed in the struggle for independence.

Tapasya or Self-Suffering

Tapasya translates to "self-suffering" and is the third major principle in Gandhi's belief system. Gandhi viewed self-suffering as a viable maneuver to confront the violence that is often leveled at those who work to remove social injustices. The willingness to endure suffering instead of re-taliating for a violent act with a violent act breaks the cycle of violence. While those fighting so-cial injustices might suffer more than those who work to maintain the status quo, Gandhi be-lieved that in the long run the world as a whole will witness less total violence.

The ability to engage in self-suffering requires considerable courage and self-control. In fact, Gandhi describes the self-discipline required of someone who follows his principles as being akin to those of a military soldier. Like soldiers, individuals who practice *tapasya* require exten-sive training to establish the needed discipline when violence is leveled at them.

Gandhi's Value System

Human values are transsituational goals which vary in importance and serve as guiding princi-ples in people's lives (Schwartz, 1992, 1994). An analysis of the value system of an individual can help explain the actions of an individual in a range of social and political situations. Schwartz (1994) has identified ten value types which have implications for understanding political orientation and political action. Closely examining the goals and princi-ples which Gandhi considered important can shed some light on his actions.

Based on the goals and principles of Gandhi, outlined above, his values seem to fall into three of the value types identified by Schwartz. The notion of the welfare of all *(sarvo-daya)* and the concern about truth and wisdom *(satya)* directly corresponds to the two self-transcendent value types of universalism and benevolence. The emphasis placed on self-discipline corresponds to the value type of conformity as defined by Schwartz. This is consistent with the research of Mayton, Diessner, and Granby, who found that individuals with pre-dispositions to nonviolent behavior placed more emphasis on universalism, benevolence, and conformity values than individuals more predisposed to violence.

Satyagraha is a method whereby grievances could successfully challenge an established political order. Bondurant (1965) has outlined the steps of a typical *satyagraha* movement, which is an activity of civil disobedience designed to confront unjust laws and policies. It would start with an effort to resolve the conflict through established channels and accepted protocol. Should these methods prove ineffective, systematic planning for the group to take direct action would begin. Following an active propaganda campaign involving demonstrations, parades, etc., a final strong appeal or ultimatum to one's opponent would be made which would explain the steps that will be undertaken if no agreement can be reached. Depending on the nature of the grievances and the specific situation, the subsequent actions taken may involve boycotts, strikes, and other forms of noncooperation such as nonpayment of taxes. Those who take part in the movement are called *satyagrahi.*

The Salt Satyagraha

The Salt *Satyagraha* was a national movement throughout India that began early in 1930 and lasted for over a year (Bondurant, 1965). Its immediate goal was the removal of the salt tax which exploited the peasants and symbolized the unjust nature of British rule. The Salt Act made it a crime to possess salt not purchased by the British salt monopoly .

Following the initial planning of the specific actions, Gandhi sent a letter to the Viceroy de-scribing the grievances regarding the Salt Act and indicating the specific nature of the plan for civil disobedience. When this ultimatum was ignored, Gandhi and other *satyagrahis* began their historic march to the sea. Careful planning and the training of the *satyagrahis* in self-restraint and crowd control made this a peaceful event. The march took over three weeks and was widely covered in the press, making the injustice of British rule known throughout the world. Shortly after arriving at the beach, Gandhi purposely broke the law outlined in the Salt Act by making salt. With his act he opened the door for others to engage in the same type of civil disobedience. Estimates of the number of Indians jailed for breaking the Salt Act exceed sixty thousand (Fischer, 1954). As the salt tax was still in place, additional levels of civil disobedience were planned and executed.

In a second letter to the Viceroy, Gandhi explained how the *satyagrahis* would demand pos-session of the Dharsana salt works. While this letter led to Gandhi's arrest, the march on the salt works still took place. 'Over two thousand *satyagrahis* took part in the nonviolent raid on the salt works. The leaders of the Salt *Satyagraha* admonished the *satyagrahis* to not resist nor raise a hand even to ward off the inevitable blows from the police. Webb Miller, a journalist for United Press, witnessed the raid and reported

In complete silence the Gandhi men drew up and halted a hundred yards from the stockade. A picked column advanced from the crowd, waded the ditches, and ap-proached the barbed-wire stockade. Suddenly, at a word of command, scores of native policemen rushed upon the advancing marchers and rained blows upon their heads with their steel-shod lathis. Not one of the marchers even raised an arm to fend off the blows. They went down like ten-pins. From where I stood I heard the sickening whack of the clubs on unprotected skulls. The waiting crowd of marchers groaned and sucked in their breath in sympathetic pain at every blow. Those struck down fell sprawling, unconscious or writhing with fractured pain or broken shoulders. Although everyone knew that within a few minutes he would be beaten down, perhaps killed, I could detect no sign of wavering or fear. They marched steadily, with heads up, without the encouragement of music or cheering or any possibility that they might escape injury or death. .There was no fight, no struggle, the marchers simply walked forward until struck down.

The raids and the carnage continued for days with stretcher bearers carrying bleeding men to the first aid station.

While the raids on the salt works ended with the approaching monsoons, civil disobedience continued in the form of boycotts and intentional acts that broke unjust laws and ordinances (Bondurant, 1965). Eventually, the salt regulations were modified in ways which removed much of the injustice forced on the poor. The impact of the thousands of localized campaigns which were part of the Salt *Satyagraha* had been successful in following the guidelines for a *satya-graha* and were effective in reaching the immediate goal.

Gandhi implemented *satyagraha* successfully in many contexts (Gandhi, 1951, 1957/ 1927). In his "experiments with truth" Gandhi field-tested and applied numerous psychological constructs in very effective ways. How can we explain the success of this method Gandhi called a *satya-graha?* The next sections of this chapter will draw on research and theory in social psychology in an attempt to explain the positive outcomes *of satyagraha.*

Attribution Theory

From Gandhi's point of view the goal of *satyagraha* was to awaken the conscience of the oppo-nent (Nakhre, 1982). Social psychologists have observed that people make attributions or try to determine the causes of their own and other people's behavior all the time (e.g. Brehm, Kassin, & Fein, 1999). According to attribution theory, when we try to understand why others are behav-ing the way they are, we often focus on the situation. However, when their behavior is vastly dif-ferent from what we would expect of people in their situation, then our tendency is to attribute their behavior to their disposition. We learn a lot about people's disposition when their behavior deviates markedly from our expectation. Ordinarily, we would expect the *satyagrahis* to respond violently to the violence of the British. Because the *satyagrahis'* nonvio-lent behavior deviates from the norm or what we would expect of people in their situation, we are likely to attribute their nonviolence to the disposition of Gandhi and his fellow Indians.

Not only were the peaceful *satyagrahis* viewed favorably according to world opinion, but there were additional psychological dynamics that could have influenced the British to focus on the unjust nature of the Salt Acts. Social psychologists have identified a set of biases and errors that people make in looking for causes of behavior. The *self-serving bias* involves the tendency of people to take less credit for failures than they do for their successes. When the *satyagrahis* provoked the British to enforce the unjust law and to engage in violent action, self-serving attri-butional biases would predict the British would continue to view themselves favorably by attrib-uting their violent actions to external situational factors. Therefore, instead of denigrating them-selves for inflicting pain on the Indians who had positive dispositional characteristics, they would attribute their violent behavior to the external situation and focus on the law that required them to commit acts which were unjust. With each additional aspect of the Salt *Satyagraha* as well as subsequent acts of civil disobedience, which were nonviolent, the self-attributions of be-ing on the moral high ground gave way to the focus on the socially unjustice policies created by the British. Fischer (1954) characterized the effects of the Salt *Satyagraha* in a manner consistent with this attributional interpretation when he said "it made the British aware that they were sub-jugating India".

Attitude Change Variables

Gandhi succeeded in getting support for his efforts from the Indian people as well as the world community. Gandhi capitalized on many of the factors identified as efficacious by researchers of persuasive communication. In particular, three factors that are found in models of persuasive communication are noteworthy.

First, Gandhi's *charismatic leadership* clearly worked in his favor. Gandhi spent considerable time traveling around India observing and listening to the concerns of the common citizen. Sub-sequently, he was able to address issues of significance in succinct ways that could be easily un-derstood. Gandhi had a message of independence for

India and the removal of social injustices, which were inspirational to nearly all Indians.

A second source characteristic of the communication model of persuasion which helped Gandhi was his *similarity* with the common people of India. He dressed and lived in the manner of an Indian peasant which made him a positive role model. He was very knowledgeable about diverse religious beliefs present in India and abroad and used this knowledge to express his non-violence in terms of Hindu, Moslem, and Christian doctrine. From the Bhagavad-Gita, to the Ko-ran, to the "Sermon on the Mount" in the Bible, Gandhi was comfortable with many different audiences. His use of traditional terms to explain his procedures and concerns increased the sup-port he received.

Third, Gandhi engaged people in his thoughtful analysis of social injustice. Petty & Cacioppo (1986) have developed the elaboration likelihood model. This model proposes that the central route to persuasion, which engages the person being persuaded in serious thought to the relevant points, results in more long term attitude change than the peripheral route, which appeals to emo-tion and results in lower cognitive engagement. Gandhi's efforts utilized the central route to per-suasion in several ways. Because *satyagraha* was so different from what people expected, the focus on the content of the message was enhanced and thus more serious thought was given to the message and a more enduring change was a result.

Negotiation Methods

Gandhi's way of dealing with the British utilized behaviors which foreshadowed the method of principled negotiation discussed by Fisher, Ury, and Patton (1991). The notions of separating the people from the problem and focusing on interests and not positions, are mainstays of principled negotiation (Fisher, Ury, & Patton, 1991). In separating the people from the problem, Gandhi was quick to remind his *satyagrahis* to distinguish the unjust laws from those who enforced them, and when harm did befall any of the British he was deeply troubled by it. Gandhi harbored no animosity toward any British individual and, on the contrary, his compassion for the hardship his actions had on the British were very genuine (Fischer, 1954). The outcome of the Salt *Satya-graha* serves as a good example of how Gandhi focused on interests of all parties instead of dig-ging in and holding onto a position. While the initially stated objective was the repeal of the Salt Act, when the British agreed to modify the salt regulations so that much of the injustice forced on the poor ended, he modified his position and accepted their proposal as it satisfied the inter-ests of this *satyagraha* (Bondurant, 1965).

Psychological Lessons from Gandhi

From the time he was thrown off the train in South Africa until he fell from an assassin's bullet in India, Gandhi acted to rid his country of social injustice. His peacebuilding efforts were strongly based on self-transcendent values combined with a commitment to principle which re-flected a conservative value emphasis. The search for truth combined with tolerance and self dis-cipline made him an ethical model who many wanted to emulate. He utilized good communication with his allies and his opponents at the interpersonal level as well as via the written word. Gandhi never lost sight of the fact that all were humans cut from the same cloth by God, and gave unconditional positive regard to all. He was an applied social scientist who used some very effective psychological principles to reach his goals.

Bibliography

Ahluwalia, B. K., 1938, *Rajaji and Gandhi,* 1st ed., New Delhi : Allora, 1978.

Ahmad, Razi, *Indian Peasant Movement and Mahatma Gandhi*, Delhi : Shabd Prakashan, 1987.

Alter, Joseph S., *Gandhi's Body: Sex, Diet, and the Politics of Nationalism*, Philadelphia : University of Pennsylvania Press, c2000.

Bakshi, S. R. (Shiri Ram), 1935, *Gandhi and Champaran Satyagraha*, 1st ed., Delhi : Akashdeep Pub. House, 1988.

Bakshi, S. R. (Shiri Ram), 1935, *Gandhi and Civil Disobedience Movement,* New Delhi : Gitanjali Pub. House, c1985.

Birala, Ghana'syamadasa, 1894-1983, *Bapu, A Unique Association,* Bombay : Bharatiya Vidya Bhavan, 1977.

Bondurant, Joan V. (Joan Valérie), 1918, *Conquest of Violence; The Gandhian Philosophy of Conflict,* Rev. ed., Berkeley, University of California Press, 1965.

Borman, William, 1948, *Gandhi and Non-Violence,* Albany, N.Y. : State University of New York Press, c1986.

Bose, Anima, 1932, *Mahatma Gandhi: A Contemporary Perspective,* Delhi : B.R. Pub. Corp. ; New Delhi : distributed by D.K. Publishers' Distributors, 1977.

Cenkner, William, 1930, *The Hindu Personality in Education: Tagore, Gandhi, Aurobindo,* Columbia, Mo. : South Asia Books, 1976.

Chadha, Yogesh, *Rediscovering Gandhi,* London : Century, 1997.

Cheney, Glenn Alan, *Mohandas Gandhi,* New York : F. Watts, 1983.

Clément, Catherine, 1939-, *Gandhi, the Power of Pacifism,* New York : H.N. Abrams, [c1996].

Clément, Catherine, 1939-, *Gandhi: Father of a Nation,* London : Thames and Hudson, c1996.

Copley, A.R.H. (Antony R.H.), 1937, *Gandhi: Against the Tide,* Oxford [Oxfordshire]; New York, NY : Blackwell, 1986.

Dalala, Candulala Bhagubhai, 1899, *Gandhi: 1915-1948; A Detailed Chronology,* 1st ed., New Delhi, Gandhi Peace Foundation [1971]

Dalton, Dennis, *Indian Idea of Freedom: Political Thought of Swami Vivekananda, Aurobindo Ghose, Mahatma Gandhi and Rabindranath Tagore,* Gurgaon, Haryana, India : Academic Press, 1982.

Dalton, Dennis, *Mahatma Gandhi: Nonviolent Power in Action,* New York : Columbia University Press, 1993.

Dandavate, Madhu, 1924, *Marx and Gandhi,* Bombay : Popular Prakashan, c1977.

DeLuca, Anthony R., *Gandhi, Mao, Mandela, and Gorbachev: Studies in Personality, Power, and Politics,* Westport, Ct. : Praeger, 2000.

Desai, Mahadev H. (Mahadev Haribhai), 1892-1942, *The Epic of Travancore,* Ahmedabad Navajivan Karyalaya [1937]

Dhanagre, D.N. 1936, *Agrarian Movements and Gandhian Politics*, Agra : Institute of Social Sciences, Agra University, 1975.

Dikshita, Gopinatha, 1907, *Gandhi's Challenge to Communism,* New Delhi, S. Chand [1972]

Documents of Non-cooperation Movement, 1st ed. Delhi : Akashdeep Pub. House, 1989.

Dutt, Shib Chandra, *Conflicting Tendencies in Indian Economic Thought,* Calcutta, N. M. Ray-Chowdhury & co., 1934.

Easwaran, Eknath, *Gandhi, the Man: The Story of his Transformation,* 3rd ed. Tomales, Calif. : Nilgiri Press, 1997.

Eaton, Jeanette, *Gandhi, Fighter Without a Sword,* New York, Morrow, 1950.

Edwardes, Michael, *The Myth of the Mahatma : Gandhi, the British and the Raj,* London : Constable, 1986.

Erikson, Erik H. (Erik Homburger), 1902, *Ghandi's Truth on the Origins of Militant Nonviolence,* 1st ed., New York, Norton [1969].

Gandhiji and Village: Papers Presented at the Seminar Held Under the Auspices of the Department of Sociology, University of Jodhpur, on October 2-3, 1980/New Delhi : Agricole, 1981.

Ganguli, Birendranath, *Gandhiji's Vision of Ideal Social Order,* Hyderabad [India] : Andhra Mahila Sabha, [pref. 1972]

Gardner, Howard, *Extraordinary Minds: Portraits of Exceptional Individuals and an Examination of our Extraordinariness,* 1st ed. New York : BasicBooks, c1997.

Gaur, V. P., *Mahatma Gandhi: a Study of his Message of Non-Violence,* New Delhi : Sterling Publishers, c1977.

George, P. V., *The Unique Christ and the Mystic Gandhi,* Tiruvalla, Travancore, S. India : Malabar Christian Office, [1934].

Ghosh, Indu Mala, 1947, *Ahimsa, Buddhist and Gandhian,* Delhi, India : Indian Bibliographies Bureau : Balaji Enterprises, 1988.

Gregg, Richard Bartlett, 1885, *The Psychology and Strategy of Gandhi's Nonviolent Resistance,* by Richard B. Gregg. With a new introd. for the Garland ed. by Charles A. Barker. New York Garland Pub. 1972

Grenier, Richard, 1926, *The Gandhi Nobody Knows,* Nashville : T. Nelson Publishers, c1983.

Guha, Ramachandra, *An Anthropologist Among the Marxists and Other Essays,* Delhi : Permanent Black ; Bangalore : Distributed by Orient Longman, 2001.

Guha, Samar, *The Mahatma and the Netaji: Two men of Destiny of India,* New Delhi : Sterling Publishers, c1986.

Gupta, Manmath Nath, *Gandhi and his Times,* 1st ed., New Delhi : Lipi Prakashan, 1982.

Gupta, S. P.K. (Sikharam Prasanna Kumara), 1931, *Apostle John and Gandhi: The Mission of John Haynes Holmes for Mahatma Gandhi in the United States of America,* 1st ed. Ahmedabad, India : Navajivan Pub. House, 1988.

Gupta, Sunil Kumar, *Gandhi-Jawaharlal Confluence,* 1st ed. New Delhi : Oriental Publishers & Distributors, 1976.

Hari Singh, 1937, *Gandhi, Rowlatt Satyagraha, and British Imperialism: Emergence of Mass Movements in Punjab & Delhi,* Delhi : Indian Bibliographies Bureau, c1990.

Horsburgh, H. J. N., *Non-violence and Aggression: a Study of Gandhi's Moral Equivalent of war,* London, New York [etc.] Oxford U.P., 1968.

Hutchins, Francis G., *India's Revolution; Gandhi and the Quit India Movement,* Cambridge : Harvard University Press, 1973.

Huttenback, Robert A., *Gandhi in South Africa; British Imperialism and the Indian Question,* 1860-1914, Ithaca [N.Y.] Cornell University Press [1971]

India Office Library and Records, *Gandhi and Civil Disobedience: Documents in the India Office Records, 1922-1946,* London : India Office Library and Records, 1980.

India, the Brightest Jewel [videorecording]/[London, Eng.] : BBC TV; Richmond, B.C. : PEMC [distributor], 1977.

Jain, Vidya, *M.K. Gandhi, Leader of the Masses,* New Delhi : Deep & Deep Publications, c1995.

Jha, D.C., 1926, *Mahatma Gandhi, the Congress, and the Partition of India,* New Delhi : Sanchar Pub. House, 1995.

Jones, E. Stanley (Eli Stanley), 1884-1973, *Mahatma Gandhi : an Interpretation,* New York : Abingdon-Cokesbury Press, 1948.

Juneja, M. M., 1945, *The Mahatma & the Millionaire: a Study in Gandhi-Birla Relations,* Hisar, Haryana, India : Modern Publishers, 1993.

Kasturi, Bhashyam, *Walking Alone: Gandhi and India's Partition,* New Delhi : Vision Books, 1999.

Kumar, Chandra, *Mahatma Gandhi: His Life and Influence,* London [England] : Heinemann, 1982.

Kytle, Calvin, *Gandhi, Soldier of Nonviolence: An Introduction,* Rev. ed., Cabin John, Md. : Seven Locks Press ; New York, NY : Distribution, Everest House, c1982.

Kytle, Calvin, *Gandhi, Soldier of Nonviolence: His Effect on India and the World Today,* New York : Grosset & Dunlap, [1969].

Lewis, Martin Deming, 1924, *Gandhi: Maker of Modern India?,* Boston : Heath [1965]

Leys, Wayne Albert Risser, *Gandhi and America's Educational Future,* Carbondale : Southern Illinois University Press, [1969].

Limaye, Madhu, *Mahatma Gandhi and Jawaharlal Nehru, a Historical Partnership, 1916-1948,* Delhi : B.R. Pub. Corp. ; New Delhi : Sales office, D.K. Publishers Distributors, 1989-1991.

Mahadevan, T. K., *Dvija: A Prophet Unheard,* New Delhi : Affiliated East-West Press, c1977.

Mahadevan, Thopil Krishnan, 1919, *Gandhi, My Refrain; Controversial Essays, 1950-1972,* 1st ed., Bombay: Popular Prakashan, [1973].

Mahatma Gandhi [videorecording] Falls Church, Va. : Landmark Media; Scarborough : Omega Films Ltd.[distributor], 1995

Mahatma Gandhi 125 years: Remembering Gandhi, Understanding Gandhi, Relevance of Gandhi, New Delhi : Indian Council for Cultural Relations & New Age International Publishers, c1995.

Mahatma Gandhi and the Indian National Congress: Studies in Gandhi's Contribution to the Development of the Indian National Congress, 1st ed. Chandigarh : Publication Bureau, Panjab University, 1988.

Mahatma Gandhi as Germans see him, Bombay, Shakuntala Pub. House [1969].

Malhotra, S.L., *From Civil Disobedience to Quit India: Gandhi and the Freedom Movement in Punjab and Haryana, 1932-1942,* 1st ed.,- Chandigarh : Publication Bureau, Panjab University, 1979.

Malkani, Naraindas Rattanmal, 1890, *Ramblings & Reminiscences of Gandhiji,* by N. R. Malkani., 1st ed., Ahmedabad : Navajivan Pub. House, [1972]

Mallac, Guy de, 1936, *Nonviolent Strategies for Today: a Handbook,* Gandhigram, Tamilnadu, India : Gandhigram Rural Institute, 1989.

Mathur, D.B., 1932, *Gandhi, Congress, and Apartheid,* Jaipur : Aalekh Publishers, 1986.

Mathur, D.B., 1932, *Prefacing Gandhi,* Jaipur : R.B.S.A. Publishers, c1988.

Maurer, Herrymon, 1914, *Great Soul,* Bombay Orient Longmans on behalf of Gandhi Peace Foundation [1969].

McLaughlin, Elizabeth T., 1923, *Ruskin and Gandhi,* Lewisburg [Pa.] : Bucknell University Press, [1974].

The Meanings of Gandhi, 1st ed., Honolulu : University Press of Hawaii, [c1971].

Mehendale, M.S., 1928, *Gandhi Looks at Leprosy,* 1st ed., Bombay : Bharatiya Vidya Bhavan, 1971.

Mehta, Ved, 1934, *Mahatma Gandhi and his Apostles,* New York : Viking Press, 1977, c1976.

Mudiraj, C.E., 1915, *Revive Gandhism and Save Democracy,* by C.E. Mudiraj. [1st ed.] [Hyderabad, A.P.] [1969].

Mukerjee, Hirendranath, 1907-, *Gandhiji; a Study,* 2d rev. ed., [New Delhi] People's Pub. House [1960]

Munshi, Kanaiyalal Maneklal, 1887-1971, *Gandhi: the Master,* Delhi, Rajkamal Publications [1948].

Muthanna, I.M., *Mother Besant and Mahatma Gandhi,* Vellore, Tamil Nadu : Thenpulam, 1986.

Muzumdar, Ammu Menon, *Social Welfare in India; Mahatma Gandhi's Contributions,* London, Asia Pub. House [1964].

Muzumdar, Haridas Thakordas, *Mahatma Gandhi, Peaceful Revolutionary,* New York : Scribner, 1952.

Nagaraja Rao, P., 1910, *Mahatma Gandhi; Centenary Lectures,* Patiala, Guru Gobind Singh Dept. of Religious Studies, Punjabi University [1972].

Naidu, Ch. M., 1939, *Salt Satyagraha in the Coastal Andhra,* Delhi, India : Mittal Publications, 1986.

Nair, Pyarelal, *Mahatma Gandhi,* Ahmedabad : Navajivan, 1965.

Nair, Pyarelal, *Mahatma Gandhi; the Last Phase*, 2d. ed., Ahmedabad Navajivan Pub. House [1965].

Namboodiripad, E.M.S. 1909, *The Mahatma and the Ism,* New Delhi People's Pub. House [1959].

Nanda, B.R. (Bal Ram), 1917, *In Search of Gandhi: Essays and Reflections,* New Delhi ; New York : Oxford University Press, 2002.

Nanda, Bal Ram, *Gandhi and his Critics,* Delhi ; New York : Oxford University Press, 1985.

Nanda, Bal Ram, *Gandhi : Pan-Islamism, Imperialism, and Nationalism in India,* Bombay ; New York : Oxford University Press, 1989.

Nanda, Bal Ram, *Mahatma Gandhi; a Biography,* London, Allen & Unwin [1959, c1958].

Nanda, Bala Ram, 1917, *Gandhi; a Pictorial Biography,* [New Delhi] Publications Division [Ministry of Information and Broadcasting] [1972].

Narain, Jai, *Gandhi's View of Political Power,* New Delhi : Deep & Deep Publications, c1987.

Naravane, Vishwanath S., *The Saint and the Singer: Rreflections on Gandhi and Tagore,* Allahabad : V.S. Naravane : Distributors in India, Lokbharti, 1995.

Nehru, Jawaharlal, 1889-1964, *Nehru on Gandhi; a Selection, Arranged in the Order of Events, From the Writings and Speeches of Jawaharlal Nehru,* New York, J. Day Co [1948].

Owen, Hugh, 1933, *Gandhi,* St. Lucia [Qld.] : University of Queensland Press ; Lawrence, Mass. : Distributed in the USA and Canada by Technical Impex Corp., 1984.

Pant, Apa, 1918-, *An Unusual Raja: Mahatma Gandhi and the Aundh Experiment*, Hyderabad : Sangam Books, 1989.

Panter-Brick, S. (Simone), *Gandhi Against Machiavellism: Non-Violence in Politics,* Bombay ; New York : Asia Pub. House, [1966].

Patel, Jehangir P., *Gandhi, his Gift of the Fight,* Rasulia : Friends Rural Centre, c1987.

Patil, V.T., 1940, *Mahatma Gandhi and the Civil Disobedience Movement : a Study in the Dynamics of the Mass Movement,* Delhi : Renaissance Pub. House, 1988.

Pattabhi Sitaramayya, Bhogaraju, *Gandhi and Gandhism: [A Study],* Allahabad : Kitabistan, 1942.

Payne, Robert, 1911, The Life and Death of Mahatma Gandhi, 1st ed., New York : Dutton, 1969.

Polak, H. S.L. (Henry Salomon Leon), 1882, *Mahatma Gandhi,* London : Odhams Press, 1949.

Power, Paul F., *Gandhi on World Affairs,* Washington, Public Affairs Press [1960]

Pradhan, Benudhar, 1931, *Socialist Thought of Mahatma Gandhi*, Delhi : GDK Publications, 1980.

Prasad, Bimla, 1925, *Gandhi, Nehru & J.P.: Studies in Leadership*, Delhi : Chankya Publications, 1985.

Prasad, Rajendra, Pres. India, 1884-1963, *Mahatma Gandhi and Bihar; Some Reminiscences,* Bombay Hind Kitabs [1949]

Pyarelal, *Mahatma Gandhi—The Last Phase*, Ahmedabad, Navajivan Pub. House [1956-58].

Raja Singam, S. Durai, *Recalling Gandhi*, Sussex, Eng. : Book Guild Ltd., 1995.

Ram Rattan, 1938, *Gandhi's Concept of Political Obligation*, [Calcutta] Minerva Associates [1972].

Ramachandran, G., *Quest for Gandhi,* 1st ed., New Delhi, Gandhi Peace Foundation, 1970.

Ramakrishnan, Padma, *Gandhi and Indian Independence,* New Delhi : Blaze Publishers & Distributors, c1994.

Ranga, N. G., *Bapu Blesses Nidubrolu,* Indian Peasant Institute [1969]

Rao, M. B., *The Mahatma; A Marxist Symposium*, Bombay People's Pub. House [1969].

Rao, Rampalli Visweswar, 1911, *Relevance of Mahatma Gandhi to our Times,* 1st ed., Hyderabad, India, Distributors: Book Lovers [1970].

Rao, U. R. (Ullal Ratnakar Rao) 1915-1969, *Let us Know Gandhiji,* New Delhi : Ministry of Information and Broadcasting, Govt. of India [1969]

Rao, U.R. (Ullal Ratnakar Rao) 1915-1969, *Mahatma Gandhi: The man and his Mission,* by U.R. Rao. Edited by G.S. Pohekar. Bombay United Asia Publications [c1971]

Rao, V.K.R.V. (Vijendra Kasturi Ranga Varadaraja), 1908, *The Gandhian Alternative to Western Socialism*, 1st ed., Bombay, Bharatiya Vidya Bhavan, 1970.

Rastogi, G.D., *Psychological Approach to Gandhi's Leadership,* 1st ed. Gorakhpur, Mrs. Girisha Rastogi; can be had from: U.B.S. Publishers' & Distributors', Delhi, 1969]

Ravindran, T.K., *Vaikkam Satyagraha and Gandhi,* Trichur : Sri

Narayana Institute of Social and Cultural Development, 1975.

Rawding, F.W., *Gandhi and the Struggle for India's Independence,* Minneapolis : Published in cooperation with Cambridge University Press [by] Lerner Publications Co., 1982.

Ray, Annadasankar, 1904, *Yes, I saw Gandhi,* 1st ed. — New Delhi : Gandhi Peace Foundation ; Bombay : Bharatiya Vidya Bhavan, 1976.

Richards, Glyn, *The Philosophy of Gandhi : A Study of his Basic Ideas,* London, [England] : Curzon Press ; Totowa, N.J. : Barnes & Noble, 1982.

Rivett, Kenneth, *Economic Thought of Mahatma Gandhi, Bombay,* Allied Publishers Private [c1959]

The Road to Indian Independence [videorecording] / Princeton, N.J. : Films for the Humanities and Sciences, c1990.

Ross, Alan, *The Emissary : G.D. Birla, Gandhi, and Independence,* London : Collins Harvill, 1986.

Rothermund, Dietmar, *Mahatma Gandhi, an Essay in Political Biography*, New Delhi : Manohar Publications, 1991.

Roy Choudhury, Pranab Chandra, 1903, *Gandhi, the man,* Mysore : Geetha Book House, 1974.

Roy Choudhury, Pranab Chandra, 1903, *International Politics,* Compiled and edited by P.C. Roy Chaudhury. [1st ed.] Ahmedabad Navajivan Pub. House [1970]

Roy-Chowdhury, Sumitra, *The Gurudev and the Mahatma,* Pune : Shubhada-Saraswat Publications, 1982.

Rudolph, Lloyd I., *The modernity of Tradition : Political Development in India*, Chicago : University of Chicago Press, [1967]

Saksena, Baburam, 1897, *Gandhiji's Solution of the Language Problem of India,* Bombay, Mahatma Gandhi Memorial Research Centre, Hindustani Prachar Sabha, 1972.

Sankhdher, M.M., 1930, *Gandhi, Gandhism and the Partition of India,* New Delhi : Deep & Deep Publications, c1982.

Savita, *Gandhi and Social Policy in India; a Sociological Analysis,* Delhi, National [Pub. House, 1970].

Seminar on Gandhi and the West, University of Mysore, 1969.

Gandhi and the West. Mysore, University of Mysore [Dept. of Post-graduate Studies and Research in English; for copies: Director, Prasaranga, 1969].

Shriman Narayan, 1912-1978, *India Needs Gandhi,* New Delhi : S. Chand, 1976.

Shriman Narayan, 1912-1978, *Relevance of Gandhiàn Economics,* 1st ed., Ahmedabad, Navajivan Pub. House [1970]

Shriman Narayan, 1912-1978, *Gandhi, the Man and his Thought,* New Delhi Publications Division, Ministry of Information and Broadcasting, Govt. of India [1969]

Shriman Narayan, 1912-1978, *Mahatma Gandhi: The Atomic Man,* Bombay Somaiya Publications [1971]

Shriman Narayan, 1912-1978, *Memoirs: Window on Gandhi and Nehru,* Bombay Popular Prakashan [1971]

Somarajan, C.N., 1945, *Role of Gandhi in Vaikkom Satyagraha,* Quilon : Raj Publications, 1986.

Steger, Manfred B., 1961, *Gandhi's Dilemma : Nonviolent Principles and Nationalist Power,* 1st ed. New York : St. Martin's Press, 2000.

Stern, Elizabeth Gertrude (Levin), 1890, *Women Behind Mahatma Gandhi,* London, Reinhardt [1954].

Suda, Jyoti Prasad, *Manu, Marx & Gandhi,* 1st ed., Meerut, Jai Prakash Nath [1967]

Swamy, K.R.N., 1930, *Mughals, Maharajas, and the Mahatma,* New Delhi : HarperCollins Publishers India, 1997.

Tähtinen, Unto, *The Core of Gandhi's Philosophy,* 1st ed. — New Delhi : Abhinav Publications, 1979.

Tandon, P.D., *Gandhi, Warrior of Non-violence,* New Delhi, National Book Trust, India; [sole distributors in India: India Book House, 1969]

Tendulkar, D.G., *Mahatma; Life of Mohandas Karamchand Gandhi,* [New ed.] [Bombay] The Publications Division, Ministry of Information and Broadcasting, Government of India, [1960-1963]

Thirtha, N.V., *Philosophy of Sarvodaya: Educational Implications,* Chandigarh, Mohindra Capital Publishers, 1969.

Thomas, T.K., *The Impact and the Challenge,* [Madras, Christian Literature Society for the Ecumenical Christian Centre, 1969]

Towards a Just Civilization : the Gandhian Perspective on Human Rights and Development, Toronto : Canadian Scholars' Press, 1993.

Upadhyaya, J.M. Mahatma, *Gandhi; a Teacher's Discovery,* Vallabh Vidyanagar, Sardar Patel University; [agent: Balgovind Book Sellers, Ahmedabad, 1969]

Uppal J. N., *Gandhi, Ordained in South Africa,* New Delhi : Publications, Division, Ministry of Information and Broadcasting, Govt. of India, 1995.

Varma, Vishwanath Prasad, 1924, *The Political Philosophy of Mahatma Gandhi and Sarvodaya*, Agra Lakshmi Narain Agarwal 1959

Vaswani, Thanwardas Lilaram, *Gandhi, Man of the Ages,* Poona, Mira [1969].

Verma, Amar Nath, 1935, comp., *Recollections of and About Mahatma Gandhi,* [Delhi, Star Publications; distributors: Newlight Publishers, 1969]

Walker, Roy, *Sword of Gold,* Bombay : Orient Longmans on behalf of Gandhi Peace Foundation, [1969].

Watson, Francis, 1907, *Talking of Gandhi,* by Francis Watson and Hallam Tennyson. London British Broadcasting Corporation 1969

Watson, Francis, 1907, *The Trial of Mr. Gandhi,* London : Macmillan, 1969.